Tactical Inclusion

FEMINIST MEDIA STUDIES

Edited by Rebecca Wanzo

Series Editorial Board
Mary Beltrán, Department of Radio-Television-Film, University of Texas–Austin
Radhika Gajjala, American Cultural Studies, Bowling Green University
Mary L. Gray, Department of Communication and Culture, Indiana University; Senior Researcher, Microsoft Research
Bambi Haggins, Arizona State University, Tempe
Mary Beth Haralovich, University of Arizona, Tucson
Heather Hendershot, Massachusetts Institute of Technology
Michele Hilmes, University of Wisconsin–Madison
Nina Huntemann, Suffolk University
Elana Levine, University of Wisconsin–Milwaukee
Robin Means-Coleman, University of Michigan
Mireille Miller-Young, UC Santa Barbara
Isabel Molina-Guzmán, University of Illinois at Urbana-Champaign
Laurie Ouellette, Communication Studies, University of Minnesota
Carrie Rentschler, McGill University
Kim Sawchuk, Concordia University
Carol Stabile, University of Oregon
Leslie Steeves, University of Oregon

For a list of books in the series, please see our website at www.press.uillinois.edu.

Tactical Inclusion

Difference and Vulnerability in U.S. Military Advertising

JEREMIAH FAVARA

© 2024 by the Board of Trustees
of the University of Illinois
All rights reserved
1 2 3 4 5 C P 5 4 3 2 1
♾ This book is printed on acid-free paper.

The appearance of U.S. Department of Defense visual information does not imply or constitute DOD endorsement.

Library of Congress Cataloging-in-Publication Data

Names: Favara, Jeremiah, 1982– author.
Title: Tactical inclusion : difference and vulnerability in U.S. military advertising / Jeremiah Favara.
Other titles: Difference and vulnerability in U.S. military advertising
Description: Urbana : University of Illinois Press, 2024. | Series: Feminist media studies | Includes index.
Identifiers: LCCN 2023034972 (print) | LCCN 2023034973 (ebook) | ISBN 9780252045721 (cloth) | ISBN 9780252087820 (paperback) | ISBN 9780252056581 (ebook)
Subjects: LCSH: United States—Armed Forces—Recruiting, enlistment, etc.—History—20th century. | United States—Armed Forces—Recruiting, enlistment, etc.—History—21st century. | Advertising—Recruiting and enlistment—Social aspects—United States. | United States—Armed Forces—Minorities. | United States—Armed Forces—Women.
Classification: LCC UB323 .F383 2024 (print) | LCC UB323 (ebook) | DDC 355.2/230973—dc23/eng/20230907
LC record available at https://lccn.loc.gov/2023034972
LC ebook record available at https://lccn.loc.gov/2023034973

For my parents, who taught me the value of being curious about the world and the importance of working to build a better one.

Contents

Acknowledgments   ix
Abbreviations   xiii

Introduction   1
1. We'll Hire You   31
2. America at Its Best   62
3. The Military Type   92
4. Make the World a Better Place   124
5. Walls Always Fall   154
   Conclusion: Beyond Tactical Inclusion   189

Appendix   201
Notes   205
Index   239

Acknowledgments

Like many academic books, this book has traveled to different cities and states, a constant companion as I navigated the academic job market. I am indebted to many people who have helped me along the way. Carol Stabile, a mentor, has become a dear friend, and her support, encouragement, and modeling of feminist scholarship have been invaluable. I had the great fortune of benefiting from the insights and guidance of C. J. Pascoe, Dan HoSang, Christopher Chávez, and Gretchen Soderlund. A number of colleagues and friends supported me during my time in Oregon: Allison Ford, Angela Rovak, Courtney Thorsson, Edmond Chang, Jamie Bufalino, Josie Mulkins, Laura Nickerson, Lauren Stewart, Margaret Rhee, Patrick Jones, Sarah Hamid, and Thea Chroman.

I benefited greatly from my time at the James Weldon Johnson Institute for the Study of Race and Difference at Emory University, where I was part of a fantastic community dedicated to racial justice. Thank you to Andra Gillespie, Kali-Ahset Amen, Rhonda Patrick, Dan Reiter, and all the visiting scholars and other fellows at the institute who generously took the time to exchange ideas and offer encouragement. Dwight Lewis and Rafa Solórzano, I cherish our friendship. I owe special thanks as well to Tanine Allison for her support and guidance. Clark Brinson gamely took on the difficult task of helping gather information on military budgets and advertising-agency contracts.

My colleagues in the department of women's and gender studies at the University of Wisconsin-Milwaukee provided a wonderfully supportive feminist community: Anna Mansson McGinty, Carolyn Eichner, Gwynne Kennedy, Katie Merkle, Krista Grensavitch, Kristin Pitt, Molly McCourt,

Melinda Quinn Brennan, and Xin Huang. An additional thanks to Anna and Krista for regular outdoor gatherings no matter the weather during the early years of the COVID-19 pandemic. Your friendship and good company really helped sustain me during a challenging time. Susan Wagner, you always had the answers or could always find them no matter the question, and I am so grateful for the work you do.

I feel so very fortunate to be in the communication studies department at Gonzaga University. It's so exciting to be among colleagues who view media and communication as radical tools in the pursuit of social justice. A special thanks to Melissa Click, who took the time to answer so many questions as I worked on finalizing the book. I look forward to working and learning with my colleagues in the years to come.

As this book and I have traveled, I've had the privilege and pleasure to work with so many fantastic students, whose curiosity and intelligence has helped me enormously. I am grateful to students in courses I've taught on media, militarization, and difference at the University of Oregon and Emory University and to students in women's and gender studies courses at the University of Wisconsin-Milwaukee, especially students in graduate seminars on feminist theory and queer theory. Their questions and insights reinforced how critical teaching and the opportunity to learn with and from students are to the research and writing process.

Many people have taken the time to read drafts, offer their thoughts, and share readings. I worked with Cathy Hannabach and Rachel Fudge, whose assistance with developmental editing really helped to focus and clarify the manuscript. Shoniqua Roach, your suggestions were so helpful at a critical point in rethinking the manuscript. Thank you to Elana Levine, Mary Vavrus, and Natalie Fixmer-Oraiz, all of whom read drafts of different chapters, offered feedback, and so generously shared their expertise. A special thanks to Tom Oates, whose steadfast support and mentorship have been invaluable. I am beyond grateful for having the opportunity to learn from such wonderful feminist scholars about the importance of intellectual generosity and community.

This book would not have been possible without librarians and archivists. Josh Rowley and other archivists at the Hartman Center for Sales, Advertising, and Marketing History at Duke University guided me to fantastic source material. Librarians at the Multnomah County Central Library in Portland, Oregon; the Knight Library at the University of Oregon; and the Golda Meir Library at UW-Milwaukee helped me track down issues of magazines, trade publications, and more. A special thanks to Daniel Dolan-Derks, Kaitlin

Cushman, and Laura Hutton at the Foley Library at Gonzaga University and to Marisa Uribe for their help with locating and scanning images.

It has been a pleasure to work with the team at University of Illinois Press. Rebecca Wanzo offered critical insights and encouragement as I worked to refine and revise the manuscript. Dawn Durante, your early support of the project has been deeply appreciated. Thank you to Daniel Nasset for your support as an editor and to Mariah Schaefer and Megan Donnan for your help getting the book over the finish line. I am grateful to the anonymous reviewers, whose feedback and suggestions made the book stronger.

A number of mentors and friends have provided support over the years. Thanks to Bethany Letiecq, Leah Schmalzbauer, Marsha Henry, and Sadie Wearing. Thanks also to Azadeh Akbari, Alex Doll, Farah Kassam, Kathryn Medien, and Milo Bettochi. I owe much to friends who have helped me get outside and get out of my head: Chaundera Wolfe, Eva Maggi, Jeff Hawe, Jess Gentner, Joe Pope, Judson Corn, Loren Kajikawa, Matt Pittman, Monica Thornton, Ocean Howell, Phil Weiss, Shane Stalling, Tracie Weiss, Tyrel Thornton, Vicky Pittman, and so many more. Your enthusiasm, patience, and care have made it possible for me to complete this book.

Lastly, I thank my family. My parents, Blaise Favara and Cynthia Favara, to whom this book is dedicated, have been unwavering in their support. Thank you to my grandmother Susan Cowell, who always took my ideas seriously even when they probably didn't deserve to be. I appreciate you welcoming me into your home, one of my favorite places on Earth and a lovely place to read, write, and relax. Darcy, my canine companion, provided a soundtrack of snores to which many of these chapters were written. And to Michelle Romano, your compassion, patience, and sense of humor sustain me.

Abbreviations

ASVAB	Armed Services Vocational Aptitude Battery
AVF	all-volunteer force
DADT	Don't ask, don't tell
ERA	Equal Rights Amendment
JROTC	Junior Reserve Officer Training Corps
MAVNI	Military Accessions Vital to the National Interest
MLDC	Military Leadership Diversity Commission
ROTC	Reserve Officer Training Corps

Introduction

My first memories of military recruiting slogans and advertisements date back to when I was in elementary school. The phrase "Be all you can be" was a cultural fixture throughout my youth, a meme that circulated through school hallways and sports fields. I have clear memories of seeing knights on television fighting their way through living chessboards and of young men braving labyrinths and gauntlets filled with fire and mythical monsters. When these knights and men reached their destination, a lightning strike magically transformed them into U.S. Marines. "Be all you can be" entered the pop-culture lexicon when the U.S. Army first used it as their recruiting slogan in 1981 and the marine corps ads I remember were featured in magazines and on television throughout the 1990s. While I can't pinpoint my first encounter with military recruitment advertising, it made enough of an impression that I can easily recall specific slogans and ads more than thirty years later. As I grew older, my relationship to military recruiting began to take a more concrete shape.

During my junior year of high school, all my classmates and I were required to take the Armed Services Vocational Aptitude Battery (ASVAB) exam, which is considered the first step toward enlisting in the U.S. military.[1] After getting my scores, I started receiving phone calls from recruiters. During these calls recruiters would ask if I'd considered joining the military, telling me about benefits associated with serving and military jobs they thought I might be interested in. The following year, just after my eighteenth birthday, I received a Selective Service card in the mail.[2] While attending Montana State University as an undergraduate, I often walked past posters hanging in the windows of a recruiting center, and recruiters would occasionally reach out to gauge my interest in the military. During the course of researching this book, I've talked to recruiters from a variety of military branches, and more than once our conversation would turn to whether I'd considered serving and the unique opportunities available to someone with my educational background and knowledge of military advertising.

Despite the consistent presence of military recruiting throughout my youth, I also recall moments in which I came to be less and less recruitable. Going to high school in a small town in rural Montana, I'd gotten good-enough grades so that teachers and guidance counselors put me into a college-bound track as opposed to friends who'd not done as well in school, didn't have the financial support to attend college without scholarships, and were seen as bound for the military. When I was in college, a recruiter knocked on the door of the house I shared with a roommate, and upon hearing that each of us had plans for after graduation, the recruiter asked if we knew any people who didn't have their stuff "as together" as my roommate and I. These moments reveal that though I might have been a desirable recruit, I was not a vulnerable recruit.

The very qualities that made me desirable to the military—my maleness, Whiteness, educational background, rural upbringing, and class privilege—were tethered to other opportunities that made it unlikely that I would want or need to join the military. As advertisements and recruiters told me that the military was looking for people like me, my social world was telling me that I didn't need to look to the military. Teachers, parents, and other adults in my life guided me toward college as my path forward, a path that many of my peers were told wasn't for them. My own experiences speak to the ways different individuals and groups are seen as recruitable, as vulnerable to the various opportunities on offer in the military.

While vulnerability is far too often cast as personal failure, a failure of effort, intelligence, or upbringing, it is a condition meted out by the state. A series of related forces, including decreased state support for public services, widening economic inequality, and gendered, racialized, and sexualized norms of productive citizenship, have constructed whole swaths of people as vulnerable, as ever at risk of slipping off the rungs of the ladder leading to a better life.[3] For those rendered vulnerable by structural forces, the military is framed as the remedy to what ails you. If you can't afford to go to college or you're struggling to get a good job, the military can help. If you are excluded from the privileges of first-class citizenship or your patriotism is in question, the military can help. If you are looking to bolster bona fides of manliness, the military can help.

Vulnerability hinges not only upon lack, lack of opportunities, resources, support, or cultural capital but also upon a promise of recuperation, a promise that joining the military offers a fast track to productive, respectable citizenship. This promise is articulated in different ways in recruitment advertisements through appeals emphasizing economic benefits, upward mobility, personal transformation, and patriotic duty. However, the promises of military service are not always fulfilled and are always contingent upon risk. The vulnerabilities that make one recruitable are doubled-down upon when recruits become soldiers and are exposed to violence, whether in the form of harassment and violence within the ranks or experiences of combat and war. As such, vulnerability functions in multiple ways in military recruiting, as a structural force taken advantage of, a metonym for recruitability, and a consequence of being in the military. Being vulnerable to military recruiting is a matter of life and death. If your life seems like a dead end, the military can offer you a path to the good life, a path littered with violence and potentially ending in death. These biopolitics of vulnerability tell potential recruits that the way to remedy the state failing you and make your life productive is to volunteer for the military and not fail the state, even if it means your injury or death.

My peers and I started on the same path, as young students in rural Montana, trying to figure out a way forward. The divergence that happened when we were sixteen and seventeen years old and were told we were either bound for college or the military had profound effects. As I navigated course schedules and picking a major, I had friends who were navigating IEDs in Iraq. As I grappled with the pressures of the post-college job search, I had friends who grappled with post-traumatic stress. While the majority of the young people I shared high school hallways with survived their tours of duty while in the military, many others did not, and those who did remain burdened with costs and consequences of state violence, not to mention the countless numbers of people who aren't U.S. military service members who have been displaced, traumatized, and killed in war.

The harsh realization of the profound consequences of being recruitable, of being vulnerable to the military path, led to the questions that animate this book. What does it mean that the U.S. military, one of the foremost instigators of violence around the world, is sold as a way to get ahead, as an opportunity to fulfill the American dream of upward mobility? What does it mean to be viewed as recruitable, as vulnerable to the appeals on offer in the military and as disposable within projects of state violence? What figures of militarization emerge when the military is sold as the solution to the vulnerabilities people face?

To answer these questions, this book focuses on recruitment advertisements and the industrial strategies and institutional policies that influence them. The analysis focuses primarily on print advertisements published in commercial magazines as one aspect of military recruiting. Military recruitment advertising is a massive endeavor, of which print advertising comprises one component among many, including advertising in other media, such as radio, television, and social media; junior reserve officer training corps (JROTC) programs in high schools; cooperation with commercial media industries in producing films, television shows, and video games; events on high school and college campuses; and the maintenance of recruiting offices worldwide. Recruitment advertisements are the primary way the military communicates with the broader public and portrays what it means to be in the military. Recruitment advertisements, though ostensibly designed to persuade recruits to enlist, also serve a much broader function in shaping perceptions of the military's domestic and global legitimacy. As cultural productions emerging at the convergence of the state and the advertising industry, recruiting ads construct and make intelligible subjects vulnerable to the project of military inclusion.

This book argues that inclusion is a mechanism of power and a cultural production predicated on vulnerability. Military inclusion takes shape through what I refer to as "tactical inclusion." Tactical inclusion is the science, art, and practice of constructing and representing subjects as vulnerable to recruiting appeals and a means of deploying inclusion to maintain state violence. Functionally, tactical inclusion is an industrial and representational strategy resulting in the making and targeting of new markets for recruiting, the creation of appeals to reach various groups, and the representation of the military as a paradigmatic American institution committed to both social progress and war. This book traces the different permutations of tactical inclusion across forty-three years of the all-volunteer force (AVF) between 1973 and 2016, during which the military was forced to meet all personnel needs by persuading volunteers to enlist. Encompassing the different branches of the military—the air force, army, coast guard, marine corps, and navy—tactical inclusion is an overarching project driven both by strategies developed to expand the target market of potential recruits and a series of political narratives about the military and its role in the nation.[4] Representations and strategies of tactical inclusion in recruitment advertising have been deployed at various times to promote views of military service as a safe economic opportunity in the wake of the Vietnam War; reassert American military, political, and cultural supremacy during the Reagan era; emphasize multiculturalism in the 1990s; justify the war on terror as a morally just and benevolent endeavor; and position the military as a key factor in promoting militarized diversity as a hallmark of progress during the Barack Obama administration.

Despite or perhaps because of these varying articulations, the material project of tactical inclusion has been remarkably successful. Recruitment advertising is arguably the most successful and innovative site for reaching Black Americans, people of color (a term I use to refer to racialized groups, including Asian Americans, Indigenous peoples, Pacific Islanders, Latinx peoples, and other non-White peoples) and women. Since the implementation of the AVF in 1973, the military has become one of the most diverse American institutions. In 2019, the most recent year with available data as of summer 2022, the military had over two million service members. Service members came from all fifty states, the District of Columbia, and American territories including Guam, Puerto Rico, and American Samoa. Three branches of the military, the army, navy, and air force, were more racially diverse than the civilian population. Although women made up less than 20 percent of service members, the percentage of women in the military steadily increased for the last decade, and women made up a higher percentage of service members in 2019 than any other year to date. Additionally, military women were a much more racially diverse group than both civilian women and military men.[5] I approach the emergence of a diverse military with a critical and cautious eye, not treating it as cause for celebration or as a sign of an inherent trajectory toward progress but, rather, as resulting from the particular cultural, industrial, and political strategies of tactical inclusion.

What follows offers an overview of the conceptual, historical, and industrial landscapes upon which tactical inclusion rests. Guided by an investment in the free market, the implementation of the AVF in 1973 altered dynamics of recruiting and intensified military advertising efforts. The AVF did away with the draft and forced the military to meet all their personnel needs by persuading volunteers to enlist, when for the first time in three decades they had the choice not to. The increased importance of advertising in persuading recruits to enlist during the AVF resulted in the formation of the military advertising industry, a coordinated network of military personnel and civilian advertising agencies. Existing at an intersection of the state and the commercial advertising industry, recruiting ads produced by the military advertising industry occupy a unique position situated in a gray area between commercial advertising and state propaganda. In discussing these imbricated landscapes—inclusion, vulnerability, the AVF, and the military advertising industry—this book provides a portrait of the terrain in which various manifestations and permutations of tactical inclusion emerged. The cultural, social, and political contexts in which different groups were deemed recruitable at various historical moments converged with the industrial logics of advertising and marketing and the needs of the all-volunteer military to create figures of militarization that reveal the promises and pitfalls of military inclusion and, ultimately, suture inclusion, as a seemingly progressive project, to militarism and state violence.

Tactical Inclusion and Vulnerability

As an industrial and representational strategy, tactical inclusion emerged in tension with vulnerability. As will be elaborated on, vulnerability arose as a guiding industrial strategy for advertisers as they sought to target potential recruits based on a variety of factors, including age, race, gender, education, and employment status, that would make it more likely that prospective recruits would choose to join the military, even if they had little or no desire to do so.[6] Tactical inclusion draws on existing vulnerabilities within capitalism and furthers them by extending vulnerability as something that not only makes one recruitable but, once included in the military, renders one vulnerable to the costs and consequences of state violence. In other words, tactical inclusion exploits and reproduces vulnerability, with vulnerability acting as both a precursor and consequence of military inclusion. To describe military inclusion as tactical highlights that it is not a benevolent gesture toward social progress but, rather, a specific strategy developed through connected logics of commercial advertising and militarism. Advertisers working on recruitment advertising built on and honed industrial strategies from commercial advertising, constructing different target groups for recruiting and subsequently representing how individuals from those groups could see themselves fitting within the military. In doing so, recruitment advertising negotiates the long-standing exclusion of women, Black Americans, people of color, and queer folks and attempts to reconcile appeals to those groups with the imperatives of a military institution defined by historical and ongoing investments in Whiteness, heteronormativity, patriarchy, and empire. In short, tactical inclusion entails creating appeals that uphold the institutional values of the military while expanding who is seen as able to inhabit and embody those values. The following discussion details the relationship between vulnerability and inclusion and the importance of each for thinking about military recruitment advertising.

Inclusion has been central to many social and political movements in the United States. From movements advocating for access to rights, including the right to vote, marry, and serve in the military, to those seeking increased representation in institutions, including media, higher education, and government, the idea of inclusion permeates liberal ideas of social progress. Couched in a variety of different terms and policies, such as affirmative action, multiculturalism, equal opportunity, and diversity, inclusion is perhaps the primary mode through which equality has been conceptualized and operationalized in American political and social life.

A number of scholars have demonstrated how calls for inclusion have come to dominate mainstream social movements and how inclusion, once granted, has failed as a redress to harm. Legal scholar and trans activist Dean Spade argues that a politics of inclusion has replaced radical reform as a model for achieving equality and ultimately functions to uphold dominant institutions and systems of meaning.[7] Drawing on critical race theory and focusing on legal systems, Spade contends that a politics of inclusion coincides with co-optation, in which the language of resistance movements is recast to legitimate the institutions and power structures they seek to dismantle. Similarly focusing on critical race theory and the legal system, Black feminist scholar Jennifer C. Nash argues that inclusion, understood as entry into an existing system, is predicated on exclusion and hierarchy and is an insubstantial form of radical politics, particularly for Black women.[8]

Other scholars have detailed how similar processes of inclusion and co-optation function in other powerful institutions. For instance, interdisciplinary scholar Roderick Ferguson explores the institutionalization of difference in the U.S. academy in the form of disciplines like ethnic studies and women's studies. Ferguson argues that the incorporation of these new forms of knowledge was made possible through a process of adaptive hegemony, in which state, capital, and academic institutions recast and incorporated difference as part of their own institutional aims and goals while continuing to discipline and exclude minority subjects.[9] Keeanga-Yamahtta Taylor chronicles the shift from exclusion to inclusion in homeownership programs in the 1970s driven by a partnership between government agencies and the real estate, housing, and banking industries. Taylor argues that this public-private partnership—a partnership not unlike that between the military and the advertising industry—resulted in predatory inclusion, a form of inclusion in which low-income African Americans were encouraged to become homeowners on exploitative and extractive terms.[10] Predatory inclusion was based upon a view of the market as a neutral equalizer and a disavowal of the racist practices that had long characterized housing and real estate in the United States. Ultimately, predatory inclusion led to continued inequalities revealing the failures of racial liberalism and dispelling notions that inclusion is necessarily a pathway to equality.[11] Feminist scholar Sara Ahmed, in a detailed analysis of inclusion in higher education, approaches inclusion as performative and as a process that legitimates institutional norms and signals an embrace of diversity without any significant redress of structural inequalities.[12] Ahmed points to the contradictory nature of inclusion, contending that being included can reproduce a politics of exclusion and that diversity is a hollow form of repair predicated on maintaining historically exclusive norms of gender, race, and sexuality.[13]

This critical work allows one to think of inclusion as a mechanism of power rooted in the maintenance of existing institutions, despite the proliferation of a politics of inclusion in social justice movements. More specifically, these scholars make clear that inclusion has been deployed in the interest of maintaining specific institutions while also being characteristic of broader political and cultural views. As American studies scholar Daniel Martinez HoSang points out, inclusion into existing institutions and structures is viewed as the sole framework for addressing inequalities within the context of U.S. liberalism and capitalism.[14] As such, inclusion is often invited by those in power as a state-sanctioned form of redress that ultimately reproduces harm and inequality.[15] Considered along with media studies scholarship addressing representational inclusion, I draw on this lineage of scholarship to critique military inclusion as an operation of power.

Given that recruitment advertising is crucial to tactical inclusion, questions of representation and visibility are fundamental to understanding military inclusion. Herman Gray argues that despite a history of representation and recognition as crucial for Black freedom struggles, a cultural politics of representation no longer leads to substantive change.[16] Recognition has become the end of a cultural politics of diversity, in which the visibility of racial difference is incorporated as a source of brand value. As demonstrated by Sarah Banet-Weiser, such a process has become the dominant mode through which categories of race and gender are rendered solely as visible representations, robbed of their political and structural significance.[17] What is left then is a hollow politics of inclusion divorced from structural changes and, ultimately, operating to maintain existing forms of power. As these scholars demonstrate, inclusion projects are guided by logics of capitalism and liberalism in which selectively expanding the scope of those included functions to promote a fiction of a neutral market and an equal society and have resonated in a variety of institutions beyond the military. However, the military and the specific articulations of tactical inclusion are worthy of specific focus due to both the symbolic and material power vested in the military. The military is one of, if not the most, trusted of American institutions, regularly eliciting higher levels of confidence from a greater share of Americans than many other institutions, including the media, schools, police forces, government, and the medical institution.[18] Additionally, military inclusion has been key to a variety of social movements.

From the aligning of an Allied victory during World War II with the recognition of Black Americans as equal citizens in the Double V campaign, to efforts seeking to allow transgender Americans to openly serve in the armed forces, the ability to serve in the military has been a long sought-after goal for groups desiring recognition as first-class citizens.[19] This is not to say that military inclusion is not contested within social movements but that it is a particularly privileged site of inclusion. The consistency with which military inclusion has been viewed as a key step in movements for equality speaks to an enduring national commitment to martial citizenship, a valorization of military service as a defining quality of national identity and an important site for the granting of full citizenship, both practically and symbolically. As noted by feminist scholar Ilene Rose Feinman, martial citizenship is rooted in a masculinist culture in which citizenship was initially only available to White, land-owning men.[20] Rights of citizenship have long been granted in exchange for military service. Promises of citizenship have been leveraged to enlist people of color in the military during times of need from the Civil War, during which the Emancipation Proclamation allowed recently freed Black men to join the Union Army and Navy, to the more recent practice of granting posthumous citizenship to noncitizen Latinx soldiers killed in the Iraq War.[21] Military service functions to mediate claims to citizenship, able to formally grant citizenship and bolster claims to symbolic citizenship while elucidating that such claims to martial citizenship do not correspond with equality and are predicated on an uneven allocation of the risks of state violence. While an array of scholarship has addressed various movements for military inclusion, including contestations and debates within such movements, little work has focused on military inclusion as an industrial and institutional strategy, as a manifestation of state power that strengthens the military.

Inclusion is an operation of power, especially in the military. From the regulation of uniforms and haircuts to the indoctrination process of boot camp, the military remakes new recruits into service members, requiring that they inherit, inhabit, and embody military norms and values. Although all institutions require a similar capitulation to existing norms and values, the military does so with a much more explicit emphasis on maintaining existing institutional values, making clear that being included in the military doesn't mean that a new recruit will change the military but, rather, that being included in the military will absolutely and definitively transform the new recruit into a new subject: into a soldier, sailor, airman, coast guardsman, or marine.[22]

These militarized subjects, the figures of the soldier, sailor, airman, coast guardsman, or marine, are historically and culturally tied to ideals of maleness, Whiteness, and heteronormativity. While the regulatory power of inclusion operates on all who join the military, that power is intensified for those not marked as ideal service members. Inclusion operates hierarchically. Those historically excluded from national spaces are viewed as "space invaders," unnatural occupants whose inclusion highlights the constitutive boundaries of the nation and the body politic.[23] As the military grappled with persuading volunteers to choose to enlist, the ideal recruit, the person most desired by the military, converged with the vulnerable recruit, the person most likely to view themselves as in need of the various promises the military offers. Somewhat paradoxically, tactical inclusion hails those traditionally viewed as ideal recruits—straight, White cisgender men—while also constructing limited pathways through which some Black Americans, people of color, women, and members of the lesbian, gay, bisexual, transgender/Two-Spirit, queer/questioning, intersex, asexual, plus (LGBTQIA+) community are encouraged to view themselves as belonging in the military.[24] In tracing the intersectional parameters through which Black Americans, people of color, women, and members of the LGBTQIA+ community have been targeted and represented in recruitment advertisements, the mechanisms of power at work in tactical inclusion are made clear. Some aspects of difference—such as race and gender—have been more easily incorporated into representations in recruiting ads provided they didn't deviate too far from historical norms of Whiteness and maleness, whereas other aspects of difference—namely, queerness and disability—have been consistently cast as threatening, as purposefully unintelligible, and as being outside the bounds of tactical inclusion. In other words, tactical inclusion is more likely to result in images of recruits that only depart to limited degrees from institutional norms of Whiteness, maleness, and heteronormativity. Tactical inclusion reveals how women, people of color, Black Americans, and queer Americans are figured as constitutive outsiders whose inclusion requires unique strategies and representational forms. Part of the task of tactical inclusion is to reach out to new groups and offer them unique pathways to becoming martial subjects while not completely abandoning ideal recruits who historically have been constructed as "natural" martial subjects.

This balance between hailing those who *want* to join the military because they can already see themselves as belonging in the military and those who *need* to join the military for other reasons, such as economic incentives, patriotic validation, and upward mobility, highlights the tactical nature of tactical inclusion. In many ways, ideal recruits—generally imagined to be straight, White men—haven't needed persuading to join the military. However, the different branches of the military regularly competed with one another to reach the most desired and ideal recruits, resulting in differing brand images of masculinity rooted in narratives of martial, economic, and technological mastery, as political scientist Melissa T. Brown aptly demonstrates.[25] Throughout the AVF, there existed a balance between targeting and appealing to ideal recruits and vulnerable recruits while not alienating either. The tensions at the center of this balance, at the center of tactical inclusion, were crafted through two primary concepts: vulnerability and propensity.

Vulnerability has been central to the development of different strategies and messages used to persuade recruits to enlist. During the early years of the AVF, in the mid-1970s, one of the first steps advertisers took in planning recruitment advertisements was to identify vulnerable target groups, followed by the development of appeals that might persuade those groups to enlist. More specifically, advertising professionals from the J. Walter Thompson agency proposed an integrated research program for the armed forces in 1973, the year the AVF was implemented. In the proposal one of the first objectives was to identify "vulnerable target groups."[26] Target groups were seen as including those predisposed to military service and those with reservations about military service but who were seen as persuadable. Vulnerability was further determined by an array of markers used to identify and define potential recruits, including gender, race, age, employment, and education.[27] Advertisers marshaled and honed industrial strategies of commercial advertising in service of creating vulnerable target markets based on demographic and psychographic segmentation.

Market research accounts for, produces, and informationalizes difference, as a variety of traits, including gender, race, geography, education, and economic background, become critical in creating target markets. Drawing on these industrial strategies, military recruitment advertising is based on the ordering of populations, the exhaustive cataloging of difference, and the use of this information to target, construct, and represent different groups as vulnerable and, subsequently, as recruitable. Demographic data is crucially important within the military advertising industry, as a mode of not only accounting for the overall size of the youth market in a given year but also for determining the composition of the market. Attitude and awareness surveys categorize youth by gender and race, gauging their opinions of the military, military service, and the different branches of the armed forces to create a taxonomy of recruitability, determined by which groups have high opinions of military service and high expectations of serving.[28] Initially only surveying young men, these surveys consistently relied on certain demographic categories—namely, gender, race, age, employment, education, and geography—to detail specific target markets for recruitment advertising and recruiting more broadly.

As such, the strategies of military recruitment advertising and, more broadly, of advertising are deeply biopolitical. Within commercial advertising, this process is primarily about selling goods, that is, about selling aspirational and fantastic visions of the "good life" bound to capitalist norms of citizenship.[29] While recruitment advertisements are certainly aspirational and fantastic, they are also uniquely bound to life and death. Vulnerability to recruiting means being vulnerable to the life-affirming opportunities sold by the military, including signing bonuses, job training, and subsidized education, as well as the life-ending risks of the military, including injury, trauma, violence, and death. Vulnerability, as a promise of life and a risk of death, has continued to shape strategies of recruitment advertising through considerations of unemployment and propensity.

Throughout the AVF, a variety of industry and government documents point to youth unemployment rates as among the most important factors influencing recruiting. When youth struggle to find jobs in the civilian sphere, military service becomes a more appealing option, and the military is more easily able to meet personnel needs. Simply put, a bad economy is good for recruiting. Considerations of unemployment mapped recruitability onto economic precarity and is one way vulnerability has manifested in recruitment advertising, the other is through the concept of propensity. Scholars and researchers have undertaken studies that measure the success and efficiency of the AVF based on the propensity to serve.[30] Propensity is a measure of the likelihood that an individual will serve in the military and does not always align with a desire to do so. Some individuals expect to serve regardless of their desire, based on perceptions that the military offers educational, vocational, and financial opportunities not available in civilian life. Although propensity certainly is tied to unemployment, it extends beyond that to address potential recruits' feelings about their life chances in a broader sense. Propensity can emerge when a young person encounters a world seemingly dominated by dead ends. In this sense, the allure of military service functions on an affective register, albeit not the enthusiastic or patriotic register that one might think. Rather, propensity speaks to a dual affective register of despair and hope, not that the military is one's first or even preferred choice but that the military is the best option for potentially attaining upward mobility.

In the face of staggering economic inequality, the dismantling of social services, and structural inequalities of gender, race, and sexuality, joining the military represents a narrow—and potentially dangerous—pathway to stability and security. What is concerning is not that people might choose the military as a way out, as a path to a better life, but the widespread acceptance that one of the only avenues for state-supported economic and social advancement is necessarily tied to empire, violence, destruction, and death. That propensity has emerged as the industrial and academic term for measuring the success and efficacy of both the AVF and of military advertising further solidifies the link between vulnerability and recruiting. The industrial logic of vulnerability, tied to unemployment and propensity as markers of precarity that make one more likely to be persuaded to enlist, makes clear that military inclusion, specifically tactical inclusion, occurs to those deemed vulnerable to it, by virtue of their biopolitical position in an unequal society.

As the AVF was implemented in 1973, forces that had excluded Black Americans, people of color, women, and queer folks from attaining economic security were being reshaped through a series of shifts associated with neoliberalism.[31] Although neoliberalism is an imperfect term, and its proliferation in critical scholarship has perhaps dulled its conceptual specificity, discussing neoliberalism allows for a consideration of shifts in economics, social policies, and ideologies that shape the social, political, and cultural world. In terms of recruitment, considering neoliberal shifts in economic thought and ideologies of gender, racial, and sexual difference shows how tactical inclusion emerged out of viewpoints privileging free markets, narratives that inequality could be overcome if individuals simply made better choices, and an emphasis on inclusion and incorporation as the goal of social movements.

As a mode of political and economic thinking, neoliberalism emphasizes free trade, free markets, and individual choice while advocating for a scaling back, including deregulation, privatization, and reductions in social provisions, of state intervention.[32] Economic policies rooted in neoliberalism were primarily instituted during the administration of Ronald Reagan in the United States, though having antecedents in the 1960s and 1970s as politicians like Richard M. Nixon and economists like Milton Friedman and Alan Greenspan offered the free market as the remedy to an array of social ills, including the problem of how to maintain the military.[33] Neoliberal policies have exacerbated economic inequalities through the diminishment of wages, attacks on labor unions, and cuts in social welfare programs.[34] When read through a biopolitical framework, the intensification of economic inequalities under neoliberalism results from particular policies as well as ideologies that perpetuate and justify the uneven distribution of life chances. Neoliberalism functions to include and exclude individuals and groups based on their proximity to a national identity defined via racialized norms of gender and sexuality.[35] Poor life chances are attributed not to systemic inequalities but, rather, to bad actors, to the poor choices, and supposedly pathological failures of racialized, sexualized, and gendered others. This way of thinking relies on a disavowal of difference and the embrace of ideologies promoting universalism and equality within the free market, a disavowal discussed under different guises including racial liberalism, colorblindness, neoliberal multiculturalism, and queer liberalism.[36] Asian American studies and gender studies scholar Grace Hong argues that neoliberalism, as an ideology, is about both repression and affirmation, about necropolitical and biopolitical forms of power operating at the same time.[37] More specifically, the disavowal of ongoing gendered, racial, and sexualized violence is based upon the selective recuperation of some minoritized subjects as a mode of justifying the death of other minoritized subjects. In other words, if one could point to a select few who had "made it" and could chalk up their success to hard work, respectability, and doing things the "right" way, all those who didn't make it or did things the "wrong" way deserved their fates of poverty, underemployment, and death. This dual working of power converges when one thinks of vulnerability and military recruiting.

Predicated, at least in part, on inequality and precarity, vulnerability also entails a promise of recuperation, a promise of productive life and affirmation associated with military service while marking one as precarious, as disposable within projects of state violence. In this sense, industrial strategies that mark some bodies as vulnerable, and consequently as recruitable, function similarly to queer theorist Jasbir Puar's conceptualization of debility, in which certain bodies are deemed available for injury, as necessary casualties in narratives of progress.[38] Nestled in tension between life and death, between biopolitics and necropolitics, vulnerability is foundational to recruitment advertising and to tactical inclusion. Focusing on vulnerability highlights the contradictory impulse of military inclusion and situates it as a particular instantiation of biopolitical and necropolitical forms of power. Drawing on the work of Michel Foucault and Achille Mbembe, Hong details how during the post–World War II period in the United States, repressive and affirmative forms of power operated in tandem, marking some lives as protectable and others as precarious.[39] Tactical inclusion functions as a manifestation of these dual forms of power. Recruitment advertisements frame the military as fostering life by ensuring economic and material benefits while also taking advantage of existing regimes of power tethered to economic inequality and racialized, gendered, and sexualized norms of citizenship. At the same time as military service is framed as productive of life, it fosters violence, destruction, and death. To be vulnerable to recruiting is to be seen as in need of what the military can offer, deserving of the promise of a better life if one makes the choice to enlist and concurrently disposable in projects of state violence by virtue of that same choice.

In developing tactical inclusion and vulnerability as the primary theoretical concepts guiding this book, *Tactical Inclusion: Difference and Vulnerability in U.S. Military Advertising* builds on an array of interdisciplinary scholarship that interrogates militarization as an important site for reflecting and producing meanings of gender, racial, and sexual difference. Gender and militarization are bound together in a complex interplay that shapes political, cultural, and social meanings of war and state violence, as detailed by feminist scholars including Cynthia Enloe, Cynthia Cockburn, and Feinman.[40] Gendered meanings of war and militarization have been influenced by intersecting dynamics of race and sexuality as well as by struggles for military inclusion. Documented in scholarship by Brenda L. Moore, Charrisa J. Threat, Allan Bérubé, Aaron Belkin, Steven Rosales, and Máel Embser-Herbert, histories and experiences of women, Black, Latinx, and queer service members reveal the racialized and sexualized contours of the military and what historian Kimberley Phillips refers to as a paradox of military inclusion, in which the military has offered more opportunity than other institutions while suppressing struggles for freedom.[41]

As feminist media studies scholars have demonstrated, media representations of war play an influential role in shaping dynamics of difference and militarization, especially since the implementation of the AVF, which was an influential catalyst for shifting ideas about military service.[42] Recruiting ads, though left relatively unexplored in critical scholarship, have played an important role in shaping gendered ideas of military service during the AVF, as noted by Wendy M. Christensen, Stephanie Szitanyi, and Brown.[43] Brown, in a trenchant analysis, details how recruitment materials for the different branches of the military constructed gendered ideas about military service and citizenship.[44] In doing so, Brown provides important insights on the deployment of varying gendered narratives to sell military service to potential recruits in the years between 1973 and 2007.[45] Much of Brown's analysis focuses on representations of military masculinity, while notably considering how women were or were not included in recruiting materials. *Tactical Inclusion* expands on this work by foregrounding an explicitly intersectional analysis and thinking about how recruitment advertising more specifically targeted, imagined, and represented those who do not easily fit the mold of the ideal recruit. An intersectional analysis of tactical inclusion reveals the crucial role the military advertising industry and the ads produced within played in crafting militarized ideals of gender, race, sexuality, and class but also in creating a broader narrative of the military as an institution invested in inclusion. In drawing on the rich body of scholarship discussed above, this book unpacks the complex relationships at the heart of the challenge of military inclusion.

In adopting a deeply intersectional analysis, *Tactical Inclusion* looks at the military not simply as an institution that creates and sustains norms of gender, race, sexuality, and class but also as an institution that communicates how such norms are tied to concerns of power and violence. In her influential work on intersectionality, Kimberlé Crenshaw uses an analogy of a basement to describe intersectionality:

> Imagine a basement which contains all people who are disadvantaged on the basis of race, sex, class, sexual preference, age and/or physical ability. These people are stacked—feet standing on shoulders—with those on the bottom being disadvantaged by the full array of factors, up to the very top, where the head of all those disadvantaged by a singular factor brush up against the ceiling.... A hatch is developed through which those placed immediately below can crawl. Yet this hatch is generally available only to those who—due to the singularity of their burden and their otherwise privileged position relative to those below—are in the position to crawl through.[46]

Although less widely referenced than the analogy of the traffic intersection, this analogy is particularly salient for exploring tactical inclusion. I read representations and strategies of recruitment advertising as particular instantiations of the hatch that Crenshaw describes, where being included functions as invitation to crawl out of the basement. Considering recruiting ads alongside military policies and advertising industry archives, *Tactical Inclusion* unpacks the multifaceted process through which those in power hail different individuals to climb through the hatch, the conditional parameters those hailed must meet, and the costs and consequences of ascending into an institution, that though able to grant material and symbolic benefits is defined by an unflinching commitment to violence.

Guided by an array of critical feminist, antiracist, and queer scholarship, including Black feminism, critical race theory, and queer of color critique,

I am also orienting what follows in service of a particular political project. This book provides a better understanding of the intersectional dynamics of gender, race, sexuality, and class at work in military recruitment advertising and tactical inclusion so that those dynamics can be challenged and resisted. As feminist scholar Marsha G. Henry points out, critical work on militaries and militarization that doesn't deeply engage with feminism and intersectionality risks reinforcing racial, gender, and class hierarchies.[47] I approach narratives of inclusion and diversity in recruitment advertisements as a call to critique, a call to, in the words of Ahmed, explore how "power can be *redone* at the moment it is imagined as *undone*."[48] Resistance to sexism, racism, heterosexism, classism, and other oppressive structures of power is paramount to feminist media studies scholarship and is made more difficult as such structures become sutured to purportedly liberatory discourses of equality, inclusion, and diversity. Tactical inclusion is the primary mode through which the military and advertisers have reconciled tensions between violence and inclusion, not only reconciling those tensions but also rendering them productive in creating politically and socially legitimate meanings of military service and concurrently expanding the pool of potential recruits. The emergence of tactical inclusion is reliant not only on vulnerability but also upon the particular contours of the AVF, to which we now turn.

The Politics of the All-Volunteer Force

In July 1973 the military implemented the AVF, doing away with the draft and instituting a model of military service in which all service members choose to enlist. For the first time since the 1940s, the military could no longer rely on a draft to help meet personnel needs.[49] The process of shifting to an AVF was shaped by years of political and social debate about military service revolving around free-market economics, obligations and rights of citizenship, American military involvement in Vietnam, and the equity of the draft. The draft figured as an important concern across the political and cultural spectrum, and its elimination was embraced by a variety of political leaders and organizations in the midst of public opposition to the war in Vietnam.[50] A number of civil rights groups, such as the Mississippi Freedom Democratic Party, the Student Non-Violent Coordinating Committee, and the National Chicano Moratorium, and prominent cultural and political leaders, including John Lewis, Shirley Chisholm, Kwame Ture, Fannie Lou Hamer, Malcolm X, and Martin Luther King Jr., publicly denounced the war and connected struggles for racial equality with antiwar movements.[51] The government was criticized for drafting Black and Latinx soldiers, whose rights were denied at home, and American military intervention in Vietnam was framed as a form of colonialism and White supremacy.[52] Such sentiments contributed to increasing criticism of the draft as inequitable and exploitative from liberals, activists, and the left. Antiwar movements also converged with movements for women's rights in the 1960s. Some movements for women's equal rights in the late 1960s advocated for increased military inclusion and were influential in shaping the eventual implementation of the AVF, whereas others mobilized in favor of ending the war and were critical of the military.[53] At the same time, conservative politicians Barry Goldwater and Nixon spoke out against the draft by mobilizing racist anxieties arising from Black Americans calls for equal rights. In 1964 Goldwater courted White voters who disapproved of Black Americans' calls for equality as part of a "White backlash."[54] In 1968 presidential candidate Nixon pledged to end the draft promising to suppress the "guerrillas in Harlem and Saigon," through the use of a racist slur that conflated a racialized war in Vietnam with militarized police responses to civil unrest in urban cities in the United States.[55]

In the midst of divergent opposition to the draft, the language of the free market emerged as the dominant voice in debates over how to supplant the draft with a different model of military service. Widespread opposition to the draft and discontent with the state, expressed by antiwar groups, civil rights movements, and politicians advocating for an expansion of the free market, provided traction for economists' proposals to replace the draft with a model of military service in which individuals could choose to volunteer in the military based on their own economic interests.[56] As noted by historian Beth Bailey, Nixon's call to end the draft just prior to the 1968 election was opportunistic, and while he may have capitalized on resentment of the draft from the left and liberals, his thinking was guided not by agreement with antiwar, Black power, or feminist critiques of the draft but, rather, by an embrace of free-market economics.[57] Nixon framed the draft as a violation of individual liberty that forced service members to pay a hidden tax in the form of wages lost while serving in the military and linked challenges to racial inequality with weakened national security.[58] In doing so, Nixon connected growing public sentiment of the unfairness of the draft and anxieties over civil rights challenges to White supremacy with economic arguments that saw the draft as antithetical to a free labor market. Shortly after his inauguration, President Nixon announced the formation of the Commission on an All-Volunteer Armed Force, known as the Gates Commission, tasked with developing a plan for an entirely voluntary military.[59] Composed of civilians and former military leaders, the commission was initially divided on the idea of an AVF. Commission members who opposed the AVF were concerned that it would undermine patriotism, reduce the quality of recruits, and disproportionately appeal to Black Americans.[60] However, driven by a belief in the free market and arguments that the composition of the military wouldn't radically change, the commission ultimately supported an AVF.

The implementation of the AVF catalyzed a large demographic shift in which the military became increasingly diverse. Scholars have argued that without the disproportionate representation of people of color, specifically Black Americans, and women, the recruiting goals of the AVF would not have been met.[61] While, prior to the AVF, Black men and other men of color were granted full military inclusion—at least according to policy, the implementation of the AVF led to a large increase in their military participation. Black Americans have served at higher rates throughout the AVF than their civilian population would indicate, and the percentage of Latinx service members—a group largely ignored in much of the scholarship on military service and recruitment—has more than doubled since the late 1980s.[62] Along with ushering in an increasingly racially diverse military, the AVF has been among the most influential shifts driving women's increased inclusion in the military.

The percentage of women in the military has grown from 2 percent to almost 15 percent during the AVF.[63] This increase has occurred along with major policy shifts that, over time, have granted women increased inclusion in the military. During the course of the AVF, women have gained admittance to military academies, access to serving on ships and to flying combat aircraft, and in 2016 full access to all military positions, including combat positions. To be clear, and as elaborated on in later chapters, these trends toward inclusion occurred, and were enabled, by concurrent conditions and exclusions, especially pertaining to dominant norms of gender and sexuality. The increased inclusion of women, Black Americans, and people of color in the military occurred as the overall size of the military decreased. In 1973 the active-duty component of the military was 2.2 million service members, decreasing to just under 1.3 million service members in 2016.[64] As fewer and fewer Americans served in the military, the burden of military service has been increasingly borne by Black Americans, people of color, and women.

While such changes were influenced at least in part by policies meant to make the military more equitable, concerns that a free-market model of military service would disproportionately appeal to Black Americans and others who were economically disenfranchised seemed to be realized.[65] Rather than taking seriously critiques of the draft as a racially inequitable extension of White supremacy coming from Black and Latinx antiwar activists or as a continuation of patriarchal war waging from antiwar feminists, framing the draft as a violation of individual liberty best remedied by market forces insulated privileged White men from the possibility of military service. While a number of mechanisms, including paying for replacements and obtaining deferments based on education, employment, and breadwinner status, had long allowed elite White men to avoid supposedly mandatory military service, a free-market model of military service solidified their ability to avoid military service as there was little incentive for those with opportunities in the civilian world to choose to join the military. The AVF left little room for considerations of fairness and ultimately viewed all potential recruits as individual rational actors existing independently of dynamics of race, gender, and class.[66] The AVF was conceived of as a model free-market institution tasked with accumulating bodies for state use. In foregrounding the free market, the shift to the AVF altered meanings of military service in which ideas of the citizen-soldier were replaced with the logic of the market.[67]

The concept of the citizen-soldier is based on the idea that soldiering is an obligation of citizenship and a patriotic duty, motivated by a requirement of service or a pressing call to action in the face of national threat.[68] As the AVF was implemented and any requirements of service were eliminated, the citizen-soldier was replaced with the free-market volunteer. The military, in essence, entered the marketplace, and the AVF was a model free-market institution, in which values of individual liberty were privileged above all.[69] The Gates Commission described the AVF as a model of military service "that minimizes government interference with the freedom of the individual to determine his own life in accord with his values."[70] In the AVF, individual freedom was valued over patriotism, relegating military service to an issue of personal choice, a shift imagined as resulting in a military where each and every service member chooses military service based on their values. However, in foregrounding the idea of military service as an individual choice while entirely disregarding the systemic and structural terrain upon which choices are made, the AVF should make us question the nature of volunteering to enlist. The volunteer service member emerges equally out of a choice to serve and a lack of other choices in an inequitable society.

While some recruits might have been motivated to serve based on a sense of patriotic duty, planners of the AVF were well aware that they could not rely on patriotism as the sole driver in motivating volunteers to enlist. Members of the Gates Commission fully embraced a market logic and argued that raising military pay and making changes to improve the quality of military life were the first necessary steps in ensuring a successful AVF. Another key step in assuring the success of the AVF was to utilize the power of advertising to persuade recruits to enlist and make them aware of the new and improved military. Coinciding with the embrace of the free market in designing and implementing the AVF, military officials quickly turned to advertising and marketing professionals to aid them in meeting personnel needs and competing in the market for new recruits.

The Military Advertising Industry

The shift to the AVF made necessary the formation of the military advertising industry. While the military had relied on advertising to reach recruits and shape public opinions for decades prior to the AVF, developing a positive public image was crucial if the AVF was to be successful, and the planners of the AVF called for large increases in advertising budgets.[71] The increased investment in recruitment advertising facilitated a competitive environment in which civilian advertising agencies aggressively sought to land lucrative military advertising contracts. In the first year of the AVF, the military's advertising budget was $68.1 million, which was distributed amongst the different branches and their associated advertising agencies. Since then, the military's annual advertising budget has grown to upwards of $500 million in 2016.[72] Consistent investment in military advertising throughout the AVF created and consolidated the military advertising industry.

The military advertising industry consists of representatives from the different branches of the military, including recruiting and public affairs units for the army, coast guard, navy, marine corps, and air force, Department of Defense advertising and market research programs, such as the Joint Advertising Market Research and Studies group and the Joint Recruiting Advertising Program, and civilian advertising agencies in charge of military advertising contracts. Each branch of the military has its own recruiting and advertising units and its own budgets, and the branches award contracts to different advertising agencies. Military personnel and advertising professionals work in close relationships to craft recruiting materials. For example, all recruiting materials produced since the 1980s by the J. Walter Thompson agency, which has been the marine corps' primary advertising partner since the 1940s, feature images of actual marines and are presented to focus groups of marines prior to publication. The military advertising industry has been responsible for creating a variety of recruitment materials, including radio spots, poster campaigns, billboards, direct-mailing flyers, print advertisements, television spots, websites, and video games. Advertisers have also helped create other recruiting artifacts, including marine corps–branded Humvees complete with sound systems and in-vehicle video game consoles and a $2.5 million bus with an interactive video exhibit extolling medical training and occupational opportunities in the army. A number of scholars have situated these endeavors within linkages among the military, entertainment industries, and media and software companies, variously referred to as the military-entertainment complex, the media-military-industrial complex, and the U.S. empire's culture industry.[73] The military advertising industry is an oft-overlooked aspect of militarization in the United States, existing at an intersection of the state and the commercial advertising industry, in which logics and motivations of each converge.

On their surface commercial advertisements serve a primarily economic function of persuading an individual to purchase a specific product or service, yet media studies scholars have pointed to the important role advertisements play in shaping cultural values. Media historians Jackson Lears and Roland Marchand contend that advertisements promote and sanction certain cultural values to create a symbolic universe defined by fantasy and aspiration.[74] Cultural studies scholar Raymond Williams views advertising as a "magic system," in which material objects being sold have to be validated via an association with social meaning.[75] Military recruitment advertisements represent social and cultural values in similar ways to commercial advertisements but do so without selling a material object. Rather than selling a product and seeking to reach an audience interested in purchasing a particular product, military advertisers define their audience based upon whom they want as service members. For military advertisers, a sale constitutes an enlistment or a contractual commitment.[76] While the military advertising industry is concerned with procuring recruits, it is equally concerned with creating awareness and shaping perceptions of the military and military service. As military recruitment advertisements sell the possibility of military service, they also sell a broad vision of what military service and the military itself mean. In this way, recruitment advertising operates as a national form of public relations, seeking to convey to the general public a positive representation of military service, the military, and the nation. As media studies scholar Roger Stahl notes, the line between propaganda and public relations has historically been blurred, as both share the goal of persuasion and, at times, coercion.[77] Military recruitment advertising echoes many of the practical and cultural functions of commercial advertising and public relations but does so within an institution where the stakes are higher than sales numbers and profits. The military advertising industry has participated in and drawn from the broader conglomeration of connected interests that comprise the military-entertainment complex but has done so with a particular interest in identifying and targeting populations seen as recruitable.

Since the implementation of the AVF, the military advertising industry has, to varying degrees, specifically targeted women, Black Americans, and people of color in recruitment advertising. Proposals put together by advertising agencies vying for military accounts have been required to include a section dedicated to the agency's capabilities in "minority" advertising. This requirement was influenced by the implementation of civil rights laws and equal opportunity laws guiding practices in civilian agencies with government contracts. Although such laws do not have the same applicability within the military, they have contributed to a military advertising industry in which advertising agencies have long subcontracted agencies specializing in targeting "minority" groups, both to adhere to legal guidelines as well as a way to identify and target untapped markets for recruiting. Determining what target markets were included as part of "minority advertising" varied in the military advertising industry and was tied to efforts to increase the numbers of Black and Latinx officers in the wake of the Vietnam War. The category "minority" has largely been conceptualized within the military advertising with a focus on race, used to generally refer to Black and Latinx markets.[78] While women were considered to be a "minority" market in some advertising proposals, efforts to reach women recruits were seen as distinct from efforts to reach Black and Latinx markets and were more likely to be considered part of "female" advertising efforts. The practice of identifying and targeting minority groups is part of a longer-standing practice of segmented marketing at work in the advertising industry. Variously referred to as targeted marketing, segmented marketing, and ethnic marketing, the practice of focusing efforts to reach particular audiences defined by race and ethnicity through specific campaigns and publications was developed in the advertising industry in the 1960s and 1970s.[79] Driven by capitalistic views of ever-expanding markets, practices of targeted marketing were viewed as ways to broaden the pool of potential recruits and create appeals designed to speak more directly and effectively to different communities. The free market ideology behind the AVF and the capitalist ideologies of the advertising industry were structurally embedded in the newly voluntary military and laid the groundwork for industrial and representational strategies of tactical inclusion.

Tracing Tactical Inclusion

Since the implementation of the AVF in 1973, the military advertising industry has created an array of material artifacts, including recruiting plans, government reports, youth surveys, and ads, making up an empirical archive of tactical inclusion. This book focuses primarily on recruitment advertisements published between January 1973 and December 2016 in three commercial magazines: *Sports Illustrated*, *Ebony*, and *Cosmopolitan*. Each of these magazines has been targeted by the military advertising industry as crucial sites for reaching and constructing specific markets and martial identities.

Sports Illustrated was founded in 1954, gaining popularity in the mid-1960s as it began to focus on major sports, such as football, basketball, and baseball.[80] As *Sports Illustrated* grew in popularity, it was increasingly viewed not as a sports magazine but as a men's magazine. More specifically, sociologist Laurel Davis-Delano argues, in seeking to sell *Sports Illustrated* to advertisers and increase the publication's profitability, the magazine's producers structured content not solely around coverage of sports but also around a hegemonic masculine identity rooted in heterosexuality and Whiteness, as evidenced by tokenistic coverage of women's sports and the annual publication of a swimsuit issue.[81] Constructions of masculinity and representations of sports, both of which have been crucial to *Sports Illustrated,* also converge with constructions of nationalism and militarism, as noted by feminist media studies scholars Thomas P. Oates and Samantha King.[82] Brown found that recruitment advertisements published in *Sports Illustrated* were influential in constructing understandings of military masculinity during the AVF.[83] With a target market primarily consisting of straight White men and content oriented toward the consolidation of masculinity, *Sports Illustrated* has been a key publication for military recruitment advertising. In fact, recruiting plans consistently targeted *Sports Illustrated* as an effective publication for reaching a high concentration of potential recruits, specifically, young men.[84]

Recruitment advertising plans also singled out *Ebony* as a useful publication in reaching Black recruits, and recruiting ads were consistently published in *Ebony* from the 1970s to the 2010s.[85] Founded in 1945 by John H. Johnson, *Ebony* played an influential role in the emergence of a Black consumer market. *Ebony* focused on prosperous and positive facets of Black life, playing a key role in struggles over media inclusion and representation for Black Americans and offering advertisers a site for promoting products to a previously untapped revenue source.[86] In contrast to other publications like *The Crisis, Ebony* focused on upbeat stories and highlighted a Black middle-class lifestyle tied to consumption.[87] Influenced by civil rights struggles in the 1960s and 1970s, *Ebony* often portrayed a conservative vision of Black respectability tied to domesticity and heteronormativity.[88] As argued by Noliwe Rooks, *Ebony* taught readers about acceptable forms of identity based on being nonthreatening consumers and ideal citizens.[89] While balancing content portraying a middle-class lifestyle defined by consumption, domesticity, and heteronormativity with content interrogating issues of racial inequality, *Ebony* was crucial for the military advertising industry and efforts to create a market of Black recruits.

Similar to *Ebony*, *Cosmopolitan* was influential in creating a new consumer market. Following Helen Gurley Brown becoming editor in chief in 1965, *Cosmopolitan* became the first magazine to target self-sufficient working women as a consumer market.[90] *Cosmopolitan* emphasized women's changing economic and social roles and reflected women's mobility and agency through representations of Whiteness, femininity, and heteronormativity.[91] Characteristics of *Cosmopolitan*'s imagined reader, including youth, Whiteness, heterosexuality, and a desire for independence, dovetailed with how advertisers imagined and targeted women recruits, especially as recruiting ads sought to portray the military as a unique site of opportunity and independence for women. Although it has not figured as prominently in the military advertising industry as *Ebony* or *Sports Illustrated*, advertisers understood *Cosmopolitan* to be an effective publication for reaching young women.

Alongside recruitment advertisements published in *Sports Illustrated*, *Ebony*, and *Cosmopolitan*, other documents from the military advertising industry are considered, as well. As recruitment advertising moved away from print advertising to adapt to a changing media landscape, ads appeared in other media, including television, websites, and social media. Archival documents, including poster campaigns, advertising plans, and account files for advertising agencies holding military contracts, provide valuable insights into the strategies developed by advertisers in coordination with military personnel. An array of government documents, including congressional reports, General Accounting Office reports on advertising and recruiting, and military demographic reports, provides critical information on political debates about the efficacy of recruitment advertising and concerns about the composition of the armed forces. The RAND Corp., a think tank started with the goal of advancing research and development to help in military planning, has produced numerous reports on the AVF, recruitment advertising, and recruiting strategies that are further explored in the industrial strategies of tactical inclusion. Also drawn on are interviews with advertisers, specifically with advertising professionals in charge of marine corps advertising from the 1980s to the late 2010s.[92] While the primary analysis of the book focuses on print advertisements as rich cultural texts in their own right, attentiveness to additional sources accounts for the industrial and political components of cultural production and situates tactical inclusion within a broader political context.

Recruitment advertising is just one aspect of a much-larger constellation of military recruiting. Print advertisements and the other documents analyzed in this book do not represent the totality of the military advertising industry's efforts during the years between 1973 and 2016. However, print advertisements published in widely distributed magazines, such as *Sports Illustrated*, *Ebony*, and *Cosmopolitan*, played a significant role in recruitment advertising more broadly and were part of national campaigns published in other magazines and in other forms of media, including poster campaigns, billboards, and television. Although other media have figured largely in recruitment advertising in the years between 1973 and 2016, print advertising occupies a privileged site in the military advertising industry. A 1980 recruitment advertising plan developed by the J. Walter Thompson agency details how magazines had a proven track record of effectiveness for recruitment advertising and offer a response mechanism—in the form of bind-in interest cards recruits could fill out and return—that other media didn't offer at the time.[93] In the mid-1990s advertisers argued that magazines were particularly important for recruitment advertising, as research indicated magazines were an important source of information for the youth market.[94] In the 2000s, even as television and online advertising became more important to recruiting efforts, magazines still offered a broad reach at a lower cost than other media.[95] This book does not claim to provide an exhaustive account of military recruiting and recruitment advertising. Rather, it focuses on select advertisements and themes that allow for an in-depth analysis of the significant strategies and representations of tactical inclusion.

The following chapters split the forty-three years of the AVF between 1973 and 2016 into five eras and trace tactical inclusion chronologically. Each chapter engages with recruiting appeals that are not wholly distinct but, rather, that reflect the messy nature of military recruitment advertising. Some campaigns and specific ads run between and across different eras. Some ads were published numerous times over several years, whereas others appeared just once. Some themes—such as an emphasis on educational opportunities—appear in different guises and were featured in recruiting ads for various branches throughout the AVF. Other themes and slogans emerged quickly and then were abruptly dropped. The fluctuation in themes, appeals, and slogans and across branches of the military can be attributed to the complex nature of the military advertising industry.

Each branch of the military guides its own recruitment advertising and awards contracts to different civilian agencies. Recruitment and advertisement budgets fluctuate based on congressional spending measures each year, and advertising contracts must be reviewed and renewed every two or three years. Some branches of the military have maintained consistent slogans, themes, and advertising campaigns throughout the AVF. The most consistent has been the marine corps, which has had the same civilian advertising partner, the J. Walter Thompson agency—renamed Wunderman-Thompson following a merger in 2018—since the 1940s and has maintained an emphasis on toughness, manliness, and the elite nature of the corps throughout its recruiting appeals. In contrast, other branches have had numerous civilian advertising partners and a variety of slogans and campaigns throughout the AVF. Advertisers regularly discussed how the various branches of the military competed with one another to reach potential recruits and imitated and copied appeals found in other recruiting materials. At the same time, each branch of the military has attempted, with varying degrees of success, to develop a unique brand image and target different kinds of recruits. The following chapters provide an account of the strategies and representations of tactical inclusion as the military has sought to meet its personnel needs.

The first two chapters focus on the years between 1973 and 1991, during which recruiting ads largely emphasized tangible benefits of enlisting. Advertising benefits of military service, including wages, employment, vocational training, technical training, and educational opportunities, was crucial to the implementation of the AVF as was expanding the pool of potential recruits. The first chapter, "We'll Hire You," focuses on the early years of the AVF from 1973 through 1980. Driven by an unprecedented investment in advertising, practices and strategies of recruitment advertising defined military service in relation to the labor market, a process I refer to as marketization. Marketization emphasizes what the military can do for potential recruits. Advertisers portrayed joining the military as comparable to working a civilian job, a well-paid, safe opportunity. Coupled with a need to expand the recruiting market, three figures—the soldier laborer, martial feminist, and good Black soldier—were constructed to portray the newly voluntary military as a solution to problems of economic stagnation, sexism, and racism. In doing so, recruitment ads framed the military as able to recuperate some working-class men, White women, and Black men from the margins of the labor market and transform them into successful economic citizens.

Chapter 2, "America at Its Best," focuses on recruiting strategies and representations from 1980 through 1991. Guided by the influence of marketization and a continued need to expand the market of potential recruits, advertisers made a series of strategic adjustments and portrayed the military not as an institution that offered opportunities to those in need but, rather, as an exceptional institution that strengthened the nation. Recruitment advertisements rearticulated the meaning of military benefits to emphasize what the military did for the nation. Framed as a corrective to perceptions of the increasingly racially and gender diverse military as low quality, recruitment advertisements emphasized a remasculinized and reinvigorated military, where ambitious and hard-working service members earned the benefits they received and were exemplars of America's global might. Through a variety of different figures, including high-tech soldiers, martial capitalists, and proud military families, recruitment advertisements showed how technology, meritocracy, and heteronormativity were indicative of a strong military and strong nation. Representations of an exceptional military were part of a cohesive project of Reagan-era capitalist democracy that bolstered claims to U.S. global hegemony and provided justifications for conservative gender and sexual politics and attacks on social welfare and affirmative action programs.

The next three chapters focus on the years between 1992 and 2016, during which advertisers were forced to grapple with the reality and visibility of war as an aspect of military service to an extent not seen in earlier decades of the AVF. Influenced initially by the Persian Gulf War and later by the war on terror, recruitment advertisements shifted toward appeals touting transformation and more intangible benefits of military service, like pride and confidence. Alongside the pressures of war, advertisers also had to continue to expand the market of potential recruits and respond to increasing cultural pressures to emphasize multiculturalism and diversity.

Chapter 3, "The Military Type," explores advertisers' efforts during the years between 1992 and 2000 to construct a multicultural military and create new military types in the wake of the Persian Gulf War. In response to the war, which at the time was the largest and most visible military intervention since the implementation of the AVF, policy changes related to gender and sexuality, and a broader industrial and cultural emphasis on multiculturalism, advertisers created ads showing how enlisting would and would not transform Black men, Latinx men, and women. Based on an embrace of combat in recruiting appeals and a push to portray the military as racially diverse, recruiting ads promised Black men and Latinx men a transformative experience, in which they could become embodiments of state authority and warrior patriots. In contrast, ads touting new positions for women emphasized how the military would not transform women but, rather, would allow and require them to remain recognizable as women within gender normativity and narratives of hetero-romance. Through representations of a military welcoming of new military types, recruitment advertising in the 1990s set the stage for portraying a multicultural military dedicated to humanitarian military operations in the Balkans, Haiti, and Somalia and around the world.

Turning to the eight years between 2000 and 2008, chapter 4, "Make the World a Better Place," interrogates how advertisers sought to provide military service with a set of compelling meanings prior to and during the war on terror. Influenced by the dismal state of recruiting in the late 1990s, subsequently made even worse by unpopular wars in Afghanistan and Iraq, recruitment ads emphasized what the military did for the world through representations of multicultural benevolence. Multicultural benevolence is a gendered and racialized formation in which representations of the military were framed as evidence of the military's moral superiority, guided by dual commitments to inclusion and humanitarianism. Images and narratives of racial inclusion, heteropatriotism, and racialized martial maternity were brought together in recruiting ads that allowed the military advertising industry to target recruits of color and provide military service with a sense of moral superiority. Recruiting ads in the 2000s revealed the paradox of tactical inclusion, in which new martial figures including Black women, multiracial martial families, and exceptional Black service members became visible as violence, combat, and death in war were increasingly a defining aspect of military service.

Focusing on the years between 2009 and 2016, chapter 5, "Walls Always Fall," explores the emergence of militarized diversity, which refers to the melding of military violence with official commitments to diversity. Shortly after his election in 2008, President Barack Obama began instituting policies opening the military ranks in unprecedented ways as part of a larger emphasis on inclusion and diversity as national imperatives. Militarized diversity was embraced as an industrial strategy and representational logic in recruiting materials that detailed what diversity did for the military. Through official language, production logics, and representations, diversity was espoused as emblematic of American exceptionalism, leveraged to reach out to an array of recruits and promoted as a justification for the ongoing war on terror. Influenced by the end of bans against women in combat and against openly gay, lesbian, bisexual, and transgender service members, recruitment efforts constructed narratives of postgender militarism and homomartial pride, both of which revealed how militarized diversity was crafted through continued investments in masculinist violence and the policing of a rigid gender binary. As the culmination of tactical inclusion, militarized diversity exposed the operationalization of inclusion and diversity not as realizations of equality or liberation but as war-fighting imperatives.

The conclusion, "Beyond Tactical Inclusion," reflects on the stakes and consequences of tactical inclusion. Under the Donald J. Trump administration and Trumpism, valorization of the military and fetishism of state violence have been key facets of White nationalist, xenophobic, misogynist, and antiqueer politics seeking to "make America great again." In contrast to vehemently exclusionary policies and rhetoric, the military has been held up as an institution committed to diversity and inclusion. Focusing on three select events taking place in the summer of 2020—the role the military played in state responses to Black Lives Matter protests, a statement issued by graduates of West Point calling for an antiracist military academy, and the murder of Vanessa Guillen—the conclusion grapples with the resonances of tactical inclusion and the consequences of a decades-long project to sell military inclusion as the realized promise of equality.

CHAPTER 1

We'll Hire You

An army ad published in *Cosmopolitan* in August 1974 shows a classroom full of soldiers at Fort Jackson, South Carolina, and calls recruits to "[j]oin the people who've joined the Army." The group of smiling soldiers shows how advertisers represented the newly all-volunteer army. The new army, pictured a year after the last American combat troops left Vietnam and following civil rights and equal rights legislation in the 1960s and 1970s, is a diverse coalition bound together by the pursuit of the same opportunities. Smiling soldiers sit together harmoniously in the safety of a classroom in South Carolina, a sharp contrast to the violence of combat in Vietnam and pervasive racial violence within the military just years earlier. The ad asks recruits to take their place in an army that is newly committed not to warfare but to helping young Americans get an education and good jobs.

Such a message is a far cry from recruiting ads featuring strong, heroic figures and patriotic appeals published during World War II and the Korean War.[1] Rather, we see a variety of young Americans—including women and men, Black soldiers and White soldiers—seated in a classroom, bound together not by a desire to serve their country but by a desire to get a college education. While recruiting ads have made appeals based on the benefits of military service since the late 1800s,[2] the implementation of the AVF aligned such appeals with a new model of military service in which, according to Bailey, "the logic of citizenship was replaced with the logic of the market."[3]

This shift towards the market was evident in the ad as it states, "You may join to learn a good job, to work in interesting places around the world, or to do something meaningful for your Country." A sense of national duty isn't entirely absent, but is last in a list of possible motivations for joining the army. The implementation of the AVF in 1973 catalyzed a trend in which recruiting ads, driven by insights from advertisers, increasingly embraced tenets of the free market. Such ads defined military service in relation to the labor market, a process I refer to as marketization. As a fundamental logic of the AVF and a crucial form of tactical inclusion, marketization led to recruiting appeals emphasizing what the military could do for potential recruits, rather than what recruits could do for their country.

Advertisers claim that the shift to the AVF was a surrender to the free market, in which power shifted from the military to potential recruits, whose views, attitudes, and goals became increasingly influential in shaping recruiting materials.[4] Narratives of choice, in which recruits could choose to enlist to get a good job, a good education, and a shot at upward mobility, proliferated in recruiting ads. The military's appeal, then, was its ability to hire, train, and educate American youth. Balancing broad appeals highlighting the market value of military service with specific appeals targeting working-class men, women, and Black recruits, advertisers constructed a vision of enlisting in the military as a way to combat economic, gendered, and racialized precarity. The army ad discussed above exemplifies how advertisers combined marketization with visions of an inclusive army as part of multipronged strategy to reach potential recruits, expand target markets, and reassert the military's legitimacy in the wake of the war in Vietnam and social movements advocating for racial and gender equality.

Beginning with a discussion of the marketization of military service as a trend consolidated both through representations in ads and strategies at work in the military advertising industry, this chapter explores tactical inclusion during the early years of the AVF. Driven by a newfound investment in advertising as a crucial tool for navigating the consumer market, ads targeted recruits through appeals based on wages, jobs, and upward mobility. Guided by recruiting plans designating vulnerable groups as persuadable recruits, recruiting ads sought to balance a historical investment in Whiteness and masculinity with the need to present military service as an economic opportunity to a broad array of potential recruits. Attempts to strike this balance led advertisers to represent the military as helping potential recruits by offering specific forms of assistance to different groups. Military service was represented as a way for men to gain economic security and as a site of equality and opportunity for women and Black men. Such representations resulted in the construction of three figures—the soldier laborer, the martial feminist, and the good Black soldier—each of whom aided the military in reaching particular target groups. Faced with an unprecedented need to persuade eligible recruits to join the military and to bolster public support for a military whose image was burdened with the practical and moral failures of the Vietnam War, text-heavy recruiting ads spelled out what military service could do for potential recruits. Joining the military could transform one's material conditions and could, ostensibly, play a role in remedying inequality. By portraying the military as a purveyor of opportunities rather than as a potentially deadly risk through convergent narratives of marketization and equal opportunity, recruiting ads set the stage for tactical inclusion as an industrial and representational strategy in the newly voluntary military.

The Marketization of Military Service

In the first year of the AVF, 405,000 Americans enlisted in the active-duty military, and by 1980 over 3 million enlistees had joined the newly voluntary military.[5] Many individuals chose to join the military, when for the first time since the 1940s they had the choice not to, as recruiting ads promoted military service as a net benefit for potential recruits. Marketization portrayed military service as a safe job, comparable with a job in the civilian sector, but set apart through a generous set of benefits, including skills training and educational opportunities. In doing so, marketization functioned to depoliticize military service and shifted representations of enlisting from a risk or duty to an economic opportunity. Marketization aided tactical inclusion by reaching out to a variety of recruits and framing military service as a first step in the pathway toward successful economic citizenship.

Enabled by the structure of the AVF and furthered by marketization, military service was no longer viewed as an obligation of citizenship but, rather, as a job.[6] This is not to say that links to citizenship were entirely severed, but they were rearticulated. Marketization envisioned military service as generative of productive citizenship marked by full participation in a capitalist economy. Recruiting ads promised a host of material and economic benefits that would direct service members toward productive and prosperous futures. Strategies and representations in recruitment advertising dictated the limits of how one could be included in the newly voluntary military, creating a view of military service as a limited pathway of recuperation for those facing economic precarity in the civilian labor market. Such a view of military service was constructed within a recruiting environment characterized by competing tensions as military officials, free-market advocates, and advertisers sought to define what military service meant in the new AVF.

Broadly speaking, military officials and free-market advocates clashed in their views of military benefits. Benefits of military service, including housing, health care, and educational programs that had previously been viewed as rewards for patriotic service, though targeted for cuts by free-market advocates, were recast by advertisers as enticements to lure potential recruits.[7] Advertisers saw military benefits as valuable incentives that needed to be made visible and largely embraced a view of military service as a job. Military officials, wanting to provide their soldiers with a sense of security, strongly opposed cuts to military benefits and were also resistant to the categorization of military service as a job.[8] As advertising became an increasingly important tool in persuading potential recruits, advertising agencies, including the J. Walter Thompson agency; N. W. Ayer; Bates and Co.; and D'Arcy, McManus, and Masius, utilized language of target markets, sales messages, and advertising awareness to discuss recruiting.

There was a tension among advertisers as they debated how to create unique brand images for the different branches of the military through what military sociologist Charles C. Moskos would later call institutional and occupational appeals.[9] Occupational appeals frame military service as a job by highlighting tangible benefits like wages whereas institutional appeals focus on intangible benefits like transformation. Occupational appeals are broad, seeking to reach a variety of different recruits by highlighting the same material benefits available throughout the military. Institutional appeals are limited, seeking to reach those desiring transformation and speaking most directly to those motivated by patriotism and service. As the largest branch of the military, and the branch in need of the most new recruits, the army overwhelmingly utilized occupational appeals to expand its target market. As Brown notes, the navy and air force similarly drew on occupational appeals in recruiting efforts in the 1970s.[10] Mirroring concerns raised by military officials and reflecting their branch culture, the marine corps was more hesitant about adopting occupational appeals and melded references to wages and benefits with largely institutional appeals based on a brand image of elitism and transformation.

While there were nuances across the brand images for the different branches, the military advertising industry as a whole embraced marketization through references to wages, jobs, and the future life military service could lead to. One in five ads in *Sports Illustrated*, *Ebony*, and *Cosmopolitan* between 1973 and 1980 detail the wages one could earn in the military, and one in three ads reference jobs. Such references contributed to views of the military as a first step on the path to upward mobility and a remedy to economic precarity.

Publicizing wages was an absolute necessity in persuading recruits. An emphasis on competitive wages was vital to the structure of the AVF and part of a multipronged effort meant to make military service more appealing to youth.[11] Advertisers saw the civilian labor force as the greatest form of indirect competition faced by recruiters and found that pay and steady employment were the most important occupational goals for their target market.[12] Ads, including for the army, coast guard, and navy, told recruits about starting salaries and take-home pay, which ranged from just over $300 a month in 1973 to upwards of $400 a month in 1980. Other ads, including those for reserve and guard units, similarly emphasized the wages recruits could earn. Ads emphasized military pay as better than ever, telling young recruits they would start with good salaries and could earn more over the course of their service.

Military service was represented as an exciting opportunity that came with a specific dollar amount. For potential recruits faced with economic insecurity, a reliable monthly wage was a tangible remedy and could be weighed against other opportunities. Recruiting ads gave military service a concrete market value that could justify enlisting as a financially motivated decision and insulate potential recruits from criticism by groups and individuals who had opposed the war in Vietnam. In the midst of an economic recession, parents and friends of potential recruits could support military service as a mode of obtaining economic independence or as a practical decision. In short, wages depoliticized military service, facilitating a form of tacit support for military service that could be justified as a primarily financial decision. One didn't have to be a patriot who wanted to be a soldier but could want or need a good job with steady pay and, as such, be willing to be a soldier.

Additionally, starting wages in the military were equal for all recruits, regardless of race or gender. While racism and sexism certainly shaped opportunities for advancement once in the military, for potential recruits the appeal of equal wages—which were a key selling point in ads targeting women, as will be discussed in more detail—could have functioned as a point of contrast with a civilian job market characterized by a large gendered and racialized pay gap that privileged White men.[13] The pervasiveness of appeals touting wages framed the choice to enlist as an economically motivated decision based on presumptions of the military as an equal playing field.

Discussing military service as a job, as a site of attainable and desirable employment, was fundamental to marketization. Air force ads told potential recruits to "[p]oint for a job with stretch and elbowroom" and that if you enlist, "[y]ou'll wind up with a rewarding job." Similarly, ads for the army told recruits to reach out to a recruiter if "you are looking for a good job" and asked recruits to "consider a job with today's Army." Ads for reserve units of the air force and army regularly referred to serving as "the most important part-time job in America."

The emphasis on referring to military service as a job reveals an important point of contrast between advertisers and military personnel. As noted by historian Jennifer Mittelstadt, military officials saw military service as an honorable and elevated way of life distinct from civilian employment.[14] Advertisers, guided by market research and an ethos informed by commercial advertising in which ads should speak directly to the desires of potential recruits, were much more comfortable portraying military service as comparable to a civilian job. Comparability, though anathema to military officials, was a crucial way advertisers could emphasize the market value of enlisting and portray the military as a safe and beneficial site of employment. A series of ads for the Army Reserve in *Ebony* and *Cosmopolitan* reveal the ways comparability was represented in recruiting ads while conveying ideas about gender (see fig. 1.1).

The ads framed service in the reserve as a second job for a variety of different recruits—including Black women and men, women and men of color, and White women and men. The ads detail a variety of occupations with clear civilian analogues recruits could choose from to gain valuable training for the civilian job market. Service members aren't referred to as soldiers but as repairmen, typists, medical lab specialists, and computer programmers. The ads portray a military where a variety of jobs were available, while revealing that not all jobs could, or should, be done by every type of service member. Women are shown working as computer programmers, military police, and radio operators, occupations that push against the gendered division of labor in the military.[15] Men, and men alone, are shown filling positions as carpenters, bulldozer operators, and repairmen, coinciding with Brown's findings linking machinery skills to constructions of militarized masculinity.[16] Additionally, no men were shown working in clerical positions or as food specialists, making clear that while military women might be able to seek out new opportunities and take on new roles, military men certainly wouldn't be taking on any "woman's work." Although marketization was based on a view of a value-neutral and equalizing market, recruiting ads reveal that the market value of military service remained bound to the gendered dynamics of the military.

Historically, the military maintained strict divisions between White men and other service members through policies of racial and gender segregation. That the two Army Reserve ads pictured in figure 1.1 and other similar ads were published in *Ebony* and *Cosmopolitan* speaks to the ways strategies of targeted advertising might have functioned to maintain gendered divisions

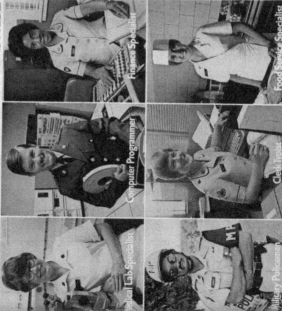

Figure 1.1. Army Reserve ads. Sources: *Ebony*, August 1976; *Cosmopolitan*, April 1976

while portraying the military as inclusive. The readership of those two publications—primarily Black people and White women—were presumed to be most receptive to visions of military service as a job open to variety of different people, whereas one can surmise that advertisers thought readers of *Sports Illustrated* might be dissuaded by such an appeal that, in the view of military officials, degraded military service.

That the ads were also able to maintain a gendered division—though seemingly not a racial division—between men and women without referencing combat, as the long held ideological center of the military most closely tied to masculine authority and power, speaks to a broader push within marketization to portray military service as a safe opportunity and rearticulations of military masculinity.[17] The Army Reserve ads show a military devoid of firearms, weaponry, and combat; even images of military police don't clearly show a firearm. Ads published throughout the early years of the AVF overwhelmingly portrayed the military as a safe opportunity for potential recruits.

Ads for the air force and army show recruits in civilian clothes on their days off and visiting tourist sites while serving in Europe. Other ads for the marines, the most combat-oriented branch of the armed forces, feature images of marines posing at the base of the Eiffel Tower and turn to images of sports, rather than combat, to tout the elite and competitive nature of the corps. Part of portraying the military as a safe opportunity entailed emphasizing benefits oriented toward life after military service. While a number of scholars have pointed to the links between discourses of military service and upward mobility,[18] such links were particularly important in assuring the success of the early AVF. By framing military service as a way to access a second job, higher education, or a job-training course, advertisers were able to distance military service from lingering connections with risks of death in combat. Recruiting ads constructed a vision of military service oriented toward a future life, an important orientation for groups who disproportionately bore the risks of combat and had faced the very real possibility of not surviving the war in Vietnam.

In the wake of a war during which the military was rightly accused of exploiting Black, Latinx, poor and working-class men and sending them to their deaths, recruiting ads portrayed military service as leading to a better life. Military service was represented as an economic benefit, both immediate and deferred, that could help American youth get good jobs, get ahead, and improve their lives. The military was represented as generative of successful citizenship via the choice to enlist and the subsequent ability to fully and effectively participate in a capitalist economy.

Marketization allowed advertisers to reach a broad array of potential recruits with a similar message: the military offers economic benefits to anyone who makes the choice to enlist. In this way, appeals touting competitive wages, steady employment, and upward mobility were ostensibly inclusive; they targeted and appealed to anyone who wanted better pay or needed a good job or the means to access an education. Marketization emphasized a vision of recruiting based not on qualities, like patriotism and duty, held by potential recruits but by opportunities recruits *didn't* have. This orientation led advertisers to recognize that those who they most desired as potential recruits—White men—might not be as easily persuaded as other groups and to develop strategies to define and target new markets who might be more easily persuaded. Historically, economic privilege has functioned to shield certain groups—namely, elite White men—from military service.[19] Marketization solidified the option for elite White men to opt out of military service, doing so under the guise of a neutral market where any inequitable distribution of military service could be attributed to individual choices. At the same time, marketization contributed to a proliferation of strategies to define and target groups vulnerable to recruiting appeals.

Surveys of potential recruits, the development of different target markets, and detailed recruiting plans all relied on transforming difference into valuable information for advertisers. Advertising plans contained detailed subplans for reaching different target markets delineated by gender, and information about age, geography, education, and race was used to inform creative strategy and media placement of recruiting ads.[20] While using information to differentiate between target markets and inform advertising strategies certainly wasn't new to the advertising industry and advertisers had for years used demographics and survey research to inform recruitment advertising efforts, such industrial practices gained a new meaning in the initial years of the AVF. Strategies rooted in marketization exploited the dynamics of labor under capitalism in which gender, race, and sexuality marked some groups as surplus labor, as excluded from the rights and privilege of first-class citizenship.[21] Marketization portrayed military service as a way to become successful economic citizens and recuperated some of those defined as surplus labor as potential service members, able to counter their place at the margins by choosing to enlist in the military.

Soldier Laborers

Recruiting appeals targeting and featuring men had to respond to the new realities of the AVF. Without the assistance of the draft, the military advertising industry was faced with a need to reach previously excluded groups while maintaining a symbolic imperative of the newly voluntary military as an institution still defined by masculine ideals. Martial abilities and the ability to both withstand and enact violence play an influential role in constructing ideals of military masculinity and of masculinity more broadly.[22] Sociologist R. W. Connell, in her groundbreaking work on masculinities, argues that the military has been absolutely crucial in defining hegemonic masculinity in American culture.[23]

Recruiting ads in the early years of the AVF portrayed military masculinity beyond associations with violence and combat. Brown's insightful study of recruiting ads found that different military branches constructed masculine ideals variously emphasizing combat, technology, business acumen, and other traits that aided in constructing distinct brand images in relation to institutional traditions and personnel needs.[24] More specifically, ads for the army sought to emphasize economic opportunities and other benefits associated with enlisting through imagery focusing on groups of men.[25] Brown contends that such representations facilitated an image of the army as a place where one could "become a man but not in the sense of an initiation rite—more in the sense of growing up, becoming responsible, gaining an economic foothold, and maturing."[26] While these various narratives are important for thinking about military masculinity, the notion of gaining an economic foothold is particularly important for the emergence of soldier laborers, a key figure in marketization.

The majority of representations in the early years of the AVF did not show military men proving their ability to fight or endure combat but, rather, their ability to take advantage of available opportunities to better position themselves in the labor market. Such representations were particularly salient in the early years of the AVF, following a critical view of soldiering that emerged during the Vietnam War driven by high rates of casualties, media coverage of the violence of the war, antiwar sentiment, and opposition to the draft. As such, warrior masculinity had little appeal in attracting many potential recruits or portraying a positive view of the military among the general public. Within the context of marketization, advertisers focused on economic opportunities to speak directly to men as an important target market and portray the military as a remedy to a convergent set of economic vulnerabilities and gendered anxieties.

The figure of the soldier laborer was exemplified in an army ad published in *Sports Illustrated* in March 1973 (see fig. 1.2). The ad featured a headline asking, "When was the last time you got promoted?" Four men—three White and one Black—are pictured on a loading dock, with hand trucks,

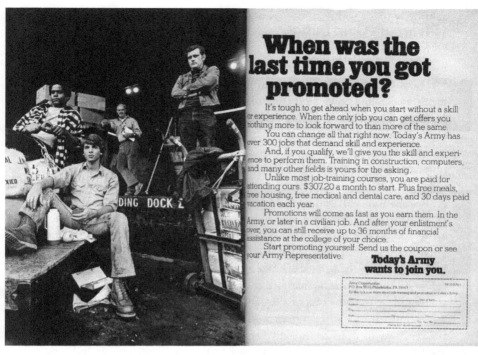

Figure 1.2. Army ad. Source: *Sports Illustrated*, March 12, 1973

pallets, and boxes surrounding them. All four of the men are wearing civilian clothes as they stare, straight-faced, at the camera. Text states, "It's tough to get ahead when you start without a skill or experience. When the only job you can get offers you nothing more to look forward to than more of the same. You can change all that right now. Today's Army has over 300 jobs that demand skill and experience." These men, on a break from their blue-collar jobs, are in need of something unavailable in the civilian labor market. These men want and need a job that can help them get ahead or get promoted, a job in the army. The ad frames military service as an attainable and beneficial job opportunity and constructs potential recruits as soldier laborers, a figure shaped by the realities of recruiting practices defined by economic vulnerability.

The initial years of the AVF coincided with the worst economic recession since the 1930s and followed the close of what Ruth Wilson Gilmore calls the golden age of U.S. capitalism.[27] Among the military advertising industry's coveted sixteen- to twenty-four-year-old demographic, unemployment in the mid-1970s was among the highest of any time period during the AVF. The ad acknowledges the difficulties young men faced, representing them as down and out. Military masculinity, then, is defined not by service to country or heroism in combat but, rather, by a feeling of economic disenfranchisement, by images of men left behind in a faltering economy and a changing workforce. Ads touting jobs for men in need framed military service as a way to regain masculine power and control not readily on offer in the civilian world. Military service was represented as a way for a young man to gain valuable experience and to change his life.

The ad portrays the army as a unique institution, able to provide secure employment opportunities men struggled to find in the civilian world: "Training in construction, computers, and many other fields is yours for the asking. . . . Promotions will come as fast as you earn them. In the Army, or later in a civilian job." In contrast to a job market where opportunities were scarce, the army offered young men an abundance of training and promotions. Part of what made a job in the army unique was a generous set of military benefits, including meals, health care, housing, and paid vacation, which Mittelstadt refers to as the military-welfare state.[28] The military-welfare state helped shape public perceptions of the AVF as a secure and comfortable employment opportunity in a stagnant economy and as an important first step on the pathway to upward mobility and successful economic citizenship. The army was not promising to turn these young men into warriors, fighters, or soldiers but, rather, into well-trained, successful workers.

Soldier laborers were promised both economic and gendered fulfillment in the army. Soldier laborers distinguished themselves from other men by enacting a form of military masculinity wherein dominance and control were not articulated via associations with combat and patriotic service but, rather, through success in the civilian labor market. This form of masculinity was inclusive of both White and Black men. Like many recruiting ads published in the early years of the AVF, we see the token inclusion of a Black man. Black men and White men were portrayed as sharing the same gendered and economic position, and racial difference was subsumed within the figure of the soldier laborer. Advertisers made choices to emphasize certain messages and target certain audiences, balancing broad appeals based on marketization and economic vulnerability with specific appeals that were defined by race or gender. In doing so, the token inclusion of a Black man and an overall emphasis on Whiteness in the ad reveals that advertisers weren't unaware of a need to create a somewhat racially inclusive vision of military service, but they did so within a context where White men were viewed as the norm and the most desirable recruits. The ad demonstrates how men's shared experiences defined by gender and class were prioritized over possible differing experiences based on race.

The figure of the soldier laborer acknowledged and highlighted economic vulnerability as a key aspect of men's experiences in the 1970s while also framing the military as the remedy to that vulnerability. This rearticulation of vulnerability as something the military helps counter rather than something the military exposes one to was crucial to marketization, especially when targeting men, who months earlier could have been drafted and sent to Vietnam. The soldier laborer showed how representations of young working-class men—including both White and Black men—who were already included in the military and overrepresented in the draft, meant something different in the AVF. The new AVF wasn't exploiting the young men or sending them to war as cannon fodder, it was giving them an opportunity they couldn't find elsewhere. This rhetorical and representational shift relied on an industrial logic based on and exploitive of economic inequality and vulnerability. Obfuscating the inequitable distribution of the risks and consequences of state violence, representations of soldier laborers framed being included in the military not as a duty or a potential risk but a choice and an opportunity. The figure of the soldier laborer was crucial in portraying the military as an institution that could bolster bona fides of manliness for men while promising them a future of productive economic citizenship rather than exposing them to risks of violence and death.

Martial Feminists

The participation of women was crucial to the success of the AVF and its implementation has arguably been the most influential policy leading to women's increased military inclusion. The almost fourfold growth in the percentage of active-duty military women between 1973 and 1980 helped the military meet personnel needs and increased the total number of active-duty military women by 106,000. Influenced by the passage of the Equal Rights Amendment (ERA) and legal cases that pushed for increased rights and equality for military women, by the late 1970s policies gave women access to military academies and did away with separate, all-women branches of the military.[29] The military recognized that women's participation could help make the AVF a success but were concerned with how an increase in military women might disrupt an institution dominated by men and masculinity and raise doubts about the military's legitimacy as a warfighting organization. As such, the military made plans to increase the numbers of servicewomen but, ultimately, saw women making up little more than 10 percent of the total active-duty force.[30] In the first four years of the AVF, the air force and navy agreed to triple their numbers of servicewomen, the army agreed to double their numbers, and the marine corps, though resistant, agreed to a 20 percent increase of women marines.[31] These goals were driven, at least in part, by a concern that there would be a lack of White male recruits.[32] In the midst of these changes, the military advertising industry developed an ambivalent approach to recruiting women.

Advertisers targeted women in publications like *Cosmopolitan*, *Harper's Bazaar*, and *Essence*. Some ads featured military women alongside military men, whereas other ads focused exclusively on women. While publication of ads in *Essence* indicated a desire to reach Black women, efforts to reach women recruits, a category mostly associated with White women, were largely conceptualized as separate from efforts to reach Black recruits. Focusing mostly on images of blonde, White, upwardly mobile women, ads published in *Cosmopolitan* implicated the military as a way for women to fulfill complementary goals of femininity, heteronormativity, and financial independence. Recruiting ads also represented the army as a unique site of equality, a place where young women could access opportunities unavailable elsewhere. Together, recruiting ads targeting women in the early years of the AVF portrayed military women as martial feminists.

Drawing on research indicating that recruiting ads should try to appeal to women's desires for equal opportunities,[33] ads framed the army as a crucial actor in the realization of liberal feminism, casting enlisting as a way to fulfill the promise of equal rights, specifically in terms of equal pay and benefits. By tempering claims to equality and opportunity with an emphasis on the femininity of military women, recruiting ads tethered representations of martial feminists to the prevailing gendered and sexualized norms of an institution steeped in rigid heteronormativity. Martial feminists, characterized by discourses of equality, heteronormative femininity, and the token inclusion of Black women, marked the military advertising industry's attempts to reach out to women and assure the general public that women would retain their femininity as they became soldiers. Cast in a tension between inclusion and regulation, representations of martial feminists were influenced by historical anxieties about military women and were carefully deployed to not overly disrupt the rigidly masculinist image of the military.

Women have long faced a complex negotiation of gender and sexuality in the military. Military women considered to be too feminine were seen as incapable of meeting the demands of a masculine institution, while women perceived as too masculine were viewed as transgressing gender norms and labeled as lesbians, a label that prior to 2010 could, and often did, result in being dishonorably discharged.[34] In her groundbreaking work on gender and militarization, Enloe contends that militaries have long relied on women and sought to control ideas about femininity, something long apparent in recruiting appeals.[35] As women were increasingly included in the mobilization for World War II, military personnel were concerned with shaping perceptions of the femininity and heterosexuality of military women in the face of critics who used accusations of sexual promiscuity, lesbianism, and gender transgression to discredit women's service.[36] As noted by historian Loren Miller, recruiting ads during World War II represented military women as paradigms of a new ideal of American femininity based on feminine appearance, Whiteness, self-interest, and consumerism, a configuration Miller refers to as martial glamour.[37] Recruiting ads published in the early years of the AVF inherited this history and sought to assure potential recruits and the general public that military women remained recognizable as women first and as soldiers second. To be clear, recruiting ads were less concerned with addressing the actual challenges military women faced than with resolving representational tensions that might threaten the military's legitimacy as an institution defined by manliness.

Representations of martial feminists were primarily featured in *Cosmopolitan* rather than in *Ebony* or *Sports Illustrated*. The selective placement of such appeals utilized segmented marketing and allowed the military to bolster its credibility among young women while not undermining its legitimacy among young men who might have viewed a gender-equitable military as less worthy of consideration. Martial feminists were represented exclusively in ads for the army and Army Reserve. As Brown contends, the army was the branch of the military most willing to feature women in recruiting materials and utilize women in their ranks.[38] Facing the greatest challenge in meeting personnel needs following the end of the draft, the army fully embraced marketization, which necessitated representing how different groups, including women, could benefit from joining the military. Ads emphasized that although there wasn't anything unique about women that made them good soldiers,[39] there was something unique about the army that was good for women.

In the first three years of the AVF, army and Army Reserve ads in *Cosmopolitan* showed military service as a way for young, White women to find careers and be financially independent. Ads targeted young women by telling them the army was the way to "take home a brand new career," "live away from home and afford it," and live "free and easy the way you always wanted." By focusing on appeals rooted in independence and professional aspirations, ads appropriated the figure of the "Cosmo girl," a fictionalized woman invented as the magazine's imagined reader in the 1960s.[40] *Cosmopolitan* targeted single working women and showed them as having needs and desires, both in terms of work and sex, that couldn't be met in the domestic sphere.[41] Feminist scholars have debated whether *Cosmopolitan* has subverted patriarchal ideologies, particularly about sex, or reinforced oppressive structures of power tied to gender, race, and class.[42] Rather than make an argument that *Cosmopolitan* and the recruiting ads featured in its pages functioned either as subversive or oppressive, I contend that the ambivalence of the Cosmo girl, a figure bound to normative ideals of White, heteronormative femininity that also challenged women's relegation to the domestic sphere, was productive for recruitment advertising, facilitating a portrayal of the military as a site of opportunity and regulation for young women.

Women represented in recruiting ads in *Cosmopolitan* overwhelmingly adhered to a specific aesthetic. Images of a smiling young, blonde, White woman were featured in ads framing the Army Reserve as a great way for women to learn professional skills for a career (see fig. 1.3). Women were often represented in civilian settings or through two paired images, one of a woman in military uniform and another of the same woman in civilian clothing, highlighting the temporary nature of military service for women. Military service was framed as a vocational opportunity, a pathway to a successful civilian career and a way to fulfill professional desires central to the Cosmo girl. At the same time, images made clear that only a certain kind of woman—young, blonde, White—was encouraged to see herself taking advantage of military opportunities. Feminist media studies scholar Laurie Ouellette argues that *Cosmopolitan* offered women class-specific positions that legitimated capitalism and encouraged women to view a reworking of their own identity as a route to upward mobility.[43] Recruiting ads functioned similarly, portraying martial feminists as fulfilling classed narratives of upward mobility by choosing to join the army and meeting expectations of heteronormative femininity.

Although the military has long been weary of portraying military women as overly sexual, recruiting ads promoted heteronormativity. An ad in *Cosmopolitan* in April 1973 makes clear that heterosexuality was a key facet of life for military women. The army ad features an image of a young White woman on "a dinner date in Chinatown," seated at a dinner table across from a young White man. They are smiling at each other. A date with a male partner was pictured as the culmination of a day off for a young woman stationed in San Francisco, California, and part of the appeal of a life of financial independence and romantic opportunities enabled by the military.

Figure 1.3. Army Reserve ad. Source: *Cosmopolitan*, February 1973

In the context of recruiting ads, women's desires to achieve independence and adhere to norms of heteronormative femininity were best achieved by joining the military. The particular contours of martial feminists signaled the concurrent desires of *Cosmopolitan* and the military, both of whom wanted young, White, straight, upwardly mobile women as their target market.

In the early 1970s, at a time when military women still served in a separate, all-women branch of the army, the women's army corps, one of the biggest challenges of reaching women recruits was overcoming a view of the military as an institution only for men. In seeking to do so, ads for the army emphasized that the army was uniquely committed to equality. An army ad in *Cosmopolitan* in 1973 and 1974 features a headline asking, "Did the last good job you wanted go to a man?" The text responds, "If it did, maybe it's because you've been looking in the wrong places. Today's Army has more than 300 good jobs for young women as well as young men. Both get the same starting salary. The same opportunities and raises. The same benefits. We'll train you to do the job you want, and we'll pay you while you learn" (see fig. 1.4). Similar to other ads from the time period, the appeal begins

Figure 1.4. Army ad. Source: *Cosmopolitan*, August 1973

with the premise that potential recruits were struggling in the civilian job market. Joining the military was framed as an employment opportunity, a way for women to access equal opportunities unlike the "wrong places" outside the military. In contrast to representations of soldier laborers, the difficulty women faced wasn't economic stagnation but sexism. Yet, the army is still the solution.

Enlisting in the army was good for women because the army believed in gender parity: military women get the same wages, opportunities, raises, and benefits as military men. In other words, joining the army could help women simultaneously combat patriarchal and economic vulnerability. While it seems implausible—and would have been against military policy at the time—to have an ad asking women if the last opportunity to be a war hero or become a decorated combat veteran had gone to a man, asking women about their experiences in the civilian labor market emphasized comparability between military service and civilian employment. The distinction between the two was that in the army women were purportedly treated as equals to men. As noted by Ahmed, discourses of equality can be marketing tools driven by the possibility of a market return.[44] The ad provides the opportunity for the military to capitalize on a two-pronged return: gaining cultural legitimacy by being seen as committed to equality and gaining needed personnel through increased enlistments from women. An emphasis on wages and equality in the ad sets up a recruiting appeal where both the military and women can benefit. The ad and the martial feminists it portrays directed politicized concerns about equal rights, labor-force participation, and wages toward a remedy of military service.

At the same time, the ad reveals how advertisers imagined appropriate occupations and attire for military women as conditions of their inclusion. Martial feminists weren't transgressing gender norms or encroaching on the masculinist culture of the army; they were young women who wanted good jobs, were fed up with sexism, and made the smart choice to look at the army as a unique site of equal opportunity. The ad directs its appeal toward women seeking upward mobility and professional opportunities, an appeal that dovetailed with the military's ideal woman recruit. In the 1970s the army held women to unique recruitment standards, requiring military women to be better educated than their male counterparts.[45]

Women soldiers were shown working in support positions as air traffic controllers, food specialists, data processors, and drivers. Two of the women are wearing skirts, a uniform component required of and restricted to women. Each of the four women is shown in distinct environments, working in different occupations. One image clearly shows a man in the background—a visual feature that appeared in other military ads in *Cosmopolitan* in the 1970s and reinforced ideas that military women worked under the supervision and command of men. Rendering army women as separate from one another indicated that although the army might include women, it was not dominated by them. By representing the four women as physically separate from one another, the ad also combatted anxieties about military women's sexuality, portraying a vision of the army where martial feminists had no direct relationship to one another and certainly not a physical, intimate, and/or sexual relationship. The martial feminists in the ad were isolated from one another, a representation protecting against accusations that the women might be lesbians, a charge long used to discredit and discharge military women. The separation of the women from one another and strict parameters of femininity detail how martial feminists were regulated even and especially as the army was represented as a site of equal opportunity.

The template of martial feminism, in which claims to equality were balanced with an emphasis on heteronormative femininity, was utilized in other ads targeting women in the early years of the AVF. An army ad in *Ebony* in 1979 and 1980 reveals both the consistency of martial feminism and the importance of regulating gender and sexuality as the numbers of military women increased (see fig. 1.5). Similar to the army ad analyzed above, the ad emphasizes, the "Army is serious about equality," and "Both men and women get the same starting pay." The ad also acknowledges that women did not have equal access to all occupations and opportunities, "several frontline combat specialties that are closed to women." Mentioning the exclusions military women faced made clear that as increasing numbers of women were enlisting, the ideological and operational heart of the military—combat—remained the province of men. Additionally, the inclusion of a reference to such exclusions in an *Ebony* ad balances visions of a gender-equitable army with a continued investment in a male-dominated military, something that could be critically important when featured in a publication viewed as having both women and men readers.

Other aspects of the ad further emphasize that military women remained invested in femininity. A quote attributed to Private 2nd Class Vicki Geiner reads, "I like being a welder, but I also like being a woman." The quote reveals how being in the army could allow women to pursue occupations traditionally associated with men, but that such opportunities didn't mean that military women lost their femininity. As more women were enlisting in the military, and a series of policy changes in the late 1970s opened up military academies and new military positions to women, the ad makes clear that military women wanted to be, and were, still women.

Figure 1.5. Army ad. Source: *Ebony*, September 1979

    Representations of martial feminists are also crafted in intersection with ideas about Whiteness and race. Each ad features images of multiple women, most of whom are White, and a single image of a Black woman. The token inclusion of a Black woman in ads featuring a mosaic of different service members is characteristic of how Black women were featured, if at all, in ads

We'll Hire You   51

in *Ebony, Cosmopolitan*, and *Sports Illustrated* during the early years of the AVF. Ads feature Black women as members of groups, visually present but unnamed and largely ignored in the text of ads.[46] That an ad published in *Ebony* features mostly White women speaks to an inability or unwillingness of advertisers to think of Black women as the focus of recruiting efforts. At the same time, both army ads of figures 1.4 and 1.5 reveal that when targeting Black women, advertisers primarily did so through appeals rooted in ideas about gender. Based on the army ads, Black women sought equality on the grounds of gender, if at all. Although making up 40 percent of army women and almost a quarter of all military women in 1979,[47] Black women were relegated to the symbolic margins of tactical inclusion in the early years of the AVF.

Representations of martial feminists were bound to marketization. Martial feminists were oppressed by patriarchal capitalism, by a lack of job opportunities in the civilian world, or by employers who failed to offer equal wages and made the choice to join the army to access equal wages and gain financial independence. However, the army turned to women recruits in the initial years of the AVF primarily because, within a free-market model of military service, they couldn't wholly rely on the male recruits they preferred. Informed by market research and the institutional imperatives of the military, advertisers crafted martial feminists as meeting the desires of both young women and the military. Rooted in the figure of the Cosmo girl and bound to parameters of Whiteness and heteronormativity, martial feminists were imagined as fulfilling the kind of life desired by young women. Martial feminists were also figured as meeting the gendered and sexualized expectations of the military, as bolstering the military's investment in heteronormative masculinity. As such, military inclusion for women—a project often cast in liberatory and emancipatory terms—was mutually constituted with regulation. The trajectory of martial feminists, as women who enlisted in the army to fulfill the promises of liberal feminism, was defined by the shifting concerns of the military advertising industry in their efforts to reach women and mold broader cultural attitudes about the role of women in the military. The tensions of recruiting women in the initial years of the AVF demonstrate the complex interplay between representations of military service, policies of inclusion and exclusion, and their relationship to broader social and cultural movements, tensions echoed in recruiting appeals targeting Black men.

Good Black Soldiers

The AVF was planned and implemented in the wake of what Moskos calls the "time of troubles."[48] In the late 1960s and early 1970s, the military was plagued by widespread violent clashes between Black and White soldiers. In 1970 there were over a thousand violent racial incidents in the marine corps alone.[49] Racial violence within the military contributed to White officers' views of Black enlisted men as agitators and to concerns that the military was an openly White supremacist organization that disproportionately sent Black and Latinx service members to their deaths in Vietnam.[50] As violence within the military shaped and was shaped by broader movements for racial equality and subsequent White backlash, distrust of the military grew in communities of color and White conservatives feared that training Black men to serve in the military was "preparing a potential enemy for war in the streets of urban America."[51] The military played a large role in struggles over civil rights, as individuals and organizations linked quests for equality with the inequity of the draft while politicians stoked fears about militant Black men to mobilize White voters. In the midst of these contestations over meanings of race and military service, the planners of the AVF insisted that the new market-based military wouldn't alter the racial composition of the armed forces.

Despite their insistence, it quickly became clear that many Black Americans were enlisting in the AVF, and there were concerns that an overrepresentation of Black Americans would lead to a "tipping point," in which a disproportionately Black military would dissuade White Americans from serving and lead to problems of military effectiveness and political legitimacy.[52] In a cultural context where the figure of the Black soldier was situated at the convergence of concerns about race, equality, and violence, advertisers made efforts to reach Black recruits in publications like *Ebony* and *Jet* and crafted ads speaking specifically to Black recruits and communities.

Broadly speaking, advertisers were tasked with persuading Black recruits to enlist through representations that could respond to a variety of seemingly disparate concerns; concerns held by Black communities, anxious White communities, and a military concerned with projecting legitimacy in the wake of the Vietnam war. To do so, recruiting ads constructed the figure of the good Black soldier. The good Black soldier is a politically and culturally legible representation of Black masculinity mutually constructed with portrayals of military service as the first step in a prescriptive pathway for Black men. Rooted in ideas of military service as a form of social uplift, enlisting was framed as a choice Black men could make to become productive citizens, role models, and family men. At the same time, good

Black soldiers functioned to serve as evidence of a purported colorblind military's commitment to racial inclusion and equality. Advertisers drew on a broader embrace of marketization and the free market to represent good Black soldiers in the pages of *Ebony* in the early years of the AVF.

Advertising historian Jason Chambers contends that John H. Johnson, *Ebony*'s founder, viewed consumption as an important social signifier and an integral facet of full citizenship.[53] The ability to purchase certain products was, for Johnson, key to broader struggles for social and political equality, and, as such, the creation of a Black consumer market was central to *Ebony*'s development.[54] In the context of a broader embrace of marketization, recruiting ads in *Ebony* mobilized existing ideas about the value the free market held for Black Americans as a sign of success and full consumer citizenship. By emphasizing economic opportunities and the better life that military service could lead to, representations in recruiting ads positioned good Black soldiers as model individuals who demonstrated how the military could help Black men.

A series of recruiting ads for the army and the navy represented the military as a remedy to problems faced by young Black men. An army ad published in *Ebony* in March 1973 features the headline "You can't get a good job without experience. We'll give you both" (see fig. 1.6). A photo shows a young Black man, dressed in sneakers, blue jeans, and a white jacket, leaning against a stack of newspapers. The stack of newspapers sits at the corner of a shopfront, with an awning touting the sale of newspapers, cigars, and candy. The man is in an urban setting, with brick buildings behind him and a cracked sidewalk at his feet. He holds a newspaper presumably opened to the classifieds section.

The text elaborates on what the young man sees in the newspaper: "There are plenty of jobs in the want ads. Unfortunately, almost all the good ones ask for experienced help. So you ask yourself, how can I get experience if no one will ever hire me? One answer lies in today's Army. We'll hire you." Similar to representations of the soldier laborer, the ad portrayed the army as the solution to economic problems. However, subtle differences reveal how recruiting ads imagined Black men as facing a different set of problems than other men. In contrast to representations of soldier laborers as workers stuck in dead-end jobs, young Black men can't get hired at all. The army, then, is portrayed as uniquely able to offer a job to young Black men as a remedy to hanging out on the street corner, hopelessly looking through the classifieds.

The idea that joining the military was a form of social uplift permeated recruiting ads. Two navy ads published in *Ebony* in 1977 and 1978 focus

Figure 1.6. Army ad. Source: *Ebony*, March 1973

on images of young Black men hanging out on basketball courts and auto shops and frame the military as a remedy to problems of idleness. Each ad contrasted "hanging loose" and "hanging out" with life in the military where young Black men could put their minds to use and earn a good salary. The ads relied on narratives of military service as a way to get Black men off the street and into the military.

A decade earlier, Daniel Moynihan, who gained notoriety with his deeply flawed analysis of Black poverty, *The Negro Family*, also known as the Moynihan Report, suggests that poverty among Black communities could be relieved by increasing Black men's presence in combat units.[55] Based on Moynihan's recommendations, the military developed the Project 100,000 program, designed to accept 100,000 men who had failed their qualifying exams for the military. Framed both as an antipoverty program and an antiriot program that could remove potential rioters from the streets by sending them to Vietnam, more than 400,000 men, including 160,000 Black men, were enlisted in army and marine corps combat units that were then sent to Vietnam.[56] Project 100,000 soldiers were disproportionately Black and disproportionately trained for combat and had a death rate twice as high as other American forces.[57]

While risks of death in combat weren't as high after the implementation of the AVF as they were during the war in Vietnam, ads framed military service as a remedy to what were seen as racialized social problems. Recruiting ads trafficked in racialized narratives of military service as a solution to underemployment, to hanging out, and hanging loose. Military service was represented as a site of normative recuperation that transformed Black men into productive citizens. Such a representation not only assumed that Black men were in need of recuperation but also drew on racial stereotypes of Black men and exploited dynamics of vulnerability, in which Black men might not have wanted to join the military but did so based on expectations that it was the best available option in the face of systemic racial inequality. Other recruiting ads expanded representations of good Black soldiers as productive citizens by showing them as role models and dedicated fathers.

An April 1975 *Ebony* ad for the air force ROTC focused on a large image of Lieutenant John Dyer standing next to his aircraft, his "sweet chariot." Dyer elaborates on his experience in the military, "I've come a long way from Atlanta, Ga. That's my hometown. But my roots are still there and my old community is still there. When I go home, the folks are happy to see me—proud of me. They say I'm doing my part in the community by showing the kids and the adults that you really can make it. You really can carve out your share of a good life." Military service was framed as an aspirational beacon; a way young Black men could "make it," get their "share of a good life," and become role models for their community. Dyer is smiling, proud of what his military service means to his family and his community. In contrast to Ture's claims of Black soldiers as "mercenaries" fighting on behalf of White colonialism,[58] the ad shows a good Black soldier with a proud family and a supportive community. Becoming a good Black soldier was about serving as evidence of meritocracy, demonstrating how the choice to join the military was an opportunity to make it. There was no risk to joining the military, only opportunity. Rather, the risk was in *not* joining the military, not making it, not getting one's share of a good life, not doing your part for your community. Any vestiges of violence, death, and war were obfuscated in the ad, replaced with a narrative of the military as a pathway through which Black men could inhabit a productive and respectable form of minoritized life and as such show their families and communities that they, too, could make it, if they made the same choice to join the military.

A series of navy ads in *Ebony* in 1975 and 1976 show how good Black soldiers joined the military to be fathers and family men. The three ads feature text portraying navy life along with a collage of photos, including photos of Black servicemen with their families. One photo is of Petty Officer Willis Lacey, smiling and hugging his wife and young child. Another shows Lieutenant Jim Gwyn seated, with his wife leaning against his right side, her arm on his leg, as their young child stands between his legs. The last ad shows Master Chief Boatswain's Mate Joseph Davis standing with two of his children as his wife is seated next to them. The text makes clear each image was of sailors with their families, saying the navy is "great for the family" and a "good life for himself and his family." Being a dedicated father and family man was represented as part of life in the navy. The ads constructed a form of Black masculinity revolving around a particular configuration of heteronormativity. Good Black soldiers were dedicated fathers, willing to join the military to provide good lives for their families.

Representations of good Black soldiers served a converging set of ideological functions. Military men were situated as notable counterpoints to stereotypes of Black men as absent fathers and burdens to the economy. Good Black soldiers valorized the military as a site of masculine recuperation where Black men could attain stable employment and reclaim positions as martial patriarchs, a view coinciding with Moynihan's beliefs about the military.[59] Black men's relations to capitalist and heteronormative respectability were framed as resulting from a singular choice, the choice to join the military and consequently become productive citizens, role models, and good fathers. As Hong notes, such a form of conditional inclusion reinforces the idea that those who don't make such choices are unworthy of life, an idea used to perpetuate and justify racial and gendered violence and neglect.[60] Such a framing allowed advertisers to portray the military as a unique site of opportunity for Black men in need of economic opportunity and assuage anxieties about militant Black men. Learning to be a good Black soldier wasn't about learning to fight but, rather, about learning to work, being a role model, and being a father.

In addition to promoting visions of the military as a way for Black men to become successful economic and patriarchal citizens, the military advertising industry developed a number of specific appeals to convince Black men that the military was an inclusive and equitable institution. Providing evidence of the military's commitment to racial inclusion and equality was absolutely crucial to recruiting efforts in the early years of the AVF. Although the military took steps to address internal issues of racial inequality and violence, including required race-relations training, the development of equal opportunity offices, and the formation of the Defense Race Relations Institute,[61] increasing the numbers of Black recruits, specifically Black officers, was seen as a key step in decreasing racial tensions within the ranks. Ads for the air force, army national guard, and navy openly discussed race. Some ads pointed to historical examples of Black success, an approach reinvigorated to a greater extent in the 2000s, whereas others focused on experiences of current service members to counter perceptions of a discriminatory and racist military. A series of navy ads in *Ebony* in 1976 and 1977 details how advertisers utilized the figure of the good Black soldier to provide evidence of the military's purported commitment to racial equality.

Three navy ads focused on past inequality to frame the "new" navy as progressive, as newly committed to racial equality. Each of the ads was directed to Black fathers, with the headline of one ad stating, "Twenty years ago, few black men would have advised their sons to join the Navy" (see fig. 1.7). The ad goes on to detail what life was like twenty years ago for Black men in the navy: "Blacks made up less than five percent of the Navy. Almost all were in the lower ranks—black chiefs were rarities, black officers virtually nonexistent." The ad then discusses how the navy has changed, telling recruits and their fathers: "It's a different Navy, and a better one. . . . The world has changed a lot in a generation. So has the Navy." The ad directs its appeal to fathers of Black recruits by acknowledging a history of racial discrimination, then asserting that the navy has progressed.

The other two navy ads echo this appeal. The headline of one ad asks, "Does a black man have a chance in the Navy?" and answers, "These days, a chance to go as far as his brains and determination will take him." The third ad features the headline, "What every black parent should know about the Navy" with text stating, "It's a lot different from when you were your son's age. . . . Now that you know it, he should too." The ads acknowledge the influence of racial discrimination and exclusion on Black men's experiences in an overwhelmingly White navy as a point of contrast with the "new" navy.

In the new navy committed to racial equality and inclusion and inspired by the changes of the last twenty years, Black fathers act as witnesses to such changes and should help persuade their sons to enlist. The resulting image is of a smiling Black father and his sailor son, both represented as good Black soldiers. While it's unclear if the father is a veteran, he is represented as a foot soldier of tactical inclusion. Black fathers, who may have served in a racist navy or not served at all, can encourage their sons to enlist and become good Black soldiers in the new navy. The ads, all of which exclusively feature images of men, reinforce a gendered notion of the military as a male-dominated institution and represent good Black soldiers as participating in a masculine lineage of military service made possible by the military's commitment to racial inclusion and equality.

Figure 1.7. Navy ad. Source: *Ebony*, October 1976

In asserting the legitimacy of the "new" military as committed to racial equality, the three navy ads represent a military where the only reason race matters is to provide evidence that it doesn't matter anymore. Such an approach introduces the notion that the military has moved beyond race, a defining characteristic of colorblindness that renders moot the impact of race in the present.[62] Together, the three ads contribute to an ideology of colorblindness as a framework that legitimates a military forced to reorient its relationship to Black recruits in order to meet personnel needs. The military's past as an institution defined by racial exclusion, discrimination, and White supremacy is framed as a resource for asserting its newfound legitimacy.

Recruiting efforts targeting Black men were largely successful in the early years of the AVF. Between 1973 and 1980 the number of Black service members in active components of the military increased by 117,202 service members. By 1980, nearly 1 out of 3 enlisted soldiers in the army were Black, an overrepresentation tripling that in the general population.[63] As unprecedented numbers of Black Americans were joining the military, recruiting ads portrayed enlisting as a tipping point of transformation. Young Black men could be stereotypes or soldiers, the choice was up to them, and the military was willing to help. Through the figure of the good Black soldier, recruiting ads produced and conveyed ideas that young Black men in need of opportunities should make the smart choice to join the military and, in doing so, become role models, family men, and productive citizens.

Tactical Inclusion in the Early Years of the AVF

The early years of the AVF were characterized by significant changes in the composition of the military, recruiting practices, and meanings of military service. Recruiting ads sought to persuade potential recruits to enlist when they had the choice not to and to convince the broader public that the military was a viable opportunity for young Americans. Paired with the new recruiting environment of the AVF, recruiting appeals foregrounded a view of enlisting as a primarily economic transformation.

As an overarching emphasis in recruiting appeals, the marketization of military service rearticulated relationships between military service and citizenship by representing the military as a crucial institution in the production of successful economic citizens. Joining the military wasn't an expression of patriotic duty but, rather, was framed as an expression of personal choice. Soldier laborers, martial feminists, and good Black soldiers didn't need to love their country, they only needed to want the opportunities the military could provide. It was by virtue of their status as surplus labor and second-class citizens at a moment of neoliberal shift and an entrenchment of economic precarity that certain populations—working-class and poor White men, Black men, White women, and, to a lesser degree, Black women—were propelled into legibility as potential soldiers. At the same time, recruiting ads delineated the normative pathways through which new recruits were included in a military that remained committed to Whiteness, maleness, heteronormativity, and capitalist success. The newly voluntary military was portrayed as an important step on the pathway to successful economic citizenship and as an advocate for gender and racial equality, a move that expanded the pool of potential recruits.

In the late 1970s immense demographic changes in the military, particularly, increased numbers of Black service members and women service members, propelled anxieties about the perception and purpose of the military. Such anxieties were expressed in debates about recruit quality, a term that technically referred to educational level and test scores of recruits but became shorthand for questioning and discrediting an AVF increasingly composed of women, Black Americans, and people of color.[64] Politicians argued that the military was drawing on the dregs of society and that the military, specifically the army, had become a safety net for the most disadvantaged Americans rather than a respected war-fighting institution.[65] Increases in civilian employment opportunities for young men made it difficult for the military to meet its personnel needs and a miscategorization of test results in the army led to the accidental admission of many soldiers who had failed to meet the minimum standards for enlistment.[66] The AVF was in a state of crisis, a crisis driven in part by perceptions of military service members as motivated primarily by the economic opportunities and benefits available in the military.

In response, there was a backlash against marketization and against representations of the military as a unique site of opportunity and equality. Mittelstadt points out how the late 1970s became a cautionary tale about the AVF and a catalyst for changes in the 1980s: "Stories of the dangers of the 1970s... were widely retold within the military as part of the larger narrative within military and defense circles that contrasted 'the dark days' of the army in the 1970s to what would soon become the story of restoration and honor of the Reagan years of the 1980s."[67]

Debates over the future of the AVF coincided with a broader narrative of national crisis. At the end of the 1970s the previous decade was viewed by some—including Nixon and Robert Bly, a writer who led the "men's movement" of the 1980s—as an era during which American men became "soft," and the nation lost its geopolitical, economic, and military resolve.[68] This perceived crisis of American manhood and the role of the military as a prime site through which to catalyze a recovery of American dominance set the stage for tactical inclusion during the next era of the AVF.

CHAPTER 2

America at Its Best

General Maxwell R. Thurman saw 1980 as the true beginning of the AVF. Called the "single most important person" in the history of the AVF, Thurman was appointed as head of the army recruiting command in late 1979 and instituted several changes that catalyzed a shift in recruitment advertising.[1] Thurman took on a more direct role in advertising and worked closely with N. W. Ayer, the army's agency partner since 1973, to help develop the army's famous slogan "Be all you can be."[2] Thurman saw the slogan as speaking to potential recruits who wanted to grow and meet their potential, a message tied to his views on recruiting more broadly. In contrast to recruiting appeals from the 1970s rooted in marketization, Thurman didn't see recruits choosing military service as a job or career but, rather, saw enlisting as a choice young Americans made to support their country.[3] Thurman opposed expanding the market of potential recruits to remedy recruiting problems, going so far to say that the army recruiting command had been "expanding the market to the bottom fish."[4] Viewing the early years of the AVF as a period during which there was an "impression that the military was becoming soft and permissive," Thurman sought to elevate the image of the army and reorient recruiting toward a focus on quality rather quantity.[5] Concerns about quality were tied to demographic changes in the military, particularly, the increased representation of women and Black Americans.[6] Thurman's main goal was to create a more middle-class and higher-educated army, a goal linked to a desire for more White middle-class men.[7] Policies and incentives, including increases in military pay and the introduction of the Montgomery G.I. Bill, were implemented to reach highly desirable and elusive middle-class recruits.[8] As changes were made to improve the image of the army, recruiting ads portrayed a renewed and reinvigorated military.

In the pages of *Sports Illustrated* in November 1986, a two-page spread shows four men, their faces covered in camouflage paint as they stand in thigh-deep water. The four men face different directions, guns at the ready, foliage and linked ammunition draped over their shoulders. At first glance, the spread looks like it could be an ad for the latest installment of the *Rambo* franchise or another action movie. However, a small logo alerts the viewer that the ad is for the Army National Guard, which the caption refers to as an "Irresistible Force." The use of the term "irresistible" speaks to a dual function of the ad's appeal. The ad contributes to an idea of the military and to the men that served in it as overwhelmingly powerful. At the same time, the idea of joining a military where, as text in the ad states, "The guns are real. And so is the adventure," is framed as an enticing appeal for young men. Complementary ideas of the military as a powerful institution and a place where young men could feel powerful themselves are brought together in an explicit expression of manliness, as the ad claims joining the National Guard "will make your momma proud she raised a man." Though visually absent from an ad exclusively featuring men, women are implicated as supportive mothers who want their sons to join the military and become men.

One month later, a second Army National Guard ad in *Sports Illustrated* further shows how women fit within the guard's "Irresistible Force." A young woman in camouflage uniform holds a small child wrapped in a blanket, as another woman also wrapped in a blanket stands beside her. A young woman's role in the army is as a humanitarian caretaker, motivated by the fact that "every once in awhile somebody looks up and says thank you."

Together, the two ads draw on tropes of strong military men, patriotic mothers, and caregiving women to articulate a vision of an exceptional military where both the United States and patriarchy reign supreme. The two ads show the crucial role representations of gender and manliness played in crafting Thurman's view of an elevated army. While Thurman's direct influence was limited to the army, his views on recruiting and an emphasis on promoting the military as an exceptional institution resonated throughout the military advertising industry as representations of technology, capitalist success, and heteronormativity were deployed to fortify arguments about the superiority of the U.S. military and distinguish U.S. capitalist culture from Soviet communist culture.

This chapter explores the adjustments advertisers made between 1980 and 1991 to target new recruits. Made in partnership with civilian agencies including the J. Walter Thompson agency, Bates and Co., N. W. Ayer, BBDO, and D'Arcy, MacManus, and Masius and others, ads foregrounded technology as a sign of military superiority, promoted the military as the paradigmatic capitalist and meritocratic institution, and restored visions of patriotic pride through images of heteronormative military families. Recruiting ads provided symbolic justification for a conservative domestic agenda while reflecting and contributing to cultural politics of the time. Narratives of protech militarism and meritocracy provided justifications for increases in military spending and, through the limited inclusion of people of color and women, suggested a multiracial and gender inclusive landscape in which social welfare and affirmative action programs were obsolete and unnecessary. Representations of military families included women within a promilitary agenda through their heteronormative relations with men, ultimately, suturing conservative gender and sexual politics to expressions of American militarism. Through a variety of different figures—high-tech soldiers, Black pilots, martial capitalists, and proud military families—recruiting ads sought to assert a vision of a reinvigorated military, a military populated by the best young people the nation had to offer, supported by proud American families and indicative of America at its best.

Remasculinization and an Exceptional Military

Throughout the 1980s and early 1990s, recruiting ads reasserted distinctions between the military and civilian life by framing the military as exceptional in two ways: as an exceptional institution itself and as a place to become exceptional. This framing coincided with what gender studies scholar Susan Jeffords refers to as remasculinization, a "revival of the images, abilities, and evaluations of men and masculinity in dominant U.S. culture" that promoted patriarchal interests and structures.[9] As Jeffords notes, a reinvigorated nation was tied to and dependent upon a reinvigorated vision of American masculinity. This is not to say that remasculinization, however, relied solely upon representations of men. Women and ideas of femininity were crucial to remasculinization, figured as constitutive outsiders against which men were defined and important for the ways they could shore up claims to masculine vigor, often through narratives of marriage and heteronormativity.[10] Similarly, racial and class differences could coexist with and bolster remasculinization, provided such differences were subsumed within a broader emphasis on the value of masculinity.[11]

The concept of remasculinization provides a foundation for thinking about tactical inclusion. An emphasis on patriarchal dominance was expressed through narratives of technology, meritocratic capitalism, and heteronormativity, each of which strengthened claims to remasculinization while showing how different figures could play vital roles in promoting and sustaining a view of an exceptional military. In the context of tactical inclusion, remasculinization revolved around the ways limited forms of difference could be incorporated into a singular vision of reinvigorated and exceptional military.

Following criticisms of marketization as sullying the military's standing in the 1970s, recruiting ads rearticulated what inclusion meant and looked like while remaining reliant upon the systematic exploitation of vulnerability at the heart of recruiting in the AVF. While military officials might have preferred to focus largely or even exclusively on recruiting educated White men, the market logic of the AVF required continued outreach to other potential recruits. Advertisers were tasked with showing an array of potential recruits the benefits of military service while also asserting that those who could or should access such benefits were deserving of them. The vision of the military constructed in the 1980s and early 1990s was of an institution that wasn't for just anyone who needed or wanted opportunities but, rather, for exceptional Americans. Images of Black pilots, martial capitalists, and proud military families targeted Black Americans, people of color, and women as potential recruits but did so with an emphasis on the exceptional ambition, skills, and pride that made them intelligible as members of the military. Recruiting ads honed the message that an inclusive military wasn't compromised in any way and was made stronger by virtue of the exceptional attributes recruits brought to and learned in the military. Differences of race and gender were mobilized in support of remasculinization and deployed to bolster views of a military defined by commitments to high-tech militarism, capitalism, and heteronormativity. Such commitments contributed to and corresponded with a series of political and cultural shifts both within and beyond the military.

In his 1980 campaign for president, Ronald Reagan painted a dire picture of a military in decline and a nation under siege from the threat of the Soviet Union. If Reagan's restorative vision for the nation was a shining city on a hill, the military was the citadel at the city's center. Throughout his administration, Reagan promoted increases in military spending, supported programs to elevate the military's status, and thought of the military as key to the resurgence of American power. Bailey and Mittelstadt have detailed how the promilitary politics of the Reagan era functioned as a corrective to crises in recruiting and the military's public image in the 1970s.[12]

Despite efforts to alter the composition of the military and increase the numbers of White men, demographics reveal a stubbornly diverse military. The overall size of the active-duty military grew through much of the 1980s, with an increase of over 125,000 service members between 1980 and 1987, before a decline in the late 1980s. To meet personnel needs, advertisers and recruiters were tasked with persuading between 223,000 and 305,000 Americans to enlist in active-duty service each year. Black service members made up between 21 percent and 23 percent of the enlisted active-duty ranks, a representation almost double that in the general population. The percentage of Latinx recruits hovered between 4 percent and 5.5 percent of enlisted active-duty personnel while the percentage of military women steadily increased from 8.5 percent to 11 percent, an increase of 46,000 women. While the percentages of White men in the military didn't change in the way military officials might have preferred, what did change was the way women, Black men, and people of color were represented as potential recruits and service members. Subjects of tactical inclusion that, in the context of the late 1970s, were viewed as burdens who had transformed the military into a welfare organization were recast as deserving subjects, as exceptionally committed to a promilitary, capitalist vision of America.

Protech Militarism and Black Pilots

Technology was indispensable to recruiting appeals in the 1980s. Representations of technology asserted the superiority of a newly modern military and signaled a desire for highly educated and motivated recruits. Ads focused on jets, helicopters, space shuttles, and satellites, framing them as important bulwarks in safeguarding America's future. In contrast to ads from the 1970s that highlighted technical skills as valuable for recruits, representations of technology in the 1980s emphasized the value of a high-tech military for the nation. The high-tech military required special soldiers, soldiers who, through the convergence of representations and military policies, were men and men alone. Influenced by practical challenges of meeting personnel needs, some ads disrupted links among technology, masculinity, and Whiteness and featured images of Black pilots. Black pilots were figured as exceptional service members and integral participants in military interventions abroad. Together, high-tech soldiers and Black pilots figured as complementary figures in promoting the manliness of a reinvigorated military.

Perhaps unsurprisingly, ads for the air force regularly featured images of military technologies in making appeals to potential recruits. Brown found that representations of technology, which offered masculine advantages of mastery, dominance, and control to male recruits, were key to air force recruiting.[13] As a crucial aspect of the air force brand, representations of technology were linked to a particular kind of recruit. The air force has been one of the most desirable branches of the military for recruits, driven in part by a perception of associations with technology, and as such, the air force has generally had little trouble attracting high-quality recruits—meaning well-educated recruits but also more typically White men.[14] Air force ads from the 1970s deployed images of jets and references to technology to portray the air force as a valuable opportunity for young Americans to learn technical skills and were as likely to show potential recruits working as mechanics and meteorologists as they were to show them as pilots. Ads published in the 1980s continued to draw on images of jets and asked recruits to join "the Air Force technology team" and "accept the challenges of modern technology."

Two air force ads published between 1984 and 1986 deployed technology-based appeals by focusing on space shuttles as key symbols in narratives of global competition. The first ad, published in *Ebony*, featured an image of a space-shuttle launch along with text telling potential recruits:

> Technology is moving faster than science fiction. And, it's more exciting. But to be part of it—to make it work—we have to learn. We have to grow. . . . We've got a choice. America's youth can watch technological developments being made. Or they can help make them. . . . America and the Air Force of tomorrow are depending on them.

Recruits were asked to join in the exciting challenge of fast-moving technology and play their part in protecting America's future. The image of a space shuttle evoked memories of the post–World War II space race, in which space travel featured as a key arena of competition between the United States and the Union of Soviet Socialist Republics (U.S.S.R.), a narrative reliant upon ideas of manliness and racialized notions of a new frontier.[15] A space-shuttle launch provided a familiar frame through which potential recruits and other viewers could make sense of the purported necessity of military technological advancement and young recruits' roles in driving it in ways that bolstered protech militarism and American manliness. While the ad focused on a specific technology—the space shuttle—to tell a gendered story, a second air force ad made explicit the manliness of high-tech militarism.

The ad, published in *Sports Illustrated* in 1985 and 1986, showed a White man holding a rifle and standing guard in front of a space shuttle, with the caption, "Our security specialists protect the doorway to the future" (see fig. 2.1). In figuring a White man as guardian of the future, the ad participated in a narrative of protech militarism crucial to formulations of masculinity in the Reagan era.[16] A number of scholars have demonstrated how material practices and ideological meanings linked to technologies are rooted in gendered power dynamics that promote men and masculinity while excluding

Figure 2.1. Air force ad. Source: *Sports Illustrated*, December 23, 1985

women.[17] The ad furthers this gendered vision of technology while also implicating representations of protech militarism as crucial for remasculinization.

The text in the ad states: "You'll be protecting what's valuable today like the F-16, the C-5A and the SR-71. And you'll also be protecting what's valuable for America's future." Best secured through investments in military technologies, namely, specific aircraft that at various times were considered indicative of America's military superiority, the future of the military, manliness, and nation converge. The image of a gun-toting White man protecting a space shuttle reinstates a traditional image of military manliness with an embrace of a high-tech future. While the ad could just have easily showed an airman working on a space shuttle, satellite, or other aircraft as an engineer or mechanic, the presence of a gun makes clear that the air force of the 1980s isn't just about technology. The ideal airman, pictured in dark green uniform and beret—colors and uniform more readily associated in popular culture with the army—carries a gun and uses it to protect the new frontier.

As an exceptional institution and the primary guardians of the nation's future, the military and White men are framed as emblematic of what is valuable about America, and, as such, worthy of investment. Reagan's increased funding of the military was geared largely toward improving technologies and weapons in quests to close perceived gaps between the United States and the Soviet Union.[18] Investing in the military was framed as an existential necessity, an imperative in reasserting global dominance. The ad attempts to convey a narrative of protech militarism and remasculinization as something Americans should support. Support for the military is support for a secure future, a future made doubly secure through the dominance it ensures globally and the gender politics it ensures domestically. The ad positions military technologies and the right kind of recruits who can protect them—namely, White men—as corresponding forces in asserting the exceptionalism of the military, resulting in a vision where securing the nation and patriarchy were conjoined.

Narratives of technology displayed a reinvigorated military that required a special kind of recruit, something exemplified in a February and March 1981 army ad in *Ebony*. Featuring an image of four faceless soldiers silhouetted against a gray sky as they rappel from a helicopter with packs and rifles visible on their backs, the ad asks, "Why should the Army be easy? Life isn't." The caption makes immediately clear that the army is a challenge, something for youth who don't want to take the easy way out. The text links this challenge to technological advances:

> In the modern Army, the Cavalry flies, the Infantry rides, and the Artillery

can hit a fly in the eye 15 miles away. It's a printed-circuit, solid-state, computerized Army. And this special kind of Army requires a special kind of soldier. The kind of young man or woman who's eager to learn tomorrow's technology, tomorrow's skills. The kind of young man or woman impatient for a challenge and hungry for responsibility.

Technology and lethality are framed as points of distinction, marking the army as different from the past, as dominant and exceptional but also as requiring special recruits. The ad ostensibly figures the special recruits the army desires as any young man or woman who wants to take on the challenge and responsibility of learning tomorrow's technologies, and the image of faceless soldiers implies a somewhat inclusive portrayal of high-tech soldiers. However, military policies in the early 1980s made clear that the high-tech soldiers the army and other branches most desired were men and men alone.

Following Reagan's election, both the army and air force secretly submitted proposals asking permission to hold recruitment numbers for women to the bare minimum in 1981 and 1982.[19] The proposals marked the beginning of the military's "womanpause" strategy, consisting of plans to lower recruiting goals for women recruits and decrease the number of women service members. With its twinned appeal based on technology and lethality, categories tied to constructions of manliness, the ad effectively excluded women from the high-tech and exceptional military.[20] Driven by personnel needs and challenges advertisers faced in reaching non-White recruits, other ads showed how Black men were represented as pilots, a specific kind of high-tech soldier.

Piloting has long been a prestigious and exclusive military occupation. The exclusivity of military piloting results from a converging set of dynamics. Associations with technology, extensive training, educational requirements, and the officer ranks have created an environment where the overwhelming majority of military pilots are White men. Military personnel, particularly, in the navy and air force, branches with the majority of military planes, have attempted and struggled to increase the numbers of Black pilots throughout the duration of the AVF.[21] The feature film *Top Gun* (1986) perhaps best evidences cultural understandings of military piloting in the 1980s. Made in cooperation with the navy, the film was the highest-grossing film of the year and followed the exploits of Pete "Maverick" Mitchell, a rebellious pilot played by Tom Cruise.[22] With the exception of a civilian woman flight instructor, who functions primarily as Mitchell's love interest, and a token Black pilot, the world of military piloting in *Top Gun* is a White man's world.[23]

While commercial media like *Top Gun* might have only included

Black men as tokens in a White man's world, recruiting ads represented Black pilots as essential figures in promoting protech militarism and U.S. global dominance. An army ad in *Ebony* and *Sports Illustrated* between 1986 and 1989 urged potential recruits to "See your future with a whole new perspective" (see fig. 2.2). The visual pairing of a Black soldier with what appears to be an AH-1F Cobra, an army attack helicopter, connects individual economic aspirations with military technology and U.S. global imperialism. The text states:

> If you qualify for the Army's Warrant Officer Flight Training Program, you'll have a lot more to look forward to than blue sky. You'll have an exciting career ahead of you. In a field where the opportunities for skilled pilots are growing every day. In the Army and in civilian life.... After you've earned your wings, you'll have an opportunity to learn how to fly some of the latest, most technologically advanced helicopters in the world.

A strategy of touting upward mobility in the form of an exciting career in or out of the military is repurposed to align with imperatives of protech militarism. Advancements in military technology provide unique opportunities for recruits, a group inclusive of Black men. The appeal on offer in the ad might be inclusive but is not universal. There is a component of deservedness and a condition to having an exciting career and accessing opportunities for skilled pilots, specifically qualifying for the army warrant officer flight training program. Warrant officers make up a very small percentage of army personnel and are trained in specific technical areas, including aviation. While military benefits have always had conditions—one must qualify for military service, then serve in the military—the ad contains a higher burden of deservedness.

A potential recruit has to apply to the program and pass training, and only then they are able to have an exciting career and an opportunity to fly the most technologically advanced helicopters in the world. The emphasis on the opportunities being available only to those who qualify reflects the exclusive nature of piloting—and of the officer ranks, which have skewed more White and male than the enlisted ranks—and contributes to a crucial narrative of representing military benefits as accessible only to those who deserve them. In contrast to representations from the 1970s that emphasized what the military could help Black men become, the ad portrays Black pilots as already being exceptional, as having cleared the high bar to become pilots, and as such contributing to a perception of the military as both an inclusive and exceptional institution.

The ad goes on to align the individual pursuit of opportunities and technological mastery with military interventions abroad, saying, "And you'll

Figure 2.2. Army ad. Source: *Ebony*, July 1987

fly these helicopters in different countries around the world . . . skimming treetops on a reconnaissance mission in Panama." The ad foreshadows the invasion of Panama in 1989, which at the time was the largest American military action since Vietnam and was designed to stem leftist and Communist influence in Central America.[24] The reference to Panama positions Black pilots as integral participants in cultural narratives of remasculinization and material practices of state violence, both of which were defined in opposition to communism. Black pilots were figured as active defenders and propagators of the American way of life through their participation in the military.

The tactical inclusion of Black pilots was also a response to particular recruiting challenges at the time. High rates of unemployment and increases in military pay in the early 1980s created a highly favorable recruiting environment in which the military easily met required personnel needs. However, as the economy improved, recruiting became more difficult and stalled in 1985. Guided by findings that those most likely to enlist were non-White and had a belief that the military could enable them to gain characteristics valued for civilian jobs,[25] advertisers struggled to speak to Black Americans in ways that spurred enlistment. Showing Black service members in positions of responsibility, such as pilots and officers, was seen as a possible solution to specific problems advertisers were having in reaching non-White recruits as the recruiting environment became more challenging.[26]

As a whole, narratives of technology operated as an important component within a gendered and racialized vision of the military. Appeals foregrounding technology spoke to advertisers' efforts to attract more high-quality recruits, an analogue for increasing the numbers of White, male recruits. Cultural narratives of technology and military policies converged to exclude women while allowing the selective inclusion of Black men in ways that reinforced the exceptional nature of the military and claims that U.S. militarism was guided by the propagation of a racially inclusive and hence, morally superior, democracy.[27] Through implicit and explicit connections with manliness and Whiteness, recruiting ads emphasizing military technologies played a key role in shaping perceptions of the Reagan-era military as a globally dominant force populated by exceptional soldiers. As representations of technology displayed the reinvigorated military and the men who served in it as capable of combatting the threat of the Soviet Union through military means, other ads engaged the military as a key institution in combatting the cultural threat of communism by portraying military service members as exemplars of capitalism and meritocracy.

Martial Capitalists in a Meritocratic Military

The success of the early AVF was predicated on the military entering the free market and persuading recruits to enlist based on their own economic interests and needs. As discussed in chapter 1, this idea contributed to marketization, in which recruiting ads defined military service in relation to the free market. In the 1980s recruiting ads continued to emphasize the economic benefits of military service but did so by imagining a different kind of recruit: the martial capitalist. In contrast to soldier laborers from the 1970s who enlisted to escape unemployment and dead-end jobs, martial capitalists used military service to become professional leaders and titans of industry. Primarily articulated through images of men, martial capitalists reproduced patriarchal power through associations with corporate control and wealth accumulation. Ads featuring martial capitalists routinely emphasized the leadership and management training available in the military, a narrative that altered the imagined economic trajectory of service members and spoke to the military's desire for more educated and upwardly mobile recruits.

While recruiting ads from the 1970s represented the military as a recuperative institution, able to transform recruits in need of opportunities into successful economic citizens, ads from the 1980s intensified the connection between military service and economic success. The military wasn't simply able to provide recruits with a good job and access to productive citizenship, it was framed as able to propel service members into the upper echelons of business and industry. Military service wasn't represented as a blue-collar job or a way to learn a trade but, rather, was tied to a different vision of successful economic citizenship defined by becoming a part of the managerial class. The military was represented as a professional training program and a model of meritocracy where a variety of striving individuals could take advantage of opportunities available in the military.

The message of martial capitalists in a meritocratic military promoted the idea that the limited inclusion of women, Black men, and men of color bolstered the moral legitimacy of the military and capitalism as complementary institutions. Additionally, martial capitalists were shown as deserving of the material benefits of military service, namely, professional training and funding for higher education, by virtue of their embrace of capitalism and success in navigating the military, which was represented as an exemplar of meritocracy. Together, representations of martial capitalists and meritocracy situated the military as the consummate American institution that provided evidence for the superiority of capitalism and provided justifications for attacks on social welfare and affirmative action programs.

In a subtle change from images of soldier laborers in the 1970s, ads in the 1980s showed the military helping men reach the pinnacles of capitalism. An army ROTC ad published in *Sports Illustrated* in 1985 and again in *Ebony* in 1987 told potential recruits that the military could help them become "captains of industry" and "top executives" (see fig. 2.3). The ad focuses on four men who served as army officers and later became leaders in the oil, steel, building, and publishing industries.

The men's trajectories that began with the army were used to implicate military service as a catalyst for capitalist success. The text tells potential recruits:

> These top executives started out as Army officers. Right out of college, they were given the kind of responsibility most people in civilian life work years for....
>
> A great way to get the training you need is Army ROTC. This is a college program that will teach you leadership and management skills, and train you to handle real challenges.
>
> If you want to prepare for a promising future in business, begin your future as an Army officer, with Army ROTC. You too might wind up a captain of industry!

Joining the Army ROTC was framed as a fast track to professional success, defined by entrepreneurship, corporate control, and wealth accumulation. Representations of martial capitalists reproduced patriarchal power. As noted by Connell, corporate control and management are gendered forms of control key to the social construction of masculinity.[28] Furthermore, men's positions within commercial and entrepreneurial capitalist culture enable a gendered accumulation of wealth that furthers material inequalities between men and women.[29] In relating military service to men's abilities to become "top executives" and "captains of industry," the ad positions the military as a relevant institution in aiding men's quests to gain economic power.

The army ROTC, due to its unique position within the military, was well suited to make appeals to martial capitalists. ROTC programs have roots dating back to the early 1800s and consist of military education classes and training as part of the college curriculum at various universities and colleges. In exchange for accepting a commission as an officer upon graduating, ROTC students can receive scholarships that cover the full cost of their higher education. Service in the ROTC is often framed as a career—a

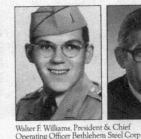

Figure 2.3. Army ROTC ad. Source: *Sports Illustrated*, September 9, 1985

distinction from ads for the enlisted ranks—and targets higher-educated recruits, including those already enrolled in college. As such, the links between military training and capitalist success elucidated in the ad coincide with broader narratives of the ROTC as the professional school of the army, directed toward recruits interested in leadership. While ROTC ads figure largely in representing martial capitalists, other ads allude to capitalist aspirations by discussing the leadership and management training on offer in the military.

Ads for the Army National Guard and the navy feature images of men in suits and officer uniforms to portray the military as a professional incubator, a place to gain important skills in leadership and management. Other ads, including for the marines and navy, talk about the military itself as a place to "[r]un your own company" or be "part of an elite management team." Brown notes that representations of business-oriented forms of masculinity were key to army advertising in the 1980s and navy advertising in the 1990s.[30] Such representations rearticulated the forms of masculinity on offer in ads and sought to reframe relationships between the military and pursuit of capitalist success. Ads create a lineage of continuity among military service, economic aspiration, and corporatization as complementary characteristics of manliness. In doing so, ads also helped the military improve public perception by representing service members as aspirational economic citizens who joined the military not as the only option at an otherwise dead end but as a starting point for managerial success. However, within the army ROTC ad that told potential recruits they could someday become "captains of industry," not all men who became martial capitalists were the same.

Three of the men, who are White, served as chairmen and presidents of Fortune 500 companies, specifically the Mobil Corp. (now known as ExxonMobil), Bethlehem Steel Corp., and Sherwin-Williams Co. The fourth man, Earl G. Graves, is Black and was listed as the editor and publisher of *Black Enterprise Magazine*, a description minimizing Graves's role as the publication's founder. The uneven positions the four men hold reflect the miscategorization of Graves's role as well as racial dynamics privileging Whiteness within capitalism, particularly, in regard to positions of corporate control and leadership. Within the project of tactical inclusion, Graves's presence in the ad suggests to potential Black recruits that though still shaped by a labor market favoring Whiteness, there is a route through which Black men can become martial capitalists. This piecemeal form of inclusion hints at a series of army ROTC ads that represent the military as a wholly meritocratic institution where service members were deserving of the military benefits they received.

A series of army ROTC ads in *Sports Illustrated* and *Ebony* between 1986 and 1987 focused on the experiences of five different service members. Two of the ads feature White men: Carl Gebo and Robert Bright, ROTC students at Notre Dame University and the University of Idaho, respectively. Two other ads focus on men of color: Timothy Cannon, a Black ROTC student

Figure 2.4. Army ROTC ad. Source: *Sports Illustrated*, October 5, 1987

at Penn State University, and Joaquin Martinez, a Latinx ROTC student at the University of Texas at Austin (see fig. 2.4). The last ad features Catherine Fahey, a White woman and ROTC student at the University of California, Santa Barbara. What is notable about the army ROTC ad series is that various individuals, who in ads in the 1970s were targeted through messages of equality and inclusion that explicitly discussed gender and racial difference, were subsumed within a narrative of sameness.[31] The ads portrayed the military as a place where anyone willing to meet the challenge of military service was able to access the same benefits and opportunities.

Army ROTC does the same thing for each of the featured student-soldiers; it provides training in leadership and management and gives an advantage in pursuing future careers. Enlisting in the army ROTC was framed as a point of distinction, both as an important credential for future professional success and as an experience that set student-soldiers apart from their peers. Being a part of the army ROTC provided something more than college alone, it provided a way for students to go to the college of their choice and become better students and leaders. The framing of the army ROTC as a better way to go to college promoted an exceptional view of the military while providing ideological support for promilitary, anti–social welfare politics.

The ad featuring Joaquin Martinez emphasizes that army ROTC classes allowed students to gain real-world experience in ways other college courses did not. Making a distinction between the ROTC and other college courses contributed to political views on the relation between higher education and military service. Thurman, the head of army recruiting, lamented increased financing of higher education without a concomitant obligation of military service, calling it a "bankrupt national manpower strategy."[32] Since his time as governor of California in the 1960s, Reagan regularly attacked higher education, cutting funding for universities, student loans, and Pell grants as part of a broader dismantling of social welfare.[33] Mittelstadt argues that in the Reagan era, "federal student aid programs symbolized the undeserving civilian users of government social welfare programs" while military programs like the G.I. Bill, and I argue the ROTC, "represented just recognition of worthy soldiers and a revered military."[34] Exceptional youth in the 1980s weren't taking out student loans or receiving grants, rather, they were serving their country and *earning* their education. The military is represented as a pathway to access state support not vilified in popular culture, and soldiers are seen as deserving subjects that should be insulated from critiques that recipients of government benefits were burdens on the state.[35] In addition to promoting a promilitary and anti–social welfare politics, the ads also foster a particular view of racial and gender difference.

Black men, Latinx men, White women, and White men alike are represented as student-soldiers. Racial and gender differences are subsumed within a broader narrative of deservedness and an image of the military as a meritocratic institution that was both multiracial and gender inclusive. In addition to not needing government assistance to pay for college, the diverse young Americans in the ads also have no need for affirmative action because they chose the military.[36] While the ads portray the army ROTC and, as such, the officers corps, as having moved beyond gender and racial inequality, such a representation disavowed the fact that both women and non-White service members had been underrepresented in the officer corps throughout the AVF.[37] A narrative of a multiracial and gender-inclusive meritocracy, where deserving subjects earned state support, coincides with ideologies promoting universalism and equality in which difference is negated as a factor in perpetuating inequality.[38] In promoting the idea that any individual can choose to join the military and subsequently succeed based on their own effort, systemic and structural inequalities recede from view, and inequalities are viewed as the effect of poor choices or lack of effort. In contrast to ads from the 1970s that explicitly discuss racial and gender inequalities, the military in the 1980s was an institution where difference only mattered as a visual marker of the military's exceptionalism.

The inclusiveness of the ROTC ads also function as a response to the shifting recruiting needs of the 1980s. Agencies responsible for navy and marine corps advertising in the 1980s pointed to a need for racially inclusive recruiting materials. Documents from the J. Walter Thompson agency and Bates Worldwide discuss targeting Black and "Hispanic" markets as part of efforts focused on expanding the officer corps.[39] Such efforts were motivated, at least in part, by a downturn in recruiting in the mid-1980s and research findings that non-White recruits were more likely to enlist and that rising unemployment among men of color could make them more recruitable.[40] Crafting inclusive recruiting appeals assuaged these concerns while contributing to a view of a reinvigorated military, where diverse recruits weren't a sign that the military was a social safety net but, rather, an institution willing to reward hard-working, ambitious Americans.

Recruiting ads situated the military and capitalism as complementary institutions, functioning together as cultural bulwarks against communism through an embrace of meritocracy. Ads featuring martial capitalists and a meritocratic military, somewhat contradictorily, emphasize the military as a site where men could consolidate power through corporate and economic control but also as an institution where exceptional women, Black Americans, and people of color could become deserving subjects. The limited inclusion of people of color, Black Americans, and women functioned to buttress the superiority of a promilitary, procapitalist politics through a nascent vision of a multiracial and gender-inclusive military.

Proud Military Families

Just as the military was a key institution in restoring American dominance in the 1980s, so, too, was the family. Throughout his administration, Reagan touted the value of family as a pillar of American society and a rampart against the threat of communism. In November 1981 Reagan instituted National Family Week, calling the family "the heart of our free democracy."[41] Reagan's emphasis on the family was linked to his embrace of evangelical Christian voters and tied to socially conservative politics that sought to reinforce heteronormative, middle-class gender norms and negate gains made by feminist movements in the 1960s and 1970s. Many conservative efforts to reinstate the traditional family at the center of American life focused on the military. Feinman contends that the defeat of the ERA was largely driven by fears that the military would become gender integrated and women would be sent to combat, developments that were seen by anti-ERA activists as unequivocally disrupting women's roles as mothers and caretakers.[42] Additionally, as Enloe notes, conservative activists viewed women's military inclusion as eroding "the gendered cultural shield" defending against communism and the Soviet Union.[43] As such, conservatives viewed women's increased inclusion in the military as a destructive and dangerous force, detrimental to the maintenance of American families and the nation as a whole.[44]

At the same time as conservatives were touting the connected value of a reinvigorated military and traditional family values, the military began to promote conservative Christian values more explicitly. Army officials developed close ties with conservative Christian leaders that intensified the military's emphasis on heteronormative gender roles.[45] Influenced by the influx of conservative Christians as a prominent political constituency and what retired air force Major General Jeanne Holm called "a deep well of resentment toward women and their growing incursion into previously all-male preserves,"[46] the trajectory of women's inclusion began in the 1970s was cut short in the 1980s. This is not to say that women stopped volunteering to serve. Rather, women continued to enlist in the military, with military women making up between 8.5 percent and 10.9 percent of active-duty service members between 1980 and 1991. However, the large increases in military women seen in the 1970s plateaued as a result of policies designed to curtail women's presence in the ranks. As mentioned, the military embarked on a "womanpause" strategy to decrease the number of women service members shortly after Reagan's election. Within the military advertising industry, this strategy manifested with the end of recruiting efforts in *Cosmopolitan* in 1983, a move that also may have been influenced by a disconnect between the heteronormative respectability espoused by the military and the more sexually liberated vision of femininity on offer in *Cosmopolitan*.

This shift in the military advertising industry coincided with policies limiting women's military inclusion. In 1981, in *Rostker v. Goldberg*, the U.S. Supreme Court upheld the constitutionality of only requiring men to register for selective service based on the grounds that the government's interest in maintaining a combat-ready military—at a time when women were excluded from serving in combat—outweighed claims to equal protection.[47] In 1982 the military doubled down on its antihomosexual stance through directive 1332.14, which framed homosexuality as a threat to the military's mission, ability to recruit, and public image.[48] The directive led to extensive witch hunts throughout the 1980s and early 1990s that disproportionately targeted women.[49] In 1988 the Department of Defense adopted a policy called the "Risk Rule," which served as a way to evaluate positions from which women could be excluded. Together, these policies represented a systematic attack on military women, supported under the guise of family values and operating as an administrative analogue to representational investments in remasculinization.

In the midst of this context, advertisers were faced with meeting a related, yet somewhat contradictory, imperative of representing the military as profamily while limiting representations of military women. In contrast to recruiting ads from the 1970s that sold a vision of the military as an equitable institution where women could gain independence and become martial feminists, ads in the 1980s and early 1990s portrayed the military as enabling and encouraging women to remain recognizable within gendered and sexualized configurations corresponding with socially conservative norms of motherhood, domesticity, and marriage. Bound by an unflinching emphasis on heteronormativity, recruiting ads variously represented women as mothers of service members, as wives, and as service members themselves. Provided they were cast as fulfilling traditional roles within proud military families, women were seen as able to fulfill select positions within a reinvigorated military.

In the summer of 1983 a group of marines and advertisers from the J. Walter Thompson agency convened for a conference to discuss the past, present, and future of recruitment advertising. The corps' brand image, developed over the previous forty years in close coordination with Thompson, was built on representations of a tough, elite fighting force and focused almost exclusively on reaching young men. As Brown notes, marine corps advertising emphasized challenge and elitism to construct a vision of the corps as a masculine rite of passage, a vision largely devoid of women.[50] However, advertisers weren't wholly opposed to representing women in marine corps recruiting materials. Over the course of the conference, advertisers and marines argued that they could improve on their quest to find a few good men by adding a sense of humanity to the corps' image and finding the heart under the "muscled body of the Corps."[51] One way to do so was to balance images of a heroic and manly corps with a sense of emotion and empathy in appeals, something demonstrated in a subsequent ad published in 1984.

Appearing in July in *Sports Illustrated*, the three-page ad begins with an image of a White, male marine drill instructor wearing a campaign hat looking straight-faced at the camera (see fig. 2.5). Beginning on the first page and continuing on the following pages, the headline states, "If there's one thing he'll teach your son, it's—pride runs in the family." A large photo shows a young White man in uniform, smiling with his parents on either side of him. His mother leans against her son, smiling as her husband reaches to touch the ornament on his son's garrison cap. The ad foregrounds the "muscled body of the Corps," embodied by a drill instructor and a message emphasizing how joining the marines enabled young men to learn directly from exemplars of manliness, quickly followed by an image of a proud military family as evidence of the heart of the corps.

The text states:

> A parent's pride in a son runs deep. From the day he's born, through learning how to walk and talk, through graduating from high school and beyond, your pride grows. But with each step of maturing there also comes concern, it's part of the blood bond that comes with family. Because parents worry about the person their son will develop into.

The ad paints an emotional picture, focusing on relationships between parents and sons. Those emotions are connected with military service:

> We want you to know we share your concern. Our Drill Instructors have a mission. To help each young man develop to his full potential. They teach him that pride in himself, his family, his country and Corps go hand in hand. And that with it, a man's potential is unlimited.

As the ad fulfilled the strategic imperative of adding humanity to the corps, it also expressed how women could be included within the gendered and sexualized dynamics of a reinvigorated and remasculinized military.

Figure 2.5. Marine Corps ad. Source: *Sports Illustrated*, July 18, 1984

The ad frames the goals of the corps and parents as one and the same; helping young men meet their potential. The corps is framed not as defending the nation but as defending families by helping raise men. Women are relegated to a specific role within a proud family, corps, and country. The woman is shown smiling, proud of her son becoming a marine. According to the ad, women aren't marines themselves and aren't concerned about their sons joining the military but, rather, are happily supportive of the crucial role the military can play in raising sons. The ad reinstates gender relations in which women fulfill roles as martial and maternal citizens, women whose domestic investment in parenting coincides with a political investment in raising patriotic children.

Patriotic mothers and sons are brought together through an expression of pride, echoing Reagan's calls for an intertwined profamily and promilitary politics that would help America reclaim its place atop the world order. Pride itself was also firmly cast within a heteronormative and militarized frame.[52] The image of a heteronormative family signaled that all was well within the military and the nation and that Americans could be proud of their military and their nation because women were back in their rightful place as patriotic mothers and the military once again helped young men fulfill their manly potential.

Other ads, including for the navy and army, also feature images of heteronormative military families that combine discourses of parenting and militarization, where parental and patriotic love converge. That heteronormative families embodied this sense of militarized pride tied the emotional orientation of recruiting appeals to a broader narrative of remasculinization characterized by the consolidation of conservative ideas about gender and sexuality. Since the development of an antihomosexual discharge apparatus in the 1940s, heteronormativity has been associated with and enforced within the military through practices and policies including family programs, recruiting practices, and military laws.[53] As a recruiting strategy, representations of heteronormativity contributed to twinned investments in family and the military as complementary and exceptional American institutions.

Enlisting parents, specifically mothers, as key actors in recruiting appeals was one way advertisers included women within representations of remasculinization; another way advertisers did so was by representing women as wives. More specifically, a series of recruiting ads for the Army National Guard published in *Ebony* and *Cosmopolitan* between 1982 and 1985 foregrounded military families and showed how women were situated both as wives of service members and as wives and service members themselves. The two ads follow the same layout, feature the same copy, and show photos of

Army National Guard officers posing with their families (see fig. 2.6). Both families are Black families, shown in front of their homes, smiling as they face the camera, a representation of convergent profamily and promilitary politics. One ad shows a male service member, with his wife and their child, while the other shows a military woman, standing with her husband. Together, the ads bolster representations of a remasculinized military while further revealing the gendered, sexualized, and racialized contours of proud military families.

In 1983 Reagan created the Great American Family Awards as a celebration of the American family and regularly included a military family among the award winners each year, a move that strengthened ties between conservative promilitary and profamily politics.[54] The ads contribute to such ties by detailing the symbiotic relationship between military service and families. Each ad describes service in the National Guard as "[o]ne of the most important jobs in America" that allows "plenty of time for your family." Service in the guard simultaneously fulfilled the linked expectations of the military and the family as similarly vaunted institutions. The ads supported a vision of a military family as an indication of American exceptionalism, made clear by the slogan "The Guard is America at its best."

Through representations of domesticity and a delineation of gender roles, the ads emphasize that military families are exemplars of heteronormativity. Each of the families is shown standing in front of their homes, implicating the domestic household as an important symbolic resource in asserting visions of an exceptional military. While the front door of each home is closed and the families stand outside, the ads foreground domestic configurations of heteronormativity as a symbol of "America at its best." This configuration is bolstered by gendered distinctions making clear the proper roles for men and women in military families. While both ads feature images of a military service member with their civilian spouse, the primary distinction between the two ads is the gender of the service member and the presence or absence of a child. The distinction between a male service member being shown as a husband *and* father and a female service member being shown as a wife but *not* a mother speaks to anxieties about parenting within and beyond the military.

Parenthood is represented as a part of a traditional-family model for a male service member, who serves as a breadwinner, while his spouse is framed primarily as a mother. Representing military men as presumably married fathers contributed to remasculinization, in which marriage functioned as a sign of masculine recovery and framed military men as exceptional sexual and gendered citizens.[55] Such a configuration is a simplistic and politically

Figure 2.6. Army National Guard ads. Sources: *Ebony*, September 1982 and May 1983

salient representation of a military family that belies the complex experiences of divorce, abuse, and desertion that many military families face.[56]

However, for women motherhood was not compatible with being in the military. A military woman is not a mother; she would not leave her child or children or ask her husband to be the primary caretaker. The military has long resisted having mothers as soldiers. Prior to 1975 military women found to be pregnant were involuntarily discharged, and guidelines in the 2010s encouraged planning pregnancies around deployment and training.[57] Representations of military women as mothers, even serving close to home, would have disrupted a narrative of remasculinization and its attendant investment in conservative gender and sexual politics while also exposing military women to criticism for failing to live up to the gendered expectations of caregiving. Both Army National Guard ads portray the military as a site of conservative social values, where men are good fathers and husbands, and woman are either mothers or service members, mutually exclusive roles promoted as markers of an exceptional nation.

Enlisting in the military, specifically the Army National Guard, was represented as a family affair, a way Black men, women, and children could meet obligations of sexual and martial citizenship. Proximity to heteronormativity, expressed through domesticity, monogamy, and procreation, has long been used to measure Black Americans' suitability as citizens.[58] As a symbol of the right way to be an American family, images of military families contrasted the exceptional heteronormative military family with civilian figures like the welfare mother and the absent father, racialized and sexualized figures framed as deviant and aberrant as part of efforts to justify attacks of social welfare programs in the 1980s. Christian conservatives used the notion of an exceptional military family to influence national policy through what Mittelstadt refers to as a "public contrast... between a supposedly moral Army family and a putatively immoral, decaying civilian family."[59] This contrast was used to attack government support for civilian families while justifying increased investments in social welfare programs for army families. The ads portray military service, along with specific conditions of heteronormativity, as a pathway for Black families to be viewed as moral families, as deserving both of recognition and of the material benefits of military service.[60] Although the ads craft a racially inclusive vision of proud military families, they also engage in representations of colorism that reinforced dynamics of White supremacy.

Colorism, a term believed to have been coined by Alice Walker in 1982, refers to discrimination based on skin color and functions both within and across racial groups.[61] While colorism has been deployed globally through a variety of colonial projects, in the United States colorism is a legacy of slavery and is deeply tied to racism and media representations.[62] In each ad the lighter skinned member of the adult couple is portrayed as being in the military. As Eduardo Bonilla-Silva and Austin Ashe note, depictions of racial diversity in media often reinforce colorism through representations of "honorary whites."[63] Proximity to Whiteness is represented as synonymous with proximity to the military, a proximity facilitating representations of Black families as symbols of America at its best. At a moment when profamily politics and associated investments in Whiteness and heteronormativity were used to delegitimize and marginalize Black Americans and people of color, militarized visions of heteronormative families marked the military as a bastion of traditional family values and a place where Black families could prove their suitability as proper sexual and martial citizens.

While it might seem that women would be less inclined to enlist in a military that represented them in such narrow terms as mothers and wives, the 1980s saw a small but steady increase in the percentage of women in the military. The increasing participation of women in the military speaks to the economic motivations that often drive enlistment, motivations that scholars have found to be influential in driving women to join the military, and doubly so for Black women who face economic disadvantages via both gender and race.[64] As women's participation in the military increased, recruiting ads constructed visions of military women that ultimately served to promote conservative gender and sexual politics as part of a broader process of remasculinization.

The Exceptional Military at the End of the Cold War

By the early 1990s the military portrayed in recruiting ads was a lethal, high-tech, capitalist, and profamily institution. Figures of tactical inclusion, including high-tech soldiers, Black pilots, martial capitalists, and military families, showed how the reinvigorated military, though largely defined by investments in manliness and Whiteness, made room for women, Black Americans, and people of color. The reinvigorated military was defined by the idea that not everyone deserved the same benefits, rather, that one had to earn them, especially when those benefits were given by the state. America at its best didn't give handouts. Rather, service members are represented as earning their benefits by virtue of their commitments to high-tech militarism, capitalism, and racialized heteronormativity. In emphasizing that service members deserve the opportunities provided by the military, recruiting ads rearticulate the dynamics of tactical inclusion and contribute to a new racial order that, as argued by literary scholar Jodi Melamed, was predicated not explicitly on color but, rather, on racialized notions of value.[65] Broadly speaking, recruiting ads throughout the 1980s constructed a vision of the military that was good for the nation, that acted as a bulwark against communism both militarily and culturally. Potential recruits, including women, Black Americans, and people of color, are rendered valuable for the military and for the nation provided they are intelligible within narrow and exclusionary parameters of remasculinization, characterized by limited avenues of racial and gender inclusion predicated on the reification of heteropatriarchal capitalism and militarism.

As the 1980s came to a close and Reagan left office to be replaced by George H. W. Bush, the emphasis on advertising a militarily and morally superior nation in recruiting ads continued in the face of a changing geopolitical landscape. The end of the Cold War catalyzed a rethinking of the military as the singular threat of communism diminished with the fall of the Berlin Wall and the dissolution of the U.S.S.R. Tasked with both capitalizing on similarities with Reagan and distinguishing himself, Bush reduced defense spending, leading to a decrease in the size of the military.[66] This decrease was referred to as the drawdown, and military officials were more concerned with getting personnel out of the military than persuading them to join it. The drawdown led to a decrease in the overall size of the military and a new set of challenges for advertisers, who struggled to persuade new recruits that the military remained a viable option for upward mobility. The recruiting landscape was then further altered by the Persian Gulf War, which was perceived by military officials and many politicians as resounding evidence of the success of the AVF.

On August 5, 1990, Bush ordered U.S. troops to Saudi Arabia as part of Operation Desert Shield, in what is now known as the Persian Gulf War. The initial deployment of 120,000 American troops grew to over 500,000 troops before the end of the war in February 1991 and was, at the time, the largest deployment since the implementation of the AVF. The Persian Gulf War was framed as an overwhelming victory that validated U.S. global power and the very concept of the AVF. Jeffrey J. Clarke, who served as chief historian for the army from 1990 to 2006, referred to operations in the war as overwhelming victories that restored the confidence and assertiveness of U.S. foreign policy.[67] In a report commissioned by the air force, the war was called "one of the most operationally successful wars in history."[68] Military historian Bernard Rostker, who served in various capacities for the Department of Defense in the 1970s, 1980s, and 1990s, contends that during the

Persian Gulf War "the volunteer force was arguably the finest military force the United States had ever sent into battle."[69] In short, representations of an exceptional military espoused in recruiting ads throughout the 1980s and early 1990s had seemed to be realized in combat.

Although Bush viewed the Persian Gulf War as a catalyst toward a "new world order" of global cooperation and peace, the war also reflected a new domestic order in the form of a diverse volunteer military where the costs of state violence were increasingly borne by women, Black Americans, and people of color. The volunteer force that served during the war was the most diverse force to date since the shift to the AVF, and the Persian Gulf War marked the largest deployment of military women in American history at the time. Although the majority of combat casualties were White men, a larger percentage of women, Black Americans, and Latinx service members were among the 143 service members killed in action in the Persian Gulf War than in wars in Korea and Vietnam.[70] When faced with criticism about the disproportionate burden borne by service members of color, specifically Black Americans, the Department of Defense, at the time headed by Richard Bruce (Dick) Cheney, who went on to serve as vice president during the George W. Bush administration, claimed that it was evidence of the military's leadership in equal opportunity.[71] At the largest scale since the implementation of the AVF, recruitability was directly implicated in risks of death and the enactment of violence in war. While the war had, at least initially, seemed to reinforce the exceptionalism of the reinvigorated AVF, the lingering effects of a highly visible war fought by an unprecedentedly diverse military led to intense political debates about gender, race, sexuality, and military service that influenced substantive shifts in recruitment advertising.

CHAPTER 3

The Military Type

In October 1994 an armed forces ad published in *Sports Illustrated* asked parents to reconsider what they thought of their children and of military service (see fig. 3.1). Below the headline, "If you never thought of your child as the military type, think again," a young woman wearing a colorful sweater and a blue skirt stands with schoolbooks in her hands and a purse slung over her shoulder. The ad touts educational opportunities and job training, an appeal consistent with recruiting ads from earlier decades of the AVF, but there is a shift in who is seen or whom the audience is asked to see as being the military type. The text concludes by telling parents, "So, if you know a smart, ambitious high school graduate who's determined to make the most of the future, maybe he or she is the military type after all." In combining a call for the audience to reconsider their ideas of the military type with a representation of a young woman as an overlooked, latent service member, the ad exemplified tensions at the heart of recruiting in the 1990s.

Advertisers with military contracts, specifically from the ad agencies Bates Worldwide and J. Walter Thompson, debated how to best target and represent young women. Advertisers working on marine corps advertising detailed a need to create recruiting materials that could reach women without "distorting the Corps' persona" in ways that would dissuade young men from enlisting.[1] Advertisers working on accounts for the coast guard and armed forces were concerned with crafting images of a "gender friendly" military.[2] Overcoming brand images and public perceptions of a male-exclusive military inhospitable to women was a challenge of reaching young women as was avoiding attracting the "wrong type" of women who were unprepared for the

Figure 3.1. Armed forces ad. Source: *Sports Illustrated*, October 17, 1994

rigors of military training or were joining for the "wrong reasons."[3] Advertisers also expressed needing to create recruiting materials better representing the racial diversity of the nation, a goal some advertisers thought was best achieved by portraying "racially neutral" service members.[4] In the midst of this context, the armed forces ad reveals one way the military advertising industry created a new military type: a light-skinned, young woman, easily recognizable within heteronormative ideals of gender, smart, ambitious, and driven to take advantage of the myriad opportunities on offer in the military.

In the 1990s the military advertising industry was influenced by a series of institutional and cultural shifts. The Persian Gulf War made clear that enlisting could potentially mean serving in combat. War changes the dynamics of recruitment advertising, often functioning to dissuade recruits motivated by tangible benefits from enlisting and the Gulf War led to a notable decline in enlistments, especially among Black Americans.[5] The war was the largest deployment of women to date, and the increased visibility of military women ultimately resulted in a series of policy shifts opening an unprecedented number of military positions to women. Political debates and the eventual institution of "Don't ask, don't tell" (DADT) in 1993 brought concerns about sexuality and military service to the forefront of the national consciousness. As advertisers were grappling with these shifts, they were also influenced by an industrial embrace of multiculturalism as a strategy to better reflect a demographically changing nation and portray the military in ways that might better resonate with American youth. Together, this cultural and political environment shaped how advertisers thought of creating recruitment advertisements. Recruiting ads had to address the challenge of reframing combat as a beneficial experience and perceptions potential recruits had of DADT while figuring out how to portray the military as a multicultural institution and how to best sell new opportunities to women.

Focusing primarily on recruitment advertising between 1992 and 2000, this chapter chronicles the military advertising industry's efforts to construct new military types through the creation and targeting of three markets: Black men, Latinx men, and women. Framed as part of efforts to more accurately represent the diversity of the nation, these three groups were largely conceptualized as discrete markets within the military advertising industry, a process that contributed to the erasure of particular groups—Latinx women, AfroLatinx Americans, and Black women, for instance—and narrowed the scope of how a supposedly multicultural military was actually represented. The creation of new military types was guided also by guarding against the wrong type of recruits through a series of exclusions. Animated by anxieties about race, gender, and sexuality, the ways certain Black men, Latinx men, and women were constructed as military types hinged upon narratives of transformation.

Recruiting ads detailed how military service could transform Black men and Latinx men into embodiments of state authority and warrior patriots. Through experiences of combat and the acquisition of traits like confidence, character, and discipline, Black men and Latinx men were made legible within brand images of warrior masculinity rooted in strict parameters of racialized citizenship. Such promises of transformation were foreclosed to women, due both to policies limiting women's participation in combat and symbolic imperatives of gender and sexuality. Women were targeted with appeals touting opportunities in the military while assuring that the military would *not* transform them. Women were represented as military types provided they stayed recognizable within narrow confines of hetero-romance and gender normativity, which reinforced heteronormativity as crucial to the military's image following the passage of DADT. While hetero-romance was largely represented through associations with Whiteness, representations of women as new military types also made room for the selective inclusion of some women of color. As a gendered, sexualized, and racialized narrative, transformation functioned normatively to tactically include some Black men, Latinx men, and women while also delineating the limits of who could be seen as the military type. Recruiting efforts to target these three groups were deployed as part of an industry-wide effort to portray the military as a progressive institution in the midst of a shifting political landscape.

President Bill Clinton suspended the policy banning gay and lesbian personnel from military service and instituted the policy known as DADT in 1993. DADT stated that known homosexuals could not serve in the military but that the military could not ask enlistees if they were gay, maintaining an idea that the military's function and mission remained rooted in perceptions of heteronormativity.[6] While DADT ultimately did little to protect gay and lesbian personnel from the military's antihomosexual discharge apparatus, it was seen as a pragmatic compromise reached between the desires of activists and the recalcitrance of the military.[7] Initially developed during World War II, the military's antihomosexual discharge apparatus encouraged service members to surveil one another, often under threat of interrogation and punishment, and help identify other service members that exhibited behaviors and traits considered to be indicative of homosexuality.[8] Women were particularly targeted by this apparatus, especially as the participation of women in the military increased and women were perceived to be taking on more masculine roles in the military.[9] The antihomosexual discharge apparatus as a whole was based on and contributed to a broader cultural environment of heteronormativity and homophobia.

The same year that DADT was included in the National Defense Authorization Act, the annual appropriations bill detailing defense spending, a policy change opened eighty thousand new military positions to women, allowing women to serve in almost 85 percent of military occupations.[10] Women were still excluded from direct ground combat positions, but the male-exclusivity of the military was challenged to a degree not seen since the 1970s. The policy was the culmination of a series of changes that opened various occupational designations to women, including service on combat ships and in combat aviation.[11] The changes were framed as a progressive response to the George H. W. Bush–era Presidential Commission on the Assignment of Women in the Armed Services. Formed in March 1992 in reaction to the increased visibility of servicewomen during the Persian Gulf War, the commission was deeply concerned with maintaining the masculine nature of the military, reinforcing White, middle-class, heteronormative gender roles, and viewed women's access to combat positions as an undeserved form of social welfare and a threat to American ideals.[12] As the commission was debating the role of women in the military, the national discourse surrounding women and gender equality—in intersection with race, class, and sexuality—was profoundly shaped by Anita Hill's testimony during U.S. Senate Judiciary Commission confirmation hearings for Clarence Thomas for the U.S. Supreme Court; the exposure of the 1991 Tailhook assaults, during which eighty-three service women and eight service men reported being sexually assaulted by aviation officers from the navy and marine corps; and the 1992 elections, which were deemed the Year of the Woman.[13] These events increased awareness of sexual harassment and violence as questions of gender equality and sexual equality rose to prominence in the national discourse at the same time as new policies pushed the military to include more women and reconsider its rigid stance against homosexuality.

To be clear, this is not to say that the 1990s marked a watershed moment for gender equality and sexual equality but, rather, that the cultural contestations and struggles of the time are important for understanding the contours of tactical inclusion. Recruitment advertisements reveal how advertisers sought to portray the military as welcoming to women at a time when it was made clear that women could be and were subject to sexual harassment and violence; the ads also show how the military sought to respond to views of sexuality and the military. While concerns of gender and sexuality dominated policy shifts, such concerns are always in intersection with dynamics of race, an intersection made clear in recruitment advertising when one considers how dynamics of gender and sexuality set the foundation for efforts to target new military types as part of a multicultural military.

Making a Multicultural Military

Drawing on trends in management and business in which multiculturalism was viewed as a way to create policies and a workplace culture that accommodated racial and gender differences, concerns about multiculturalism proliferated across the advertising industry in the 1990s.[14] Articles in *Advertising Age* focused largely on different non-White markets, emphasizing the spending power of African American, Hispanic, Asian American, and Native American markets and various advertising strategies to reach them.[15] Advertisers were concerned that ads targeting the mass market—a market defined by an unnamed norm of Whiteness—could alienate and offend non-White consumers and advocated for campaigns that didn't simply include representations of non-White consumers but consisted of specific themes and messages relating directly to targeted markets.[16] Some advertising professionals saw their role as reflecting the racial diversity of the nation and creating campaigns that acknowledged and celebrated difference.[17] Companies and corporations utilized a variety of images, including the melting pot and the rainbow, as metaphors for difference to expand their markets in ways that, ultimately, ignored material inequalities of race, gender, and sexuality.[18]

The advertising industry's approach to multiculturalism coincided with what cultural studies scholar Stuart Hall called commercial multiculturalism, an ideology based on the premise that recognition of diversity in the marketplace would resolve problems of difference through individual consumption rather than any substantive redistribution of power.[19] Other scholars have detailed how multiculturalism, as a racial order, contributed to the superficial recognition of racial difference while ignoring and making worse systemic inequalities.[20] Within multiculturalism, race was primarily thought of as an issue of recognition, a view that allowed for the proliferation of representations of racial difference in media.[21] As noted by feminist scholar Neda Atanasoski, multiculturalism was also tethered to militarism and was "essential to the fantasy of the United States as an antiracist nation" engaged in military interventions that were framed as emancipatory endeavors.[22] These insights help to contextualize the emergence of multiculturalism within the military advertising industry and subsequent representations in recruiting ads. In terms of tactical inclusion, multiculturalism was a particular articulation of targeting and managing difference as valuable for state violence and was a way of ensuring, to paraphrase Black feminist and activist Angela Davis, that though soldiers may look different from one another or from what they used to look like, they could still be productive members of the military all the same.[23]

A 1994 report from a marine corps recruiting conference detailed the challenges of embracing multiculturalism:

> [T]he personality of the Marine Corps has traditionally been more a white, male institution. Teens, on the other hand, expect to see multi-cultured

diversity. If the prospect sees a Marine Corps that does not reflect African-American influences, if he or she does not see women in leadership roles, if he or she does not see the same path to success for everyone regardless of who they are or what they look like, then he/she may not view the Corps as being "progressive." The communications dilemma then becomes one of demonstrating that the Corps is indeed culturally diverse.[24]

The central dilemma faced by the corps was indicative of a broader set of concerns across the military advertising industry as advertisers sought to challenge and expand ideas of who could be seen as the military type. Broadly speaking, advertisers framed the portrayal of a multicultural military through reconsiderations of the "minority market" and renewed efforts to reach women.

In devising their marketing strategy for 1993, Bates Worldwide, responsible for armed forces and coast guard advertising, detailed a need to target minorities and women and that the "minority market" couldn't be thought of as Black only.[25] Other advertisers, including those developing strategies for the navy and marine corps, indicated a need to expand their thinking of the "minority market" beyond the Black/White binary that had dominated recruitment advertising during earlier decades of the AVF. Historically, the term "minority market" was used to refer to Black and Latinx recruits, especially when referring to recruiting materials targeting non-White recruits for the officer corps. However, influenced by an imperative to better reflect the nation and portray a multicultural military, efforts to reach the "minority market" in the 1990s consisted of targeting Black, Latinx, and women recruits. In the face of competing with the other branches for recruits, advertising plans for the coast guard sought to represent the coast guard as an "equal opportunity" employer and constructed their target market as 75 percent minority—a category defined as Black and Latinx—and 60 percent women.[26] An armed forces campaign quickly capitalized on policy shifts opening positions to women to "create awareness of new Armed Forces career opportunities for women."[27] Advertisers from the J. Walter Thompson agency, in their annual reports on marine corps recruiting in 1994 and 1995, discussed how, as a result of teens' expectation of seeing cultural diversity in media, women and people of color needed to be better represented in recruiting materials.[28] While terms like "multiculturalism" and "diversity" often operate as empty terms meant to signal political commitment devoid of concrete action,[29] the emergence of these terms in the military advertising industry led to tangible efforts to target women, Latinx men, and Black men. The development of more-robust recruiting plans to reach these groups was also driven by demographic shifts.

Market research in the 1990s showed a changing composition of the recruiting market. Advertisers were primarily concerned with the increase in Latinx youth, as the percentage of Latinx individuals in the civilian population had doubled since the 1970s. The growth in the Latinx market was framed alongside a declining propensity among Black Americans, attributed in part to the Persian Gulf War. Although some advertisers considered small-scale efforts to reach out to Asian Americans and Indigenous Americans, the task of representing and recruiting a multicultural military centered on reaching Latinx and Black Americans. Advertisers sought to reach "across cultures and ethnic groups" to portray various branches of the military as accepting of new military types.[30]

The military struggled to meet recruiting goals throughout the 1990s. In the history of the AVF, 1993 was among the most difficult recruiting years, and difficulties in recruiting continued through the rest of the decade.[31] The overall numbers of Black active-duty service members declined by over a third through the 1990s, with a decrease of 144,500 service members. During the same time, the percentage of Latinx service members increased from 5 percent to 8.5 percent with 10,681 more Latinx service members serving in the active-duty ranks by the end of the decade. The overall numbers of military women fluctuated through the 1990s, but the percentage of women service members steadily increased from 10.9 percent in 1990 to 14.7 percent at the end of the decade, the highest percentage of military women to date.

Shifts in the racial and gender composition of the military occurred as the overall size of the military declined by over 650,000 service members, a decrease catalyzed by the post–Cold War drawdown. The military advertising industry was still tasked with persuading between 167,000 and 203,000 new recruits to enlist each year between 1992 and 2000. Despite the Clinton administration's "Reinvention of Government" that sought to cut government spending, including defense spending cuts, advertising and recruiting budgets were increased in the late 1990s in the midst of what some military personnel referred to as a recruiting crisis.[32] For the first time since the implementation of the AVF, the army and navy failed to meet their annual recruiting goals in 1998.[33] In the midst of the most challenging recruiting environment of the AVF to date, converging influences of the Persian Gulf War and an emphasis on portraying a multicultural military, the 1990s were defined by a reconsideration of who was seen as and who could become the military type.

Combat Legibility

The Gulf War forced advertisers, potential recruits, and the broader public to grapple with the realization that the primary function of the military was to wage war, a reality largely ignored in recruitment advertising. Enabled by a symbiotic relationship between the military and media industries, particularly television, the Gulf War was a media event that marked an unprecedented entanglement of war and entertainment and brought Americans within proximity to war more than at any previous time during the AVF.[34] Surveys of American youth conducted in the early 1990s by J. Walter Thompson, the agency in charge of marine corps advertising, indicate that the war had a largely negative effect on recruiting. Although the war had a positive effect on young people's attitudes toward the military, the risk of getting shot and/or killed was seen as a distinct disadvantage of military service, particularly in the combat-oriented marine corps.[35] By the mid-1990s, there was recognition that deployments in the Persian Gulf and Somalia had a negative effect on propensity, particularly for youth who enlisted to gain a marketable skill.[36] The military advertising industry was forced to grapple with the specter of combat, a specter that was increasingly present in the minds of potential recruits and that recruiting ads had spent years warding off in efforts to build the AVF.

Advertisers were also negotiating changing patterns in the enlistment of Black recruits, a group the military had become disproportionately reliant upon to meet personnel needs. In 1990 Black service members made up almost a quarter of all enlisted service members, the highest percentage at any point during the AVF. Black women were even more overrepresented than Black men, with Black women making up almost half of all army women in the mid-1990s.[37] Despite their overrepresentation, Black women remained largely absent from recruiting appeals, and military officials responded to concerns about the decline in propensity among Black Americans with renewed recruiting efforts targeting Black men. In the midst of a larger trend of declining interest in military service, the propensity of Black Americans dropped by 60 percent in the first half of the 1990s, a decline attributed, in part, to concerns among Black youth about the dangers of serving in combat.[38] Such concerns were justified given that Black service members made up 17.2 percent of all casualties during the Persian Gulf War although Black Americans made up 12.1 percent of the civilian population.[39] The increased risks of injury and/or death faced by Black service members during the Gulf War also belied recruiting promises emphasizing economic and occupational opportunities, both of which are irrelevant if one doesn't survive their military service. The military advertising industry's efforts to target Black recruits, specifically Black men, reveal the ways new military types were constructed through converging imperatives, namely, the need to construct a multicultural military and to grapple with the specter of combat as a more visible aspect of military service. In other words, advertisers were tasked with representing the military as both a multicultural and war-waging institution.

As representations of combat proliferated in media coverage of the Gulf War, recruiting ads embraced symbols associated with combat, including firearms, camouflage, and combat uniforms—officially referred to as battle dress uniforms at the time. Ads for the army regularly discussed valuable traits recruits could learn in the military, such as teamwork, initiative, determination, and self-discipline, in association with images of male soldiers in combat uniforms driving tanks and running with rifles in hand. Ads spoke of service in combat positions as giving soldiers' future careers "a little firepower" and as "the learning and growth experience of a lifetime" that "feels like nothing else you've ever experienced." Rather than a potentially deadly risk or an experience that could and did lead to physical and mental injuries, service in combat was portrayed as a unique experience, as a rush even, and as a positive transformation. Coinciding with Brown's reading of such appeals as solidifying links between manliness and military service, this transformation was importantly promised to men and to men alone.[40] While reflecting military policies restricting women from serving in ground combat positions, gender-exclusive representations of the transformative benefits of combat reinforced the notion that the ideological and symbolic heart of the military remained associated with men. Such representations were notably inclusive of Black men. At the convergence of combat and multiculturalism, Black men were made legible as warriors and embodiments of state authority.

Published in *Ebony* and *Sports Illustrated* between 1996 and 1998, one army ad represents service in a combat position as a way for young Black men to learn transformational traits (see fig. 3.2). The ad features two images: a smaller image of Sergeant L. Peterson, a twenty-three-year-old Black tank crewman, and a larger image of two tanks and a helicopter. Peterson's face is partially visible behind his tactical goggles, while a bright muzzle flash in the larger image indicates a soldier firing a machine gun. The close-up of Peterson's face and the pulled-back image of soldiers in combat are brought together through a narrative of what the army can teach Black men and the benefits of those lessons: "You'll learn to be focused. So when you get $40,000 for college, you'll be ready." The experience of combat, and the personal growth it purportedly enables, provide Black men with the skills to be successful college students.

Figure 3.2. Army ad. Source: *Sports Illustrated*, February 9, 1998

Other ads subtly rearticulate promises of what the military could do for Black men through a similar language of personal transformation, imagery associated with combat, and a framing of the military as a pedagogical institution of the self. In doing so, recruiting ads construct narratives about who Black men needed to become to be recognizable as military types and legible as worthy subjects.

Two army ads, published in *Ebony* between 1990 and 1994, show Black men as military police and drill sergeants. The first ad focuses on an image of a Black man wearing camouflage fatigues, crouching in a green field with a map in his left hand as he points to something out of frame with his other hand. An armband wrapped around his left upper arm reads "MP," designating his position as military police.[41] The text begins with the phrase, "You're in charge," going on to connect the soldier's position as a MP with authority and personal transformation:

> As an Army Military Policeman you'll set the standard for excellence. When you're required to make split second decisions of critical importance entirely on your own, you develop something invaluable: self-confidence and discipline. With these qualities, you'll always be one step ahead, whether you go into civilian law enforcement or any other field.

The soldier's status as an MP makes him exceptional, he "sets the standard for excellence," while also helping develop invaluable traits like self-confidence and discipline. By developing these specific traits, Black men, who are presumed to not have self-confidence or discipline prior to joining the army, transform to occupy positions of authority. The ad also aligns excellence, a term tied to Whiteness in U.S. culture, with militarism and policing, providing an avenue for Black men to embody excellence when aligned with the state.

A second army ad similarly represents the military as a space where Black men develop transformational traits and occupy positions of authority (see fig. 3.3). The headline reads, "Once you've faced this man, a job interview is no problem." A Black soldier wearing a campaign hat—a broad-brimmed hat worn by drill sergeants—and a camouflage shirt, arms folded across his chest, stands in front of a training obstacle. The ad details how this soldier will prepare new recruits:

> There you are, sweaty palms and all, wondering what your Drill Sergeant will ask next. And you know your answer better be right. Because the Sergeant doesn't play. But in the end, chances are you'll thank him—because he'll help prepare you for any situation that comes your way.

The ad represents a common trope of a military drill sergeant; a tough, demanding leader driven by a desire to best prepare his trainees, who come to view his toughness with gratitude. The sergeant is in a position of authority, tasked with transforming and shaping new recruits into well-trained,

Figure 3.3. Army ad. Source: *Ebony*, December 1991

hardened, disciplined soldiers. Although the army ad doesn't contain the explicit "few good men" rhetoric made famous in marine corps advertising, it articulates a similar promise of masculine transformation; one that helps to "build your character and self-confidence along the way." That the figure of the drill sergeant is embodied by a Black man draws on cultural narratives associating Black men and excessive masculinity, which though often framed as violent and sexually threatening is channeled into alignment with the state when figured as part of the transformative process of becoming a soldier. While both ads briefly mention the G.I. Bill as a tangible benefit of military service, they foreground the personal transformation Black men can access via the military, a transformation that results in Black men becoming aligned with state interests and embodying state authority.

To be a drill sergeant not only places the soldier in a position of actual authority but also in a position of symbolic authority. The drill sergeant embodies masculinized values of toughness, determination, and discipline and is an arbiter who dictates how recruits become soldiers and determines which recruits become soldiers. To be a military policeman places the soldier in charge of other soldiers, in charge of maintaining law and order within the military and well positioned for a career in civilian law enforcement.[42] MPs and drill sergeants are not just included in the military; they are embodiments of its authority. Black men are represented as firmly aligned with the state, tough men in charge who "don't play" and go on to work in law enforcement. Black men are represented as the military type provided they address a presumptive lack of certain personality traits, including discipline, self-confidence, and character, by joining the military and transforming who they are. While lack is central to advertising more broadly, in recruitment advertising this lack is expressed as an innate characteristic of Black men, who are constructed as unruly subjects, legible through a dichotomy of unworthiness and worthiness that, though expressed as being about personal transformation, ultimately pivots along submission to and alignment with state interests.[43]

Through combat and alignment with state interests, Black men are situated in recruiting ads on a trajectory culminating in the successful enactment of upwardly mobile, focused, driven citizenship. However, the increased life chances and right to life at the end of that trajectory are predicated on an increased exposure to the risk of injury or death. Black men are hailed as worthy subjects, as recognizable to the state, through a simultaneous exposure to possible death in the present and a promise of future life. The right to life comes with a prerequisite increased risk of death. This conditional acceptance and inclusion are certainly indicative of military service more broadly, yet for it to be represented so clearly in a recruiting ad marks a notable distinction from recruiting appeals during earlier decades of the AVF.

Black men were brought into proximity to the ideological heart of a combat-oriented military in recruiting ads in the 1990s. Drill sergeants, military police, and men in combat are certainly not new military types;

rather, they are consistent with long-standing ideas of soldiering tied to violence, toughness, and warrior masculinity. But showing Black men as these military types was new. In showing that Black men could join the military to become military policemen and drill sergeants and acquire traits like discipline, confidence, and character, recruiting appeals frame the inclusion of Black soldiers through a narrative of recuperation and regulation. The normative power of inclusion, as a process that requires capitulation to existing institutional norms, is sold as opportunity. Joining the military and being transformed by it made Black men legible as manly warriors, firmly aligned with the interests of the state. In the face of widespread police violence and criminalization, the transformation on offer in the military functions as a protection against vulnerability to state violence. Any tentative protection offered by enlisting requires vulnerability to the violence of combat and warfare. In other words, for Black men the threat of state violence awaits on either side of tactical inclusion, yet one form of state violence is rendered as legible, instructive, and productive.

Translating Transformation

From the naturalization and subsequent drafting of twenty thousand Puerto Ricans during World War I to the consistent increase in Latinx service members during the first twenty years of the AVF, Latinx Americans have long served in the U.S. military. Despite the historical presence of Latinx service members, the military advertising industry's efforts to recruit Latinx in the first two decades of the AVF were sporadic. In the mid-1970s, advertisers for the navy and marine corps published Spanish-language ads in newspapers and explored opportunities in the "Spanish-Mexican market" in California, a term used to refer to Spanish speakers.[44] In the late 1970s and early 1980s, Latinx men were targeted along with Black men in direct mailings to "minority" college students as part of efforts to diversify the officer corps, and a small number of army ads published in the 1980s focused on service members with surnames indicating Latinx heritage. The Latinx market was largely conceptualized and targeted with a focus on reaching certain geographical areas and creating recruiting materials in Spanish and as part of "minority" advertising for the officer corps. Such efforts encapsulate the primary ways the military advertising industry constructed the Latinx market, a market almost exclusively associated with men.

Throughout the first two decades of the AVF, recruiting plans considered the Latinx market and the female market as distinct, a distinction mirroring the ways the Black market was thought of and reinforcing gendered norms in recruitment advertising. Furthermore, the majority of efforts to reach Latinx recruits were subsumed within what archival documents refer to as the "minority" officer market. Such efforts were shaped by the racialized and gendered history of combat, particularly in the wake of the war in Vietnam. As the shift to the AVF was planned, there were concerns that a disproportionately White officer corps couldn't adequately lead enlisted men, especially enlisted men of color, and would contribute to racial resentment within the ranks.[45] As such, diversifying the officer corps to include more Black men and Latinx men and better reflect the enlisted ranks was crucial. Historical links among combat, men, and the Latinx market were also shaped by cultural narratives of Latinx men as predisposed toward military service. Historian Steven Rosales points to the role understandings of machismo played in directing Latinx men toward military service prior to the AVF.[46] Jorge Mariscal contends that there exists a form of "warrior patriotism," in which Latinx men, specifically Chicanx men, are driven to military service through converging narratives of assimilation, patriotism, and masculinity.[47] Together, these historical, industrial, and cultural forces influenced recruiting efforts targeting Latinx men in the 1990s.

Broadly speaking, in the 1990s advertisers targeted the Latinx market with advertisements in three kinds of publications: general-interest publications, professional publications, and educational publications. The most consistently targeted general-interest publication was *Vista*, a Sunday newspaper supplement described as having an editorial focus on traditional family values and Latinx culture. Ads for the coast guard, navy, and marine corps were featured in *Vista* in the eight largest Latinx markets, a selection that based on census data at the time most likely consisted of Los Angeles, New York City, Miami, the San Francisco Bay area, Chicago, Houston, San Antonio, and Dallas–Fort Worth. Alongside advertising in those specific markets, advertisers sought to reach upwardly mobile Latinx recruits in professional and educational publications. Magazines like *Saludos Hispanos* and *Hispanic Times* were utilized by advertisers to target college students interested in career development and were largely distributed in placement offices at colleges and universities. Other publications, including *Hispanic Student USA* and *College Preview*, were mailed directly to high school guidance counselors and targeted high school students interested in higher education and developing long-term career goals.

While ads in these publications could ostensibly reach both Latinx women and Latinx men, the primary way advertisers sought to reach the Latinx market was by translating ads into Spanish. As such, broader trends of emphasizing combat as a transformative experience for men and messages ensuring that women would retain their femininity once in the military, as will be discussed in further detail, carried over into efforts to reach Latinx recruits. In increasing efforts to reach Latinx recruits and frame them as military types, the military advertising industry shaped the Latinx recruiting market by including Latinx men based on exclusions rooted in ideas about recruit quality and warrior masculinity. Alongside a deployment of the Spanish language as a binding force cohering a presumably monolithic Latinx market, a widespread practice in advertising more broadly,[48] the military advertising industry's focus on educational and professional publications was directly linked to their quest for high-quality recruits and officers. The segmentation of the Latinx market and the narrow focus of publications not only presumed a racial and cultural distinctiveness of markets but also spoke to a particular anxiety regarding quality when constructing and targeting Latinx men.

As discussed in chapters 1 and 2, language of recruit quality was often mobilized as an analogue for anxieties about increased numbers of service members of color. While all recruits are expected to meet the same standards based on education and entrance-exam scores, perceptions of quality were more present in industrial strategies focused on reaching non-White recruits. By preemptively constructing a Latinx market focused almost exclusively on professional and educational publications, advertisers built a racialized industrial logic. Advertisers were primarily interested in a narrow subset of the Latinx market, an interest rooted in assumptions that the majority of Latinx youth were not up to military standards. The guiding strategy for the Latinx market in the early 1990s was to target already exceptional individuals. Such a strategy marks a departure from ads in the 1970s that showed the military as a transformative institution for working-class White men in dead-end jobs and reveals how the Latinx market was conceptualized as a racially and culturally distinct market in contradictory ways: simultaneously desired by and seen as predominantly undesirable by advertisers.

In the later years of the 1990s, the military, specifically, the army, relaxed its educational entrance standards to accommodate increasing interest in military service and the disproportionate high school dropout rate among Latinx youth.[49] Through the 1990s the pathway through which Latinx recruits could be seen as the military type shifted from demonstrating a commitment to education and career development aligning with capitalist forms of citizenship to demonstrating patriotism through fidelity to warrior masculinity. The most successful branch of the military in persuading Latinx recruits to enlist in the 1990s was the marine corps.

Throughout the mid-1990s the marine corps developed "Hispanic" versions of their ads, produced in Spanish. In 1996 advertisers from the J. Walter

Thompson agency created an ad "Transformation," which had a "Hispanic" version. In their advertising plan, advertisers describe "Transformation" and its appeal:

> As with previous Marine Corps spots, *Transformation* distinguished the Corps through the use of metaphors and symbolism. The spot features an immense labyrinth filled with obstacles that must be overcome before the protagonist earns the right to be called a Marine. As a Marine he is heroic. His transformation is real. It is substantive. It has been earned. Strategically, *Transformation* leverages the intangible personal growth benefits that distinguishes the Corps from any other option. It builds on the mystique of becoming a Marine and of one's personal transformation into a more complete person.[50]

The ad and advertisers' description of it situate the corps as a site where Latinx men could fulfill a transformative promise of assimilation rooted in a particular form of masculinity. In the ad the protagonist, a light-skinned man dressed in khakis, tank top, and an unbuttoned shirt uses a blend of ingenuity and physical strength to reach the center of a labyrinth. He uses his belt to scale a wall and escape quicksand and removes his shirt to cover his face as he leaps through a wall of flames. He then pulls a sword from a glowing orb to defeat a knight in armor in hand-to-hand combat and, raising his sword to the sky, is struck by lightning and transformed into a marine. The obstacles overcome to earn the title of marine represent qualities associated with the brand of warrior masculinity that had long been central to the corps' brand image. In translating the ad to Spanish, advertisers extended this promise of warrior masculinity to Latinx men and conveyed a transformational pathway through which Latinx men, and racial and cultural meanings attributed to them, were reinscribed.

The promise of transformation on offer in the ad is a promise of assimilation, a mode of redefining Latinx men not as immigrant threats but as literal protectors of the nation. For Latinx men seen as desirable by advertisers and who see themselves as desiring the challenges portrayed in the ad, earning the title of marine meant becoming a Latinx warrior patriot, whose commitment to individual transformation and achievement also signaled a patriotic commitment and an assertion of American fidelity. While promises of citizenship and national belonging have long animated the complex dynamics of racialization and military service underlying Latinx Americans contributions to the military, the portrayal in the "Transformation" ad was particularly salient in the mid-1990s.

Developed in 1995 and distributed as part of the corps' 1996 and 1997 advertising campaigns, "Transformation" followed on the heels of acrimonious debates regarding immigration. HoSang and media studies scholar Roopali Mukherjee each discuss the central role Proposition 187, a ballot measure passed in California in 1994, played in reordering the national debate on immigration and meanings of race in the 1990s.[51] The ballot measure outlawed public benefits for undocumented immigrants and their families and was framed as the "Save Our State" measure pitting White, innocent, law-abiding Californians against racially and culturally subordinate Latinx immigrants, specifically, Mexican immigrants, who were seen as unworthy subjects. Although Proposition 187 was found to be unconstitutional and overturned in 1998, it animated the national debate on immigration and contributed to widespread anti-immigrant sentiment. Concerns about immigration and legal documentation of citizenship shaped the context in which recruiting ads were produced and distributed. However, the military advertising industry did not explicitly delineate between Latinx citizens and Latinx noncitizens. Rather, as ads like "Transformation" demonstrate, recruitment advertising took part in shaping citizenship as a symbolic category tied more closely to ideas of gender and race, leaving it to the military to sort out who was actually qualified for military service based on citizenship requirements. In the midst of racialized debates about worthiness, the "Transformation" ad constructed some Latinx men, specifically, those seen as adhering to attributes of warrior masculinity and a commitment to patriotic service, as the military type, as transforming themselves into worthy militarized subjects, in which earning the title marine functioned as a pathway to earning the title American.

While the narrative of the ad in terms of its promise of warrior masculinity and national belonging is, perhaps, not surprising, it reveals how the logic of multiculturalism undergirding recruitment advertising in the 1990s recognized racial difference via narrow parameters of assimilation and incorporation. It is by virtue of the ability of Latinx men to transform themselves into the military type that allowed an increasingly important Latinx market to become legible to military advertisers. As Latinx men made up a larger and more desirable share of the recruiting market, recruiting ads represented them as legible within the confines of warrior masculinity and as vulnerable to appeals rooted in such a vision of military service. Vulnerability to tactical inclusion for Latinx peoples also hinged on questions of race and legitimacy. Advertisers indicated that if potential recruits have concerns about legitimacy, joining the military can solve that problem, a sentiment echoed in the experiences of Latinx youth who join junior ROTC programs in high schools.[52] Such a sentiment is predicated on processes of racialization in which Latinx people are presumed to not be fully American and frames military service as a choice of self-recuperation, a pathway to validation and legitimacy. Vulnerability to tactical inclusion and to anti-immigrant and racist sentiment converges, and military service offers a bulwark against one form of vulnerability as a Latinx person in a White supremacist nation alongside exposure to another as a soldier tasked with participating in state violence.

Recruiting efforts targeting the Latinx market intensified in the late 1990s, building on the efforts developed by marine corps advertisers and proliferated by Louis Caldera, the secretary of the army from 1998 to 2001. Caldera was deeply concerned with the gap between civilian demographics and military representation among Latinx and recommended increasing the army's Spanish-language TV budget, expanding JROTC programs to more high schools with large Latinx enrollments, and reaching out to high school dropouts to assist them in attaining their general equivalency diplomas (GEDs) and as such becoming eligible for military service.[53] As discussed by Irene Garza, Caldera's efforts eventually led to the development of widespread Spanish-language recruitment campaigns in the 2000s and helped to solidify the Latinx market as crucial for the military advertising industry and the ongoing viability of the AVF.[54]

Still a Woman in the Military

In 1995 Bates Worldwide issued a press release announcing the Joint Recruiting Advertising Program's first-ever ad campaign aimed at women.[55] The press release celebrated the campaign, referring to it as groundbreaking, and detailed its efforts to reach young women. The campaign consisted of two versions of the same ad, one featuring a Black woman, Kiesha Johnson, and another featuring a White woman, Sarah Morrison. The ad was published in a variety of magazines geared toward young women readers, including *Teen, Seventeen, Elle, Vibe, Mademoiselle,* and *Ebony,* among others. The campaign reveals the relationship among policy changes, an embrace of multiculturalism, and representations of women in recruiting materials, a complicated relationship that signaled as much about the military's anxieties regarding gender and sexuality as it did about its purported embrace of women.

The ad features images of young women in school settings with their peers and details new military opportunities for women: "[T]he military is opening more jobs to women, in more fields than ever before. Now you may be eligible for one of the new positions in aviation, or serve at sea aboard a carrier or cruiser. Over 50,000 new jobs have opened to women in the last year alone." New policies facilitated a representation of the military as a space where women were welcomed and had access to an array of opportunities, claims that are certainly debatable given pervasive experiences of discrimination, harassment, and violence faced by military women. The choice of publications, including publications understood as targeting White women and Black women, and the fact that there were two versions of the ad demonstrate how the campaign sought to reach out to women as military types while constituting the market of young women recruits as racially diverse, albeit within the narrow context of a Black/White binary. Furthermore, images in the ads show young women as parts of racially diverse friend groups, a way of signaling the multiculturalism youth expected to see in media.

As the ads sought to advertise new opportunities for women within a visual rubric of multiculturalism, the influence of gendered and sexual anxieties was made most evident by the imagery and headline of the ad, which read "In four years, you won't recognize yourself." While the ad promised young women a transformative experience, young women were shown in familiar high school settings and recognizable within dominant configurations of femininity, smiling, with long hair, and wearing jewelry. Despite promises of unrecognizable transformation, women were largely represented as new military types by staying the same: by staying recognizable as women. This is not to say that women weren't promised benefits like professional and personal growth but that such benefits were consistently framed alongside assertions of martial normativity.

Emerging in recruiting ads in the 1990s, martial normativity was composed of representations of a rigid gender binary and hetero-romance, both of which delineated the parameters of sexuality and gender through which military women could be seen as military types. These parameters ensured that women didn't have their femininity or heterosexuality compromised by being in the military. A series of ads for the coast guard, army, armed forces, and navy targeted women while foregrounding new opportunities and ascendant parameters of martial normativity for women recruits.

Beginning in 1994 a series of three coast guard ads in *Ebony* focused on narratives of equality and opportunity to persuade women that they were, in fact, the military type. The ads follow the same layout: eight small photos frame a large block of text, which contain messages about opportunities for women in the coast guard. One ad reads, "Of the twenty three different career opportunities in the Coast Guard twenty-three of them are for women"; another reads, "Save lives on rescue missions.... Patrol against environmental crimes.... Seize drug smugglers.... A woman's work is never done."

As the only noncombat branch of the military, the ads emphasize that coast guard women face no official exclusions. The coast guard's unique status allowed the ads to frame their mission, with threads of humanitarianism, environmentalism, and security, as feminized, as a form of "woman's work." Such a framing not only signaled an embrace of femininity antithetical to appeals espoused by other branches of the military but also constructed coast guard women as what gender studies scholar Inderpal Grewal refers to as "security feminists," women whose quests for equal opportunity are empowered by the state and their inclusion within it.[56] Grewal points to the ways security feminism, though largely associated with White women who were fearful of non-White and foreign others, incorporated other subjects, as well, especially as people of color were hailed in projects to diversify the military and other government agencies.[57] Images in the ads reflect this intersectional dynamic, showing a racially diverse mosaic of coast guard women, bound together by quests for equal opportunity and participation in national security. However, the third ad details how women's inclusion in the coast guard, regardless of race, was restricted by requirements of gender normativity and legible femininity.

The third ad features an image of a men's bathroom symbol on a woodgrain door directly beneath text reading: "In the Coast Guard there's only one restriction for women" (see fig. 3.4). The use of a bathroom—a space fraught with gendered readings and policing of bodies, particularly for transgender, genderqueer, and gender nonconforming individuals—made clear that women in the coast guard were required to identify and be recognizable as women.[58] While recruiting ads from the 1970s and 1980s utilized representations of heteronormativity and femininity to ensure that military women were recognizable as women first and as soldiers second, the coast guard ad draws on the image of a bathroom sign to openly detail a connection between a rigid gender binary and military service. In situating legible femininity within the gender binary as the *only* explicit restriction for women in the coast guard, the ad reveals how, for women, being the military type means being a particular type of woman. The ad tells women, "[L]et the Coast Guard open doors for you. Most doors, anyhow," asserting that although the coast guard was a space of opportunity for women, that opportunity was limited within a narrow gendered frame. Published in 1994 the coast guard ads were planned prior to policy shifts opening new military positions to women and reflected a particular advertising strategy for meeting personnel needs in the midst of a difficult recruiting environment.

The 1992 recruitment advertising plan for the coast guard, developed by Bates Worldwide, sought to portray the coast guard as an "equal opportunity" employer.[59] Part of this effort entailed crafting the coast guard's target market as 60 percent women, a remarkable goal considering women made

Figure 3.4. Coast guard ad. Source: *Ebony*, February 1996

up just over 11 percent of the military as a whole at the time. The focus on women reflects the coast guard's desire to be viewed as an equal opportunity employer but is also indicative of a particular strategy for meeting recruiting goals. Targeting women allowed the coast guard to reach out to potential recruits that weren't traditionally seen as the military type and, as such, were overlooked or excluded from appeals other branches made. As an industrial strategy, the designation of an "equal opportunity" market resulted in ads framing the coast guard as a unique bastion of liberal inclusion for women, a market conceived within a multicultural frame. As noted, each ad featured images of women of color and White women serving in the coast guard, an indication of the convergence of a strategy to reach a "majority minority" market defined both by gender and race.

While the ads might appear, on their surface, to celebrate the coast guard's unique commitment to gender inclusion, they result from an explicitly gendered market-based strategy driven by the military advertising industry's overall investment in heralding young men as the most desired recruits. This representational similitude reveals the crucial role industrial logics play in shaping discourses of liberal inclusion, that while often framed as being about rights are deeply informed by market-driven industrial logics and, in the case of recruitment advertising, projects of state violence. What began as a particular marketing strategy on behalf of the coast guard continued in other recruiting ads through the construction of martial normativity, which centered on a political and cultural investment in straightness based not on military women's actual sexual practices but, rather, on a visual rubric of gender normalcy and narratives of hetero-romance.

The visual rubric of martial normativity, influenced by a broader push toward multiculturalism, was crafted via racialized representations, as well. Representations of racially diverse coast guard women are imbricated with a codification of the gender binary as a condition for military women, an intersectional power dynamic reflecting both the incorporative project of tactical inclusion and the ways women of color have long been measured against gendered and sexualized norms tethered to Whiteness. Narratives of hetero-romance, while allowing for the limited inclusion of Black women in some ads, were largely represented in association with White military women, reflecting a broader historical suturing of heteronormativity and Whiteness. Ads for the army, armed forces, and navy, while not able to tout women's full—yet conditional—inclusion, constructed this visual rubric of martial normativity while capitalizing on policy changes opening new positions to women as part of recruiting appeals.

An army ad published in *Sports Illustrated* in 1995 focuses on what army life was like for women (see fig. 3.5). The heading reads, "There's something about a soldier," with text going on to state:

Especially if you're a woman.
Because you'll find yourself doing the most amazing things. Like being

a flight Crew Chief or a Topographic Surveyor, or any of the nearly 200 skills the Army offers.

You'll also find yourself doing some very familiar things. Like getting into aerobics, going to the movies or just being with friends. The point is, a woman in the Army is still a woman.

The ad makes clear that being a woman in the army is especially unique. All soldiers have something, but women *especially* have something. Women in the army have opportunities to do both amazing and mundane things that cast them in a balancing act between being soldiers and being women. Images in the ad detail two sides of this balancing act. One image shows a White woman in an aircrew helmet and a helicopter visible behind her. The woman's position in aviation marks her as a soldier trained in a technical skill as the visibility of her lipstick and makeup maintains that learning such a skill and occupying such a position will not disrupt or foreclose her commitment to a feminine gender presentation.[60] As Brown notes, the image emphasizes the woman's femininity and assures that enlisting wouldn't make women unrecognizable as women and, importantly, wouldn't make military women undesirable to men.[61] The second image reveals how hetero-romantic desirability and perceptions of femininity are mutually constituted. The image shows a smiling woman, presumably the same woman, in civilian clothes, and a man, also in civilian clothes, who has his arm over her shoulder. Part of what allowed army women to still be women was to spend off-duty time with men. While appeals during World War II were wary of representing military women spending off-duty time with men due to concerns that military women would be perceived as sexual companions for male service members,[62] the 1995 ad openly shows a military woman doing so.

As one of two images in the ad, the notion of military women engaging in hetero-romance is central to martial normativity. Furthermore, hetero-romance is a clarion call, signaling how the women seen by advertisers as the military type were the type of women for whom dating men was one of the familiar things that women could and wanted to continue to do in order to *still* be women in the army. Ads for the armed forces and navy further contributed to the central role hetero-romance played in constructing martial normativity by representing hetero-romance as both a precursor to military service and an important step in a successful military career for women.

An armed forces ad in *Sports Illustrated* in 1996 features the slogan, "Now might be a good time to talk about where to go after the prom." The ad features an image of a young, smiling, straight couple—there were two versions of the ad, one featuring a White couple, the other featuring a Black couple. Having two versions of the ad reflect a strategy of "coloring" ads,

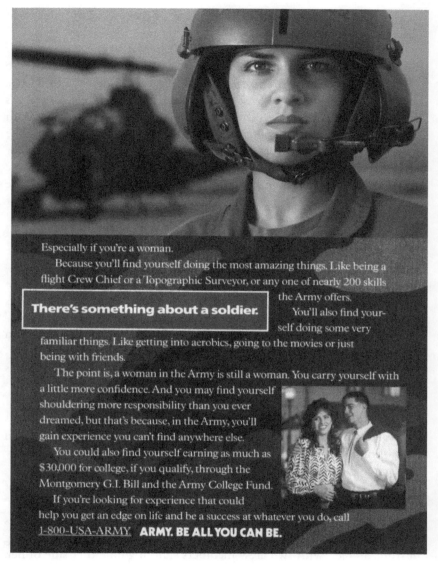

Figure 3.5. Army ad. Source: *Sports Illustrated*, June 5, 1995

in which the message remains the same while images of Black and White individuals are swapped.[63] Within this strategy, hetero-romance permeates the ad. Each young woman is wearing a necklace, corsage, and floor-length dress, her date's arm around her waist. Each young man is wearing a tuxedo, a boutonniere pinned to a lapel, and a bow tie. The slogan of the ad alludes to cultural narratives of parents having discussions with their children about safe sex laden with heteronormativity and is explicitly paired with images of differently gendered couples.

This hetero-romantic configuration was linked to the possibility of military service: "After the prom, after graduation, what's next? Now is the time seniors and their parents look to the future, a good time to update your ideas about the U.S. Armed Forces.... The advantages for today's ambitious young people are substantial." The ad goes on to state that both members of the straight couple can take advantage of the opportunities in the armed forces, "In over 200 career fields, they'll have an equal opportunity for advancement and get more responsibility, faster. Exciting new careers have opened for women.... After the prom, they have a date with the future." The ad contributes to the idea that being straight is part of what makes a recruit the military type. Hetero-romance is a precursor to military service.

The ad took on a particular resonance in the wake of DADT, as advertisers began asking youth their views on homosexuality on annual surveys, and the antihomosexual discharge apparatus was necessarily oriented toward perception and visibility. More specifically, attitude and awareness surveys in the mid-1990s asked youth if they agreed or disagreed with the statement, "It's good that homosexuals can now serve in the military," and between 49 percent to 55 percent of youth disagreed.[64] Advertisers, specifically those from the J. Walter Thompson agency who worked on marine corps advertising, argued that "the recent attention given to homosexuals in the military has not helped the image of the military."[65] Guided by market research, advertisers then had an incentive to represent the military through narratives of hetero-romance. In showing young, straight couples as ideal military types and framing the military as the next heterodate after prom, the ad foreclosed the notion that the military would even need to ask these recruits if they were gay and these recruits would certainly have nothing to tell.

A 1999 ad for the navy continued an emphasis on the importance of hetero-romance for military women through a focus on Loree "Rowdy" Hirschman, a pilot and officer in the Navy (see fig. 3.6). The ad features an image of Lieutenant Commander Hirschman in her flight suit, posing in front of a jet, with two crew members standing on either side of her. A timeline traces Hirschman's naval career with milestones like attending university through the navy ROTC, graduating college with a bachelor's in mathematics, attending flight school, and landing on an aircraft carrier. In many ways, the ad offers an unprecedented celebration of a woman's military achievements. Alongside references to educational opportunities like the ROTC program and the G.I. Bill, Hirschman's timeline details how she became a pilot. The next timeline entry following her first landing on an aircraft carrier, among the most difficult tasks asked of a naval aviator,

Figure 3.6. Navy ad. Source: *Sports Illustrated*, August 30, 1999

is her marriage to a fellow navy pilot, which given the time of publication was a marriage to a man. Hirschman is an exemplar of martial normativity, in which martial and marital achievements converge to construct a form of legible femininity aligning with the heteronormative parameters of the military, made more politically and culturally salient with the passage of

DADT and its emphasis on perceptions of gender normalcy. That the navy ad was the only recruiting ad published between 1973 and 2016 in *Sports Illustrated*, *Ebony*, or *Cosmopolitan* to explicitly mention marriage speaks to the particular gendered and sexual anxieties animating women's tactical inclusion. Explicit representations of heterosexuality as a crucial element of martial normativity for military women in the 1990s speaks to the influence of the specter of the dyke as a figure haunting advertisers as they sought to portray women as the military type.

Straight women who go to prom as teenagers are the type of young women who could have a date with the military, who once in the military want to continue doing familiar things by spending off-duty time with men and who excel in the military by deftly combining marital and martial achievements. At each step of a military woman's trajectory, recruiting ads take care to ward off the specter of the dyke, a present-absence consistently negated in representing military women. Building on sociologist C. J. Pascoe's incisive discussion of masculinity and sexuality, the specter of the dyke is the constitutive outside against which martial normativity was constructed.[66] Martial normativity is reliant on the repudiation of queerness and masculinity and, as such, the disavowal of queer and masculine military women, who though present in the military are only rendered intelligible in recruiting ads through their absence. The tenets of martial normativity—hetero-romance, assertions of womanness, legible femininity—delineate the boundaries between military types and women who by virtue of their queerness, involvement in same-sex relationships, or embrace of female masculinity were framed as the wrong type of women for the military. That the specter of the dyke emerged as such an influential present-absence in recruitment advertising as the military was presenting women with an unprecedented array of opportunities and occupations signals a fundamental tension between regulation and inclusion that resonates with the passage of DADT.

Although DADT was purportedly designed to prevent homosexuality from being a barrier to military service, the numbers of discharges for homosexuality actually increased following its implementation, and women were disproportionately represented among those discharged.[67] While not discounting the very real effects DADT and the associated atmosphere of homophobia had on military men, the concurrent inclusion of DADT and the policy change opening military positions in the 1994 National Defense Authorization Act had particular implications for military women. The pairing of the two policies is similar to what Chandan Reddy calls "freedom with violence," in which rights are granted in alignment with state authority over violence and militarism and is indicative of incorporative projects that protect and affirm certain select modes of gendered and sexualized life.[68] The twinned effects of DADT and opening military positions to women were central to the development of martial normativity as a regulatory and prescriptive set of gendered and sexualized norms upon which women's military service was predicated.

Antihomosexual policies have long been deployed in the military to punish women not seen as properly adhering to expectations of martial normativity. A 1992 report prepared by the army's inspector general and the Equal Opportunity Office states, "The prohibition against homosexuals in the Army results in a subtle 'billy club' for anyone to use against single women in the Army. When they turn down a 'date' with another soldier it is often whispered unjustifiably, that she is a 'lesbian.'"[69] Military women have detailed the complex negotiation they must undertake in attempts to strike an institutionally acceptable balance in regards to sexuality and gender presentation, a task highly linked to appearance and bodily characteristics.[70] Gender studies scholar Carol Cohn contends that DADT was more concerned with the visibility of lesbian and gay service members, which posed a problem for a military deeply invested in constructing and maintaining clear visual distinctions between military women and military men.[71] DADT, though framed at the time as an inclusive and progressive policy, continued to punish military women seen as not adhering to martial normativity and in emphasizing visuality affirmed a particular enactment of femininity as required for women to be seen and to see themselves as the military type. Recruiting ads in the 1990s were a crucial site through which the military advertising industry constructed an optics of gender and sexuality that defined the boundaries of which types of women were legible within the parameters of martial normativity and which were not.

In framing some women as the military type, recruiting ads made visible the gendered and sexualized boundaries of tactical inclusion through which women were inculcated in how to present themselves as the military type, a representation affirming certain gendered and sexualized subjects through a dual association with violence. Opening more military occupations to women exposed them to violence, both as participants in military operations and as potential survivors of sexual and gender-based violence within the ranks. In the wake of the Persian Gulf War, the Tailhook assaults, and reports of harassment and rape at the army's Aberdeen Proving Grounds in 1996, increased efforts to recruit women reveal, at best, an ignorance of the role military culture plays in perpetuating sexual violence and, at worst, a callous effort to expand the market of potential recruits with no regard for what that means in an institution defined by misogynistic violence.[72] Policy shifts and representations of martial normativity made women both increasingly legible and vulnerable within tactical inclusion, vulnerable to the disavowal of gender-based violence within the ranks, and the consolidation of links between participation in state violence and equality.

The Multicultural Military at the End of the Millennium

The desire to portray the military as multicultural, both as a response to demographic shifts and changing expectations among American youth, was leveraged to expand the scope of military recruiting and mark new military types as vulnerable to recruiting appeals. The increased vulnerability of women, Latinx men, and Black men, though consistently framed as new opportunities, coincided with an increased exposure to violence. The highly visible presence of women in the Persian Gulf War blurred the lines between combat and noncombat positions and showed that military women were, in fact, exposed to the violence of war while the exposure of widespread sexual violence revealed the danger military women faced within the ranks. Although the Persian Gulf War was viewed as a resounding victory, it had the effect of reiterating links between recruitability and bearing the burden of state violence.

That the multicultural military and these new military types emerged as the costs and consequences of state violence were more visible and pervasive than at any previous point during the AVF reveals the ways that the proliferation of tactical inclusion is bound to the proliferation of violence. Women, Latinx men, and Black men all became increasingly and newly visible as valuable new recruits and service members as violence in war became more a part of the military experience and more salient in narratives of the military. By virtue of an accompanying series of exclusions guarding against the wrong military types, each of these groups was tactically included by way of its willingness to be transformed—in the case of Black men and Latinx men—or to stay the same—in the case of women. The resulting representation of new military types contributed to and justified a narrative of U.S. military violence as guided by humanitarian impulses.

Shifting away from explicit discussion of jobs and skills training and emphasizing narratives of personal transformation along with policy shifts, the military advertising industry transformed the ways the military was represented in the 1990s. Portrayals of the military as dually committed to multiculturalism and combat took on important cultural and political meanings as U.S. military interventions were increasingly framed as humanitarian endeavors. The decade began with the Persian Gulf War, a war framed as a humanitarian rescue of Kuwait and a loyal defense of Saudi Arabia, and was further marked by a series of military actions framed through a humanitarian lens. Military operations in northern Iraq, Somalia, Haiti, North Macedonia, Bosnia and Herzegovina, and Kosovo were all presented to the American public as humanitarian endeavors and moral imperatives. Articulated together in a chain of meaning, the multicultural military, representations and realities of combat, and supposedly humanitarian military operations reveal the influential role recruitment advertising played in the construction of what Atanasoski refers to as humanitarian militarism, a form of militarism defined by narratives of moral development exemplified by democracy and multiculturalism.[73] Ideas of a military equally committed to multiculturalism and humanitarian militarism set the stage for recruitment advertising and tactical inclusion in the 2000s, as advertisers quickly found themselves grappling with ways to sell military service during an era of perpetual war.

CHAPTER 4

Make the World a Better Place

On September 20, 2001, just over a week after attacks in New York, Virginia, and Pennsylvania, President George W. Bush addressed Congress and proclaimed the nascent war on terror to be "civilization's fight," saying, "This is the fight of all who believe in progress and pluralism, tolerance, and freedom."[1] In the following years, as Bush oversaw airstrikes in Afghanistan and the invasion of Iraq, he spoke of dropping "food, medicine, and supplies" alongside bombs and characterized the war on terror as the definitive ideological struggle of the twenty-first century, a moral imperative in the face of amoral extremism, tyranny, and barbarism.[2] This narrative sought to perpetuate a discourse of wars in Afghanistan and Iraq as benevolent endeavors, driven by a desire to liberate oppressed peoples and secure the spread of American democracy. Under the guise of American exceptionalism, the war on terror normalized extralegal detention, surveillance, destruction, torture, and death, displacing millions and killing hundreds of thousands, all of which was framed as the necessary cost of spreading freedom.

Numerous scholars have interpreted this framing, which was echoed by other politicians, pundits, and military officials, as an expression of gendered, racialized, and sexualized forms of imperialism. Anthropologist Lila Abu-Lughod and media studies scholars Carol Stabile and Deepa Kumar detail how media and political discourses contributed to an Orientalist view of Afghan women as oppressed "others" in need of rescue, a view productive of colonial feminism and deployed to sell the war to the American public.[3] Puar argues that the emergence of homonationalism, a nationally sanctioned form of homosexuality tied to Whiteness and the pursuit of empire, incorporated some queer subjects into the nation through a juxtaposition with the racialized figure of the queer terrorist and promoted a view of the United States as sexually exceptional.[4] Both Cynthia A. Young and Erica R. Edwards contend that representations of Black women and men were crucial to expressions of American empire as defined by multiracial democracy, a narrative that provided further justification for the war on terror.[5] Engaging with examples from across the mediascape during the 2000s, these insights make clear the role media and cultural production played in promoting and justifying the war on terror through seemingly progressive narratives espousing the purported gendered, racial, and sexual tolerance of the United States.

Three months after Bush ordered the military to conduct airstrikes in Afghanistan, an army ad in *Sports Illustrated* focused on Special Forces Weapons Sergeant Roderick Robinson (see fig. 4.1). Robinson, a Black man, is shown in camouflage fatigues along with two of his fellow Special Forces soldiers, both White men. The gradient soft focus of the image guides the viewer's eye to Robinson, whose position in the army is framed as an expression of American exceptionalism and benevolence: "I am a Special Forces Soldier—the best of the best. This is my team. My specialty is weapons. The other guys are experts in medicine, engineering, and communications. We all speak two languages. Whenever the world calls the U.S. Army for help, we are the ones who answer." Sergeant Robinson is portrayed as the best the military and the nation have to offer, a member of an elite team, and a symbol of the twenty-first-century military.

Although published in *Sports Illustrated* in January 2002, the ad featuring Sergeant Robinson was produced in 2001 and planned as part of the army's "army of one" campaign, driven by a rebranding of the army's image and an emphasis on portraying soldiers as warriors.[6] At the turn of the millennium, the military's image was defined by multicultural benevolence, where America's standing as a global power was tied to the exceptionalism of the military, its soldiers, and the moral imperatives guiding them. Emerging prior to its deployment by politicians and pundits as a justification for the war on terror, multicultural benevolence was expressed through a variety of intertwined representations. Multicultural benevolence is a configuration of military service characterized by images and narratives of racial inclusion, heteropatriotism, and racialized martial maternity, all of which allowed the

Figure 4.1. Army ad. Source: *Sports Illustrated*, January 7, 2002

military advertising industry to expand the recruiting market and connect military service to narratives of humanitarianism and moral superiority.

Multicultural benevolence was a rearticulation of tactical inclusion as deployed in the 1990s. Rooted in a larger cultural emphasis on multiculturalism, tactical inclusion in the 1990s was guided by the creation and targeting of new military types. In the first decade of the twenty-first century, multicultural benevolence leveraged figures of tactical inclusion to portray the military as guided by a new mission. The military had long sought to appeal to recruits by emphasizing what the military could do for them. Ads sold the military to potential recruits based on what they could do for the world. Multicultural benevolence was indicative of the military advertising industry's efforts to draw on visions of inclusion and diversity to persuade recruits and garner broader support at a moment of increasing state violence. Developed as an industrial strategy, multicultural benevolence was incubated in the military advertising industry to portray the military as a diverse and morally righteous force dedicated to making the world a better place.

Beginning with a discussion of multicultural benevolence as an industrial strategy and political discourse, this chapter focuses on the eight years of the George W. Bush administration to explore representations created by the military advertising industry to expand recruiting efforts and provide military service with a compelling set of meanings during the war on terror. Multicultural benevolence, while crucial to broader political and cultural discourses of the war on terror, was not wholly determined by them. Rather than viewing multicultural benevolence as arising from an epistemic or ideological break catalyzed by the war on terror, this chapter details how the specific context of the early 2000s—increased military spending, a restructuring of the wartime military, recruiting difficulties, and increasingly unpopular wars—led different figures of tactical inclusion to become newly visible as exemplars of multicultural benevolence.

Constructed at the convergence of racial diversity and heteronormativity, representations of heteropatriotic families espoused multiracial heteronormativity as a domestic formation crucial to the military's global mission. A number of ads looked to historical examples of Black service members to create a racialized lineage of military service in efforts to reach Black recruits and portray the military as a leader of movements for racial equality through a lens of nostalgic exceptionalism. More specifically, representations of exceptional Black soldiers were deployed to connect military service in the twenty-first century with a sense of moral clarity tied to a selective history of World War II as a righteous war bolstered by the military's purported investment in racial inclusion. Black women, a group overrepresented in the AVF but largely ignored in recruiting materials, were made visible to an unprecedented extent in the 2000s. Ads represented Black women as exemplars of martial maternity, in which military service and support for the military were represented as pinnacles of successful mothering. Together, these recruiting appeals and new figures—heteropatriotic families, exceptional Black service members, and Black martial mothers—gave shape to multicultural benevolence.

Multicultural Benevolence and the War on Terror

The events of September 11, 2001, and the subsequent war on terror were profoundly influential in shaping discourses and practices of militarism in the twenty-first century. However, in order to interrogate multicultural benevolence, one must consider the broader dynamics surrounding the war on terror, including a shifting recruiting environment, plans to restructure the military, and the larger mediascape. Multicultural benevolence was constructed in response to recruiting challenges of the late 1990s and gained a particular cultural and political resonance as the war on terror intensified and increasingly shaped how potential recruits, and Americans in general, viewed military service.

The military struggled to meet personnel needs at the turn of the century, with the late 1990s constituting what some referred to as a recruiting crisis.[7] Recruiting struggles at the time were considered a threat to the ongoing viability of the AVF, and some politicians publicly brought up the possibility of reinstating a draft.[8] Both the navy and army missed recruiting goals in the late 1990s, and the air force experienced unprecedented struggles in meeting its recruiting goals.[9] These shortcomings were attributed to several factors. Overall numbers of American youth were decreasing due to broader demographic trends, many youth didn't meet the educational requirements for military service, and more American youth who did meet those requirements were choosing to attend college.[10] Additionally, there were fewer adult veterans who could speak to youth about their own experiences of military service.[11] In response, funding for military advertising doubled in the five years between 1998 and 2003, and advertisers increased segmented marketing efforts and developed more expansive efforts to include special events and online advertising alongside more traditional advertising on television and in print.[12]

Several branches of the military reworked their brand images. With the exception of the marine corps, which had minimal struggles with recruiting compared to other branches—a distinction attributed to both the small numbers of their ranks and consistent messaging rooted in warrior masculinity—the other branches overhauled their advertising partnerships in attempt to reverse poor recruiting trends.[13] Advertising agencies Campbell Ewald and Leo Burnett Worldwide were awarded new contracts for the navy, air force, and army in 2000 and quickly rolled out new slogans and campaigns.[14] The army's long-standing slogan "Be all you can be" was replaced with "An army of one," the navy adopted the new slogan "Accelerate your life," and the air force asked new recruits to "Cross into the blue." New recruiting campaigns sought to rework the messages at the heart of their appeals. The marine corps' relative success in meeting recruiting needs led to their messaging, rooted in ideas of personal transformation rather than in tangible benefits, being emulated by other branches. As advertisers sought to reframe military service, they were also grappling with perceptions that the military failed to provide equal opportunities to all service members.

A 2000 survey of American youth found that perceptions of the military as discriminating against women and people of color had risen since the early 1990s and reached levels not seen since the 1970s.[15] A large part of the recruiting downturn in the late 1990s was attributed to decreasing propensity among Black Americans and reaching out to other groups, including women and Latinx, was seen as a potential remedy. While American youth were suspect of the military's claims to equal opportunity, research found that the motivations guiding enlistment were shifting. A study of youth attitudes in 1999 found that, in contrast with earlier years of the AVF when many recruits were motivated by economic factors, youth motivated by patriotism and a desire for adventure were most likely to enlist.[16] In the early 2000s youth were also driven to enlist by a desire to help others.[17] Additionally, young women indicated that working in an environment free from racial and sexual discrimination was crucial when considering future opportunities, including military service.[18] Together, these factors present prior to 9/11 created an incentive for advertisers to promote a vision of a military defined by multicultural benevolence.

In the weeks following September 11, a patriotic fervor swept much of the nation. For instance, there was a massive increase in the purchase and display of American flags. Retailers sold out of flags, and producers shifted operations to meet the unprecedented demand.[19] At the same time, the state enlisted media industries to promote patriotism and foster support for the wars in Afghanistan and Iraq. Hollywood films like *Behind Enemy Lines* (2001) and *Black Hawk Down* (2001) and television series like *Combat Missions* (2002) were produced in cooperation with the military and promoted promilitary narratives.[20] The military also became a partner in producing video games, including the popular game *America's Army*, which was an unabashed recruiting tool.[21] An array of news stories and other media showed how women and Black Americans, both within and beyond the military, could play a role in supporting the war on terror and helped portray the military as a postfeminist and postracial institution.[22] In the midst of this cultural environment infused with patriotic and nationalist fervor, defined in part by claims of racial, gender, and sexual inclusion, and despite the proliferation of promilitary media, recruiting continued to be difficult.

In 2005 Ray DeThorne, the brand manager for the army's advertising account at Leo Burnett, acknowledged the difficulty of recruiting during wartime, saying that despite a surge of patriotism, "there was no surge of people rushing in saying they wanted to join the Army."[23] The war in Iraq, in particular, had a negative effect on recruiting, and a RAND report found that each year of the war was associated with a 34 percent decline in high-quality enlistments.[24] The war had an even greater negative effect on efforts to recruit Black service members, a group that had become indispensable to the AVF.[25] A study of youth motivations in 2003 and 2004 found that youth were increasingly concerned about the risks of military service, including the risk of having to fight in combat, getting injured, or being killed.[26] Such concerns were certainly justified. Between 2001 and 2008 over four thousand American service members were killed in Iraq and Afghanistan.[27] Over four thousand veterans of Iraq and Afghanistan died of suicide, drug overdose, car crashes, and other causes after being discharged from the military.[28] Tens of thousands of service members were wounded while serving, post-traumatic stress disorder and traumatic brain injury were common among veterans of wars in Afghanistan and Iraq, and 21 percent of women veterans in 2008 were diagnosed with military sexual trauma resulting from being raped and sexually assaulted while serving.[29] Tens of thousands of military contractors and allied forces, including Afghani and Iraqi security forces, were killed, as were hundreds of thousands of civilians.[30] To enlist in the military in the 2000s made one especially vulnerable to and complicit with the consequences of state violence.

As such, recruiting ads overwhelmingly avoided any mention of the war on terror. Brown found that 9/11 and the war on Afghanistan had little perceptible effect on print ads for the air force, army, navy, or marine corps.[31] Some ads, including those for the army and marines, showed soldiers and marines in combat and alluded to war through historical comparisons with earlier wars that portrayed soldiers and marines as protectors and heroes.[32] A few ads published in *Sports Illustrated* and *Ebony* similarly alluded to war through narratives of heroism and national security. An ad for the air force, in *Ebony* in October 2002, directly references the attacks of 9/11. The ad features an image of a bomb painted with logos for New York Police and Fire Departments and the words "NYPD," "Vic says hi," "God bless America!" and "Hurts, doesn't it!" Framing ongoing bombing campaigns in Afghanistan as retribution for the attacks in New York City on September 11, the ad is an anomaly in the broader landscape of recruitment advertising, which largely continued with campaigns developed prior to the beginning of the war on terror. The war on terror contributed to existing recruiting difficulties and a broader cultural embrace of militarism was at odds with recruiting ads that sought to assuage concerns youth had about the risks and consequences of enlisting during wartime. The war also coincided with a massive increase in military spending and a restructuring of the military.

Brown University's Costs of War Project found that appropriations for the war on terror rose each year between 2001 and 2008.[33] Part of the increased spending on the war on terror was tied to a shift in the organization of the military and in how war itself was understood. Two weeks after September 11, then secretary of defense Donald H. Rumsfeld described the war on terror as a "new kind of war" combining military force, border security, and cybersecurity in an unending conflict without fixed rules.[34] Part of Rumsfeld's vision entailed restructuring the military into a more mobile and higher-tech force better equipped to quickly respond to conflicts around the world.[35] While Rumsfeld's calls to restructure the military gained resonance in the immediate aftermath of 9/11, it built on existing calls to reorganize the military in the late 1990s. General Eric Shinsheki and secretary of the army Louis Caldera worked to transform the army into a more agile and flexible force and reframe what it meant to be a soldier.[36] That both men were men of color—Shinsheki was the first Asian American four-star general and Caldera was the first Latinx man to serve as army secretary—connected plans to transform the army with perceptions of the military as a unique site of opportunity for men of color.

Calls to restructure the military led to a context where, in contrast to wars in the twentieth century, the war on terror did not catalyze an increase in the size of the military. In the eight years between 2000 and 2008, the size of the active-duty military stayed fairly consistent, vacillating between 1.36 million and 1.42 million service members. The military advertising industry was tasked with persuading between 152,000 and 183,000 new active-duty recruits to enlist each year.[37] Initially driven by recruiting challenges and market research, the development of multicultural benevolence continued unabated through the war on terror. Faced with trying to persuade recruits to enlist in the midst of two increasingly unpopular wars, advertisers melded select representations of racial and gender inclusion with appeals framing the military as a force for good, dedicated to transforming the lives of service members who, in turn, could join the military and make the world a better place.

Heteropatriotic Families

In January 2001 an armed forces ad in *Sports Illustrated* featured an image of a soldier in uniform with his parents standing on either side of him, each with an arm on his shoulder, smiles on their faces as they lovingly look at their son. The soldier son, whose last name is Alvarado, indicating Latinx heritage, is positioned at the center of the family. As the first in a series of seven ads, the ad set the template for representations of military service as the culmination of successful national heteronormativity for racially diverse families and of the military as a multiracial institution dedicated to making the world a better place.

Each of the seven ads shared similar imagery and, at times, identical captions, slogans, and text. Images of service members surrounded by their families, including parents and younger siblings, dominate each ad (see fig. 4.2). Each ad positions the service member at the literal and figurative center of the family unit with captions, as dictated by the gender of the service member: "She's/He's not just my daughter/son. She's/He's my hero." A small American flag and the slogan "Today's Military. Proud Parents. Bright Futures" appear in the corner of each ad. Text in each ad details that military service was an "opportunity to make the world a better place," a distinguishing feature of military service. Combining expressions of altruism with parental and patriotic pride, the ads represent service members and the families and nation they come from as racially diverse mosaics bound together by heteropatriotism.

While images in each ad focus on service members, the ads are targeting parents of potential recruits. Featuring quotes from parents of service members, each ad asks parents to "[v]isit our website with your teenager" and emphasizes how parents should feel confident about the military's "structure for success." The call to "Proud Parents" was an industrial strategy developed in response to the recruiting environment at the time. Influencers—a term advertisers use to refer to adults, such as parents, coaches, teachers, and school counselors—were targeted in recruiting materials since the shift to the AVF in 1973 but were especially important in the early 2000s.

At the turn of the twenty-first century, the share of the population with military service experience was at the lowest it had been at any point during the AVF. In 2000 roughly 25 percent of the U.S. population had served in the military, in contrast with 47 percent during the 1970s.[38] Studies on the efficacy of recruiting found that decreasing numbers of veterans were linked to recruiting difficulties.[39] In the 2000s military officials argued that adults who had never served didn't have accurate perceptions of military service and, thus, were unable to adequately explain the benefits of military service to youth.[40] In the midst of wars in Afghanistan and Iraq, recruiters found the opinions of parents to be paramount in persuading youth to enlist.[41] At a moment when many parents didn't have firsthand knowledge of military service but were likely aware of the risks of enlisting during wartime, the ads emphasized pride as the primary emotion associated with having a child in the military.

In the ads, parents of service members exclaim, "We're so proud, we could burst," "We tell him how proud we are of what he's done," and "It's been one proud moment after another for us." In other ads, parental pride was more explicitly tied to having a child enlist, distinguishing the military from other options their children might have pursued. Parents in one ad said, "Kevin had a choice: college or the military. . . . We're very proud and happy about

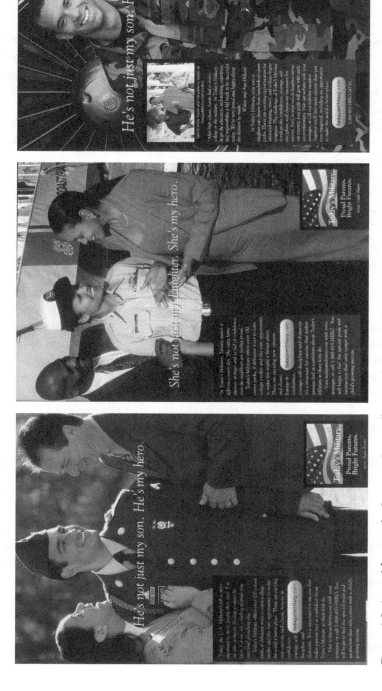

Figure 4.2. Armed forces ads. Sources: Sports Illustrated, January 29, 2001; Ebony, April 2001; Ebony, November 2001

the decision he made." In another ad parents explained how having a son in the army led to "a feeling of pride you can't find anywhere else." The military was framed as a unique bastion of pride, setting military service apart from other options, specifically, attending college. Other ads connected parental pride with explicit support for the military's mission, featuring parents' statements: "He knows the work he does in Today's Military is important," and "The job the US military does is something we can all be proud of." As the prevailing emotion associated with military service, pride in one's child and in the military converged, collapsing being a good parent with being a good patriot.

In addition to sharing pride in their military children, each ad shows families that similarly adhered to a particular version of heteronormativity. We see images of straight couples, generally standing on either side of their son or daughter, smiling as they look at their child with their hands around their child's shoulders or on the child's back. The parents are picture-perfect representations of socially conservative heteronormativity. All the men have short hair and wear suits or collared shirts neatly tucked in. Women are shown with purses over their shoulders, visible jewelry, and long-sleeved sweaters and blazers. Within these parameters of heteronormativity, racial diversity is constructed as a key marker of the twenty-first-century military.

Families of color and White families are shown as similarly engaging in productive, patriotic parenting, their children proudly serving in the military to make the world a better place and functioning as symbols of the nation's "bright future." One ad shows an interracial couple, a first among recruiting ads published in *Ebony*, *Sports Illustrated*, or *Cosmopolitan* since 1973. What emerges in the ads is a representation of racial difference as valued within heteropatriotism where having a child in the military is the culmination of productive parenting. In other words, an overarching emphasis on heteronormativity and patriotism allowed for racial difference to be made palatable in recruiting ads. In terms of tactical inclusion, the ads show how racial inclusion is predicated on conditions not only of heteronormativity but also fidelity to militarism and patriotism and was deployed at a moment when the military was struggling to meet personnel needs. Such representations of heteropatriotic families were significant in delineating intersectional parameters of tactical inclusion and held particular meaning in the early 2000s.

Heteropatriotic families obfuscated any vulnerabilities, whether in the form of economic vulnerability and need of military benefits or vulnerability to risks of violence. In the ads, supporting a child's choice to join the military isn't an acknowledgment that one might need military benefits to access education, job training, or upward mobility or a disavowal of the potential dangers of military service but, rather, an expression of one's parental, familial, and national pride. In the ads, there was no room to question state violence and official military policy. Similar to ways the "Support our troops" rhetoric that dominated popular discourses surrounding the war on terror diverted attention away from political critique and collapsed concern with the well-being of service members, so too did representations of proud heteropatriotic families.[42] The risks and consequences of military service and of state violence, more broadly, are reframed as generative of pride and a sense of moral clarity.

In the months preceding and just following the attacks of 9/11, readers of *Ebony* and *Sports Illustrated* would see a multiracial collection of proud parents, all supportive of their child's decision to enlist in the armed forces and make the world a better place. By representing a racially diverse collection of military families, the military advertising industry was taking part and, perhaps, leading the way in constructing what Puar refers to as "an exceptional multicultural heteronormativity" at the turn of the twenty-first century.[43] Portraying a variety of military families also expanded the recruiting market in important ways, allowing advertisers to reach out to parents and youth from different racial groups and backgrounds in one appeal. Images of racial diversity were bound together and made intelligible as patriotic not only through the explicit pride expressed by parents but also through shared representations of heteronormativity. If so many different American families supported their military children and the military's mission, opposition to the military was then framed as opposition to racial diversity, family, and the "bright future" of American youth and the nation. As the armed forces ads used a call to the future to assert multicultural benevolence, other ads turned to the past to portray the military as having long been an inclusive and benevolent institution.

Nostalgic Exceptionalism and Black Soldiers

In February 1999 a marine corps ad in *Ebony* featured an image of a Black marine in dress uniform, standing at attention, with the headline, "During Black History Month, we honor those who have served with honor" (see fig. 4.3). The ad was the first published in *Ebony*, *Sports Illustrated*, and *Cosmopolitan* to recognize Black History Month. Begun as Negro History Week in 1926 by historian and educator Carter G. Woodson to foster recognition of the accomplishments of Black Americans, Black History Month was acknowledged nationally in 1976 and was quickly co-opted by corporations to target the Black consumer market.[44]

Figure 4.3. Marine corps ad. Source: *Ebony*, February 1999

Black History Month was framed as a connection between contemporary service members and their historical predecessors:

> It was August of '42. They arrived hot and tired, but each had that look of determination. They numbered 13 men, but they were the first African Americans to earn the title Marine. Many have followed in the footsteps of

those proud few. During the month of February, the United States Marine Corps salutes the contributions of African Americans to its proud and distinguished history.

The thirteen Black men who first became marines are known as the Montford Point Marines, named after the camp in North Carolina where they trained. At the time, the corps did not welcome the men. White drill instructors were hostile, at times using racial slurs, and the corps ensured that at no point would a White marine receive an order from a Black marine.[45] Black marines regularly encountered segregation and racism off base and recalled living in tents while White marines slept in barracks.[46] The idea of Black men being marines was so inconceivable at the time that a Black marine reported being arrested for impersonating a marine while on leave, and other Black marines recalled marine corps camera operators being told to turn their cameras away from Black marines on Iwo Jima, the site of a major battle in the Pacific theater, ensuring that the corps would remain a White institution in the visual record of World War II.[47] The ad disavows the historical realities of military life for Black marines, glossing over the White supremacy that shaped their inclusion in the corps. The ad constructs a narrative of nostalgic exceptionalism, remembering the Montford Point Marines, who served in spite of segregation and racism in the corps, as beacons and embodiments of the corps' mission. In doing so, nostalgic exceptionalism valorizes the military institution and selectively articulates the history of Black military service in a way that, to paraphrase W. E. B. Du Bois, tells a story of a perfect military and a noble nation.[48]

Cultural memory serves an important function in making sense of militarism and promoting support for the military. American studies scholar Robert K. Chester argues that connections between cultural memory and militarism reworked meanings of race in U.S. history as part of a broader project of racial incorporation following World War II.[49] More specifically, Chester focuses on the story of Dorie Miller, a Black messman who received the Navy Cross for his heroism when he manned a machine gun, shot down an enemy aircraft, and moved his captain to safety during the attack on Pearl Harbor in 1941. Tracing Miller's status as a historical figure, Chester contends that the varying ways Miller was remembered—as a heroic figure in the Black press and a symbol of the military's racial exclusion in the 1940s then as a symbol of the military's purported commitment to racial inclusion at select moments in the 1970s, 1990s, and 2000s—functions as a form of retroactive multiculturalism.[50] Rooted in a selective memory of World War II and notions of martial citizenship, retroactive multiculturalism constructs non-White servicemembers as ideal democratic subjects and positions the military at the center of an allegedly postracial nation.[51] Media studies scholar Tanine Allison, in an exploration of film techniques and video games, similarly argues that World War II is crucial to cultural memories of war.[52] For Allison, nostalgia for war, a longing for an ideal past defined by a narrative of World War II as a virtuous war guided by American ideals and emblematic of American military superiority, was crucial to media representations of war in the late 1990s and 2000s.[53]

Drawing on these insights, recruiting ads published in the 2000s constructed a form of nostalgic exceptionalism through a selective memory framing the military as a postracial institution and as a leader in movements for racial equality. Postrace is an iteration of national scripts about race, a racial project predicated on representations of racialized bodies as no longer aligned with subordination and characterized by an inability to see race as linked to social or cultural disadvantage.[54] Postracial representations are particularly well suited to practices of recruitment advertising as colorblindness, with its inability to mention or discuss race, makes little sense for ads celebrating Black History Month or recruiting appeals speaking directly to Black Americans as Black. In their quest to reach Black Americans and to assert multicultural benevolence as the guiding imperative of the military's mission in the 2000s, recruitment advertisements had to acknowledge race. The question then became how to do so.

Race was represented as a legacy in the military and used to create a lineage of Black military service that valorized the contributions of Black service members and, more important for tactical inclusion, the military itself. An army ad published in 2006 features a mosaic of current and past Black soldiers and discusses connections between "the past, present and future contributions of African-American soldiers." A marine corps ad published in 2007 claims, "Today, African Americans throughout the Corps proudly continue the legacy of the Montford Point Marines" and asks recruits to "find out how you can continue the legacy of African American service." The ads discuss race solely through its association with a proud, patriotic legacy of service. While the pride associated with military service has an affective appeal and political resonance based on connections between military service and struggles for equality, to frame the experiences of Black service members as something the military has long celebrated requires eliding vulnerabilities and violence.

Violence from within and beyond the ranks has long been a defining feature of military service for Black Americans, stemming from a White supremacist culture in which Black service members were treated as disposable in times of war and were subject to discrimination, harassment, and assault within the ranks. Through stories and images of past service members, recruiting ads emphasize pride and legacy as the primary modes of recognizing race and attribute the valorization of Black service members to the unique character of the military. In other words, according to nostalgic exceptionalism, Black service members succeeded and would succeed not in spite of the military but because of it. Such ads constructed and represented a version of military history that, at best, told a partial truth and helped to enlist Black recruits at a moment of need for the military and a moment of increased risk for service members. Obfuscating the violence Black service members faced and continued to face at the time was crucial to recruiting efforts during the war on terror. A series of ads for the air force focused on World War II to frame the military as a leader in both warfare and racial equality. In more explicitly referring to World War II and positioning the military as a leader in movements for racial equality, the ads further nostalgic exceptionalism and frame the war on terror as a continuation of a legacy of morally righteous warfare.

The three ads, published in *Ebony* and *Sports Illustrated*, each focus on the Tuskegee Airmen. A group of Black aviators trained in Tuskegee, Alabama, in 1941, the Tuskegee Airmen were the first Black men allowed to serve as military pilots. Sepia-toned photographs of the airmen and their planes, images of the Distinguished Flying Cross (an award granted to service members who distinguish themselves in aerial flight), a blue air force logo, and text are all arranged on a background of dented metal plates bordered by screws and rivets (see fig. 4.4). The text—discussions of the airmen, their participation in World War II, and references to military policies from the 1940s—and aesthetic elements—creased and tattered photographs, dented metal plating, and heavy type font mimicking a typewriter—give the ads a nostalgic quality. This aesthetic aids in representing World War II as a morally righteous war during which the military provided opportunities for the Tuskegee Airmen to distinguish themselves, both proving the capabilities of Black service members and the military's commitment to racial inclusion and equality.

One ad discusses Lieutenant Charles B. Hall and how "[i]n 1943, while flying over the coast of Sicily in his P-40 Warhawk, he downed a German Focke-Wulf 190 fighter"; the ad goes on to discuss the exceptional combat record of the Tuskegee Airmen: "They flew more than 15,000 sorties. They destroyed hundreds of German aircraft. And they took home 150 Distinguished Flying Cross medals. In fact, the Tuskegee Airmen had an unsurpassed combat claim: In World War II they never lost an escorted bomber to enemy fighters." In addition to celebrating the combat accomplishments of the Tuskegee Airmen, the ads situate such accomplishments as militarized

Figure 4.4. Air force ads. Sources: Ebony, May 2002; Sports Illustrated, June 10, 2002; Ebony, September 2002

quests for racial equality. Headlines for the ads read, "Before the air force shattered the sound barrier, these airmen shattered the race barrier," "They escorted bombers into Europe and equality into America," and "Did the civil rights movement start in the streets of America or in the skies over Europe?" Racial equality is represented as a militarized endeavor, in which military technological superiority coincides with shattering the race barrier, and participation in state violence is at the vanguard of equal rights.

The facts that the Tuskegee Airmen were formed only after pressure from Black leaders and that the conditions of their training deep in the segregated south were protested in the Black press are conveniently elided in the ads. The service of the airmen, which certainly was of critical importance for proving the capabilities of Black service members and an integral part of the Double V campaign initiated by the Black press, is framed as evidence of the military's commitment to equality. One ad briefly mentions how the airmen encountered racism and segregation at the time, but, ultimately, the ads implicate the military as a cooperative partner in facilitating the Tuskegee Airmen's position as symbols of both racial equality and American military superiority.

One ad refers to the airmen as "units created to prove the capability of black combat pilots and crews" and contends that "President Franklin D. Roosevelt gave them a chance to become heroes." Another ad states, "The many achievements of the Tuskegee Airmen spoke volumes, and President Harry Truman listened. In 1948, he desegregated the armed forces. It was the first step toward true equality in America." The ads represent a simplistic history of the military's views toward training and deploying Black pilots. The Tuskegee Airmen served under rigid segregation, were consistently faced with commanding officers that attempted to discredit them, and engaged in acts of protest against racist policies in the military.[55] The ads participate in twenty-first-century representations of World War II through what Allison calls a "triumphalist teleology" in which "[t]he war was good because we won, and we won because we were good."[56] In the case of the ads, the goodness of the war and of America is predicated on a nostalgic and exceptional history of the Tuskegee Airmen, in which the military was willingly at the vanguard of racial progress.

Such a narrative was deployed not simply to celebrate the Tuskegee Airmen but to persuade recruits as the military was engaged in wars in Afghanistan and Iraq. Each ad concludes by telling potential recruits, "Thanks in part to the Tuskegee Airmen . . . the world of opportunity and honor is available to everyone. They made the most of their opportunity. What will you do with yours?" By hailing potential recruits to take advantage of a "world of opportunity and honor," the ads provide a meaningful narrative of military service at a moment when the military was struggling to meet personnel needs and was trying to bolster public support for the war on terror. Narratives of racial equality, references to defeating Nazism, images of Nazi planes being shot down, and calls to potential recruits are woven together in a lineage of moral clarity. The ads consolidate a set of meanings about race and military service during World War II—a military committed to equality, a morally righteous view of war, and militarized equality as the harbinger of greater equality—and resources those meanings to persuade potential recruits to enlist.

While a number of Black service members and other service members of color have served with distinction and proven themselves to be exemplary soldiers, nostalgic exceptionalism deployed stories of Black service members to emphasize the exceptional nature of the military. The military was portrayed as a unique site of opportunity and success for Black Americans and an institution defined by a commitment to racial inclusion and equality. Ads for the navy and Army National Guard similarly focused on the past contributions of Black service members in the 1970s. That such narratives reemerged at the turn of the century speaks to renewed anxieties about selling the military to wary recruits. Declining Black enlistments, the war on terror, and increased risks of injury and death forced advertisers to abandon appeals rooted in upward mobility and economic advancement in favor of narratives of nostalgic exceptionalism, in which military service was framed as a way to carry on a proud legacy. Black recruits were asked to participate in a racialized legacy of military service and to view the military not as a risk or economic opportunity but as a pathway to participate in a decidedly Black martial lineage, one only made possible by a selective retelling of the contributions and consequences of military service for Black Americans.

As advertisers acknowledge, a good war is good for recruiting, and visions of World War II as a good war, defined by the military's commitment to racial inclusion and equality, were crucial to selling military service to Black Americans at the beginning of the twenty-first century.[57] By looking to the past, recruiting ads frame war as a righteous endeavor and connect the ongoing war on terror with a sense of moral clarity. Past inclusion, which is evidence more of Black Americans' ongoing struggles for full citizenship than of an accommodating military, became a symbolic resource for tactical inclusion, and vulnerabilities, both past and present, were reframed as legacies to be celebrated and continued.

Black Women and Martial Maternity

No group has been more overrepresented in the AVF than Black women. Between the 1970s and the 2000s, 15.7 percent to 35.3 percent of active-duty enlisted women were Black women.[58] Black women service members have been concentrated in the army, at times making up almost half of all army women.[59] The overrepresentation of Black women during the AVF is connected to a broader history of Black women's experiences in the military. Black women were encouraged to serve as part of the Double V campaign and were even targeted in recruiting materials during World War II but once in the military were subsumed into categories of either Black men or White women and encountered racism and sexism.[60] Military policies for women have long been predicated on a White, middle-class model of feminine respectability, which put a greater onus on Black military women to meet the institutional and cultural demands of the military.[61] For example, policies around hairstyles, in particular, have required Black women to adhere to White beauty standards framed as professional expectations of service.[62] Black women veterans recount experiencing barriers to military promotion, including racial isolation, superior officers viewing them negatively, and experiences of sexual harassment and assault.[63] Despite these experiences, Black women still serve at higher rates than other groups.

Scholars have largely pointed to the economic opportunities available in the military as driving Black women's enlistment. Many of the economic vulnerabilities driving enlistment are exacerbated for Black women, making them highly vulnerable recruits and among the groups with the highest propensity for military service. Phillips contends that the military has operated as a de facto jobs program for Black women since the implementation of the AVF.[64] In a study of gender and racial representation in the military, M. W. Segal et al., point out that Black women's overrepresentation in the military might result from their being doubly disadvantaged in the civilian labor market.[65] Black women have indicated that they choose to serve because jobs in the civilian sphere were difficult to find and that they received equal pay and more benefits in the military than elsewhere.[66] Furthermore, some research has found that Black women report higher feelings of satisfaction with military service than other groups.[67] Post-9/11, women veterans reported feeling that their military service had helped them be more prepared for employment in the civilian sphere.[68] However, Black women are more likely to be concentrated in administrative and support positions while in the military, positions that Moore argues provide less technical training and lead to lengthier terms of service, and employment in the civilian sphere remains difficult to find even after having served.[69] What emerges from this research is a mixed view of Black women's military service, a view resulting in part from the lack of research on Black military women and an overarching failure to account for intersecting dynamics of racism and sexism.

This might explain the relative inattention paid to Black women among advertisers, as Black women's high rates of enlistment might have been taken as a given. Advertising plans rarely mentioned Black women, instead focusing on recruiting women and Black men as discrete target markets, an intersectional erasure that, as Brown points out, carried over into official military demographic records.[70] However, the paucity of representations in recruiting materials and the particular ways Black women have been portrayed in recruiting materials indicate that advertisers haven't envisioned Black women as ideal soldiers. While having been selectively targeted in recruiting materials dating back to World War II, very few recruiting ads in *Ebony*, *Cosmopolitan*, and *Sports Illustrated* focus on or made direct appeals to Black women.[71]

Just as recruitment materials used inclusive representations to expand the market of potential recruits and promote particular narratives of the military, Black women have strategically used the military in attempts to achieve different goals and aims, including economic mobility and educational opportunities. Despite disparate outcomes, the perception that the military provides opportunities for social advancement in ways that civilian employers do not is powerful and fundamental to tactical inclusion. Given their high rates of enlistment and the dual work representing Black women in recruiting materials could mean for advertising the military as both racially and gender inclusive, their underrepresentation in ads speaks to a symbolic imperative of representing the military as an institution committed to Whiteness and manliness in which representations of Black men or White women allowed recruiting ads to keep at least one foot firmly tethered to patriarchy and Whiteness.

A small number of recruiting ads did, however, focus on Black women, naming them as service members, focusing on their service, or portraying them as mothers of service members. The majority of these ads were published in *Ebony*, and Black women were represented in recruiting ads between 2000 and 2008 to an extent not seen in previous decades of the AVF. Given the dearth of positive representations of Black women in media and the unrecognized service of Black military women, one could read the ads as engaging in an overdue affirmation of Black women's military service. The ads represent Black women as exemplary citizens, patriots, and mothers, a positive set of representations in a media and cultural environment where Black women have more typically been represented through controlling images used to perpetuate and justify marginalization, oppression, and violence.[72]

Recruiting ads capitalized on racialized and gendered discourses to make Black women more visible as service members at a time when costs of serving were at their highest since the implementation of the AVF, personnel needs were difficult to meet, and portraying the military as inclusive was crucial to justifying the ongoing war on terror. Rather than attempting to classify increased representation of Black women in recruiting ads as wholly positive or negative, I read such representations as generative for tactical inclusion, as evidence of the selective deployment of images of Black women to promote a view of a military defined by multicultural benevolence. While some ads represent military service as a transformational experience for Black women that provided them with self-confidence, a number of ads focus on Black women as martial mothers. Black military mothers, through their own military service and support for their military sons, were represented at the convergence of commitments to parenting and to the military. Black military mothers were framed as exemplars of a twenty-first-century military dedicated to transforming service members and the world.

A Naval Reserve ad, published in *Ebony* in 2003 and 2004, represents a Black woman as a national mother, whose service is guided by a commitment to caring for both children and country (see fig. 4.5). The ad tells potential recruits, "You will be counted on," and features an image of a Black woman in medical scrubs, a stethoscope hanging around her neck as she leans over a bassinet. She is looking down at an infant, with her right hand touching the infant's face and the infant's hand wrapped around a finger on her other hand.

The text states, "You are there when people need you the most. In the Naval Reserve, you can do your part for your country as you gain valuable experience that will help advance your career and enhance your life. In exchange for your commitment, you will receive immeasurable benefits and rewards." A closer look at the image reveals the intersectional dynamics of martial maternity. The lighting illuminates the baby's pale skin, which seems to glow in contrast with the Black woman's face, which is veiled in shadow. The ad situates martial maternity as an inverse of global motherhood, a term feminist media studies scholar Raka Shome uses to describe the transnational phenomenon of White women caring for and adopting children of color from underprivileged parts of the world.[73] Martial maternity is characterized by the same humanitarian impulses and ideas about femininity but is embodied by a Black woman caring for a light-skinned baby.

In the ad, the way for Black women to serve their country and enhance

Figure 4.5. Naval Reserve ad. Source: *Ebony*, January 2004

their lives is by taking care of other people's children. This narrative not only limits how Black women are imagined in the military but also tethers Black women's service to gendered and racialized narratives of care work. Black military women are shown participating in a continuation of racialized care work in which Black women and other women of color have long worked caring for the children of other women, namely, White women.

The image trades on long-standing tropes and the controlling image of the mammy and situates it within a militarized and patriotic context. As Black feminist scholar Patricia Hill Collins notes, the image of the mammy is rooted in restricting Black women to domestic service and functions normatively to evaluate Black women's behavior.[74] The Black woman in the ad is represented as a national mother, a sign that Black women can play their part in caring for the nation by caring for babies. Martial maternity becomes a metric through which Black women's patriotism is evaluated. Black women's adherence to racialized and gendered dynamics of caregiving renders them intelligible while also making them vulnerable to recruiting and state violence at the onset of the war on terror.

A second Naval Reserve ad demonstrated how martial maternity represented Black women not only as symbolic national mothers but as mothers themselves. Published in *Ebony* in May 2004 (see fig. 4.6), the ad features a large image of a Black woman in jeans and a red, hooded jacket. She is seated on the ground, roasting marshmallows with her two children on either side of her, her son seated next to her and her daughter leaning against her, her arm wrapped around her mother's neck. The family appears to be on a camping trip; a tent, gingham tablecloth, and cooler are visible in the background, and the caption tells potential recruits, "You will stay connected."

For Black mothers, commitment to family and country converge: "When you join the Naval Reserve, you can remain connected to everything you hold important in your life. Our force is filled with proud individuals securing better futures by structuring their lives around family, duty, career, and country." A similar combination of family, career, and country was utilized in other recruiting appeals in earlier decades of the AVF. However, the Naval Reserve ad marks the first, and only, ad to do so by focusing on a single mother. In representing a Black, military, single mother, the ad reproduces a narrative of Black single motherhood, often used to pathologize Black women and their sexuality, and rearticulates it to enlist Black women as valuable and valued contributors to the war on terror. A two-pronged narrative of security supports a vision of the military as an empowering institution and a crucial actor in securing the safety of the nation. Structuring life around "family, duty, career, and country" provides economic security to the woman and her children while bolstering national security. The concerns and priorities of single motherhood and soldiering converge.

Martial maternity was tethered to domesticity, which itself was mobilized as a precursor to military service. The qualities of Black motherhood framed as existing prior to joining the military—expressed in the naval reserve ads as a desire to secure a better future, stay connected to family, and be there for those in need—are marshaled as evidence that Black women, with their

Figure 4.6. Naval Reserve ad. Source: *Ebony*, May 2004

exceptional commitments to care, are particularly suited for service in a military purportedly invested in caring, as well.[75] This alignment speaks to the ways that an overarching investment in multicultural benevolence as an industrial strategy in the 2000s coincided with a particular appraisal of Black women's visibility and worth in constructing representations of the twenty-first-century military.

In representing Black women as able to join the military and continue their mothering work, whether as caregivers for others' children or as single mothers, martial maternity expanded the market of potential recruits and the cultural imagination of who was seen as recruitable at a moment when the military struggled to meet personnel needs. Martial maternity is the military advertising industry's version of what Edwards refers to as the "black normal," a set of discourses that places Black women "at the center of discourses of nation in an age of global counterterror" through images conforming to gendered ideals of citizenship and incorporation into U.S. empire.[76] Representing Black women as valuable contributors to the military reveals how the military advertising industry played a role in the proliferation of pronatalist discourses post-9/11 that, as feminist media studies scholar Natalie Fixmer-Oraiz argues, played a crucial role in reformulating boundaries of motherhood and reproduction in the interest of national security.[77] Portraying military women as caregivers and single mothers softened the military's image at a moment when the wars in Afghanistan and Iraq were increasingly unpopular, and focusing on Black women showed a related investment in racial inclusion. As symbols of the military's entangled multiculturalism and moral exceptionalism, Black women's visibility in recruiting ads added further justification for ongoing military interventions. It also firmly tied Black women's recruitability, or, more accurately, the visibility of their recruitability, to notions of respectability, articulated as a dual commitment to family and country.

Pragmatically, martial maternity allowed advertisers to target Black women in a variety of ways, as potential service members themselves and as mothers of potential service members, a target market focused on in ads for the marine corps and army. Published between 2006 and 2008, ads for the marine corps and army focused on Black single mothers of service members to portray Black women as already on the frontlines of creating dutiful and strong military men. Each ad features an image of a Black woman with her service-member son and details how Black mothers prepare their children to be good soldiers. The marine corps ad shows a Black woman wearing a red shawl over a white shirt standing arm-in-arm with her marine son. The caption reads, "Boot camp started long before recruit training with us," and text is addressed to the mother, "Thanks to you, your son is well-behaved, respectful, and courteous. You taught him to stand up straight, know right from wrong and to always respect his elders. And that nothing in life worth having ever comes easy. In short, you've given him the qualities we look for in a U.S. Marine." Black women's hard work as mothers is celebrated as an antecedent to military service. The ad perpetuates a narrative of parenting based on traits long valued in the elite and combat-oriented corps, traits that have critical implications for Black parents and children. As noted by Black feminist poet Audre Lorde, concerns of parenting for Black women have long been interwoven with fears of violence and how their children will fare in a country rife with the extralegal killing of Black people.[78] Tenets of respect and courtesy, seen as imperatives in attempting to safeguard Black youth against police violence and racism, more broadly, are recast as precursors to military service and increase Black men's vulnerability to tactical inclusion. In short, the ad tells Black mothers to raise their sons to be respectful and courteous so they might not be killed by the state at home but can then kill and die for the state abroad; on either side of respectability, vulnerability to state-sanctioned death looms.

Black mothers are represented as initial and instinctive drill instructors, playing an important role in preparing Black men for military service. However, the ad also acknowledges that Black mothers may need some persuading to support their sons joining the military, "Now, give him a chance to serve his country with honor—where he'll develop character traits like self-discipline, leadership skills, and the ability to keep his cool under pressure. All thanks to you. And you thought you were just being a good parent." If Black mothers' parenting is the critical beginning, the military will finish the job of raising young Black men. The ad implies a missing piece of the parenting puzzle—the absent Black father—while situating the military as being able to complete the picture and ensure the successful development of young Black men. In an analysis of recruiting ads, Christensen argues that ads targeting mothers reinforce gendered logics of military service, in which mothers are seen as obstacles to enlistment in need of persuasion.[79] The marine corps ad portrays Black single mothers both as obstacles to enlistment—"Now give him a chance to serve his country"—and as crucial actors in creating the kind of men the military wants. Martial maternity is framed as reluctantly critical in preparing Black men to join the military, a narrative echoed in an ad for the army.

An army ad, published eleven times between *Ebony* and *Sports Illustrated* from February 2007 to July 2008, focuses on a picture of Specialist Gary Warren, a Black man serving in the army, and his mother. Specialist Warren, in a camouflage combat jacket and a black beret, faces the camera with a straight face and his arm around his mother, who is wearing a red blazer and white shirt as she smiles at the camera. The ad is directed at parents of potential recruits with a caption, "Sometimes being strong is as simple as being supportive." Text in the ad implores parents to "take a listen" if their sons or daughters want to discuss joining the army and goes on to tell parents, "You made them strong. We'll make them Army Strong." The ad echoes the appeal of the marine corps ad discussed above, in which the military builds upon the parenting work of Black single mothers to take strong young men and make them "Army Strong." Christensen argues that such ads produced a "new kind of compliant black citizen subject" through assumptions that Black single mothers need help raising productive citizens.[80] The army ad draws upon ideas of the value of military service, mentioning job opportunities and money for college, within its appeal to Black single mothers. The ad also draws upon narratives of Black single women raising men, a concern that has long animated racist policies and cultural symbols that have situated Black single mothers as outside the bounds of racialized heteronormativity.[81]

Ads constructing martial maternity as a form of Black single motherhood in which Black women prepare and support their sons joining the military were recruiting for the army and marine corps. These two branches were most likely to send personnel to Iraq and Afghanistan in the early 2000s and had higher percentages of casualties and deaths than other branches.[82] Joining either the army or marine corps in the years the ads were published was more likely to mean serving in combat and facing a significantly higher risk of injury and death than joining the navy, air force, or coast guard. This is an important distinction that speaks to the narrow parameters through which Black women's martial maternity was imagined. While White women have long been hailed to participate in patriotic motherhood by raising their sons to be productive citizens,[83] Black single mothers were hailed to raise their sons to be infantrymen, to join the enlisted ranks in combat-oriented branches, and as such to shoulder the burdens and consequences of state violence. Even when Black mothers and their sons fulfill the criteria of respectable martial citizenship, the specter of death and violence is inescapable. Black single motherhood is rendered intelligible when respectability and responsibility coincide with vulnerability and violence. Black women's vulnerability to tactical inclusion is hereditary, passed down to their sons, who when raised "right" make perfect soldiers to fight in the war on terror. Martial maternity hinges on a representation of Black single mothers' value in providing their sons for use by the state, an instantiation of Black motherhood that follows in the wake of chattel slavery.[84]

The specter of violence haunting recruiting ads is situated alongside the affective and economic inducements of military service. Having a child join the military or joining the military oneself can mean an affirmation of citizenship long denied to Black Americans and can materially lead to an upwardly mobile career. Black women became focal points in recruiting ads at a moment when military service was more intimately tied to war and violence than at any other point during the AVF. While war and violence are, of course, the primary function of the military and as such constitutive of military service at any point in time, the specter of injury and death was more culturally salient and widespread during the war on terror. Advertisers targeted Black women as paradigmatic figures of multicultural benevolence and asked Black women to sit at the meeting point of promises of life and risks of death. Black women's intelligibility and value for the military and nation rested upon their being hailed as ideal subjects of tactical inclusion, imagined to comfortably balance opportunity, vulnerability, and violence.

The Twenty-First-Century Military

The eight years between 2000 and 2008 laid bare the risks and consequences of tactical inclusion at a scale not seen in earlier decades of the AVF. Serving in the military in the early years of the twenty-first century entailed a high likelihood of being deployed and serving in combat, particularly for soldiers and marines. At the same time, the size of the military was smaller than it had been during any other large-scale war in the twentieth century, resulting in fewer service members and their families carrying the burden of war. Service members faced multiple deployments, extended deployments, and involuntary extensions of their terms of enlistment, all of which protracted the danger of serving during the war on terror and reverberated to effect service members, their families, and their communities as they grappled with death, injury, trauma, and emotional pain.[85]

Risks of violence and death do not end when service members come home, with lingering effects contributing to high rates of domestic violence, risky behaviors, and suicide, all of which are perceived as individual problems but are exacerbated by the systemic neglect of service members and veterans.[86] The violence of war, to be certain, does not simply come to bear on U.S. service members. While the Department of Defense does not include civilian deaths in their reporting of casualties, Brown University's Costs of War Project estimates that 8,497 civilians were killed in Afghanistan between 2001 and 2008 and that 126,000 Iraqi civilians were killed between 2003 and 2011 from direct violence of the war.[87] The material success of tactical inclusion meant that the most diverse military to date was engaged in wars responsible for immense casualties.

In the midst of this proliferation of violence, the military was portrayed through an emphasis on multicultural benevolence, and visions of a diverse military were key to justifying the ongoing wars as guided by moral clarity and an unflinching investment in American democracy. New figures of tactical inclusion—heteropatriotic families, exceptional Black service members, and Black military mothers—allowed recruitment advertising to reach both new and existing markets through appeals bound together by a vision of the twenty-first-century military as committed to inclusion and benevolence. Vulnerabilities, whether in the form of economic vulnerability to recruiting appeals or vulnerability to violence within the military, were recast as sources of pride in one's children, family, predecessors, and nation. The call to join the military was deeply personal in the early 2000s, a call that when answered meant exposure to the very real vulnerabilities of serving during wartime.

The industrial and representational logic of multicultural benevolence, designed to both provide military service with a compelling set of meanings before and during the war on terror and to expand the market of potential recruits, remained a potent strategy for reaching recruits in 2008, when Barack Obama was elected as president. While the recruiting landscape was changing, due to shifts in the media environment and an economic recession, the emphasis on representing a diverse and exceptional military continued, as did ongoing wars in Afghanistan and Iraq. However, the meanings of a diverse military changed as Obama espoused a vision of a progressive and inclusive military as a hallmark of hope and change.

CHAPTER 5

Walls Always Fall

In March 2015 the marine corps released a thirty-second video ad "Wall" (see fig. 5.1). The camera slowly moves past a dust-covered vehicle and a cart draped with colorful rugs and zooms in on a wall made of mud, stones, and sticks, set in the middle of a sandy desert. A voiceover, interspersed with sounds of a goat bleating, tells viewers, "Walls are barriers. They divide, separate, segregate. We've seen walls before." An explosion abruptly blasts a hole in the wall; a burst of flames propels dirt and debris into the camera, momentarily blacking out the screen. As the dust clears, the voiceover continues, "They always fall." Marines in combat gear, guns at the ready, come pouring through the newly breached wall as helicopters fly overhead, and a tank rumbles across the lush green grass on the far side of the wall. The ad mobilizes a stark contrast between a vaguely Middle Eastern desert and the lush green landscape beyond to represent the corps' mission as one of breaking down walls, both literal and metaphoric. The official description of the ad states, "Our nation has a history of breaking down barriers—from social injustice at home to the injustice of our enemies abroad. The United States Marine Corps fights for and defends the ideals that move our country forward. In every mission, every day, Marines protect what matters most to our nation with honor." The mission of the marine corps is to fight injustice,

Figure 5.1. Marines rushing through a breached wall in "Wall" (2015). Source: "Wall," https://www.youtube.com/watch?v=1nV_H6wpTVA, March 19, 2015

manifest as metaphorical walls of separation and segregation at home and as a literal wall abroad. Tools of warfare, such as explosives, tanks, helicopters, and guns, become tools for achieving social justice, for propelling the nation forward toward progress.

The ad analogizes movements for social justice with military violence in an expression of American exceptionalism, in which ideals of militarism and equality are seamlessly intertwined. Images of the military as a wall-breaking organization firmly committed to social justice resulted from an embrace of militarized diversity in the years between 2008 and 2016. In many ways the years of the Obama administration represent the zenith of tactical inclusion, during which diversity became the lingua franca for recruitment advertising and the military, more broadly. Almost immediately following his inauguration, Obama began instituting policies that opened the military ranks in unprecedented ways and explicitly melded military violence with an official commitment to diversity, a configuration I refer to as militarized diversity. Militarism and diversity were framed as mutually constitutive, as integral to a larger progress narrative espoused by the Obama administration and to specific policy changes leading to the increased inclusion of women, lesbian, gay, bisexual, and transgender service members while intensifying a vision of state violence as a liberal quest guided by American exceptionalism. Focusing on the eight years of the Obama administration, this chapter interrogates the ways policy shifts and recruitment advertising converged to refine and intensify the scope of tactical inclusion and solidify diversity as militarized practice.

Broadly speaking, the major policy changes ushered in by the Obama administration instituted an official military definition of diversity, fully opened the ranks to women, and embraced select forms of sexual difference as an aspect of militarized diversity. Diversity was considered an institutional and national imperative, and a variety of recruitment materials emphasized what diversity could do for the military: how diversity could strengthen the military and leverage a diverse populace to fight the ongoing war on terror. The end of the combat ban on women was viewed as a possible remedy to recruiting challenges and resulted in representations of military women as empowered by the military through a rhetorical and symbolic erasure of gender, a representation of postgender militarism. Although postgender militarism asked military women to leave their gender behind, the military remained deeply invested in gender normativity and the gender binary, an investment that shaped recruiting efforts targeting lesbian, gay, bisexual, and transgender (LGBT) Americans.[1] Influenced by the repeal of DADT and the end of the ban on transgender service members, local and regional events and recruiting efforts constructed homomartial pride, a combination of militarized imagery and symbols of gay pride that ultimately functioned to regulate queerness and detail the narrow forms of sexual difference acceptable within the military. Together, these manifestations of militarized diversity characterized tactical inclusion during the Obama era.

Building on earlier industrial strategies, namely, an emphasis on multicultural benevolence as the primary narrative of recruitment advertising in the 2000s, advertisers honed a set of strategies in response to the Obama administration's emphasis on militarized diversity and a fragmented mediascape characterized by an increase in digital and social media. To be clear, militarized diversity did not emerge nascent and fully formed following Obama's election. Rather, the current of tactical inclusion converged with the political and cultural context of the first decade of the twenty-first century to bring together such messages under the banner of militarized diversity. This chapter focuses on a particular collection of recruiting ads, military events, and public relations materials bound by their messaging, as tied to specific policy shifts and an investment in militarized diversity that appeared in various media forms. Before discussing different manifestations of militarized diversity, the chapter details how militarized diversity emerged as an industrial strategy and its resonance within a broader political and cultural narrative of progress.

Recruiting during the Obama Era

During the years of the Obama administration, several important factors influenced strategies and practices of recruitment advertising. As had held true throughout the AVF, economic factors, in particular the 2008 economic recession, played an important role in influencing recruiting and led to the most favorable recruiting environment in decades. Strategic imperatives of the ongoing war on terror created an opportunity for advertisers to both highlight the contributions of and more directly target women and recruits of color. At the same time advertisers were shifting their thinking on reaching potential recruits through different media forms, including digital and social media as well as experiential and event-based advertising, and considering how to best develop messages and appeals that could travel across the mediascape. In the midst of these changes, political influences and shifts in military policy were crucial in shaping recruitment materials and the development of militarized diversity.

The year 2008 was a banner year for military recruiters. It was the first year that all branches had met or exceeded their recruiting goals since 2004 and was the best recruiting year for the marine corps since 1984.[2] In 2009 the Pentagon's head of personnel claimed that it was the best recruiting year since the first year of the AVF in 1973.[3] The recruiting challenges that had plagued the late 1990s and the first decade of the twenty-first century seemed to have been overcome. The highly favorable recruiting environment was attributed to three converging factors: a decline of violence in Iraq, the passing of a new G.I. Bill, and the 2008 recession.[4] As noted in chapter 4, the war in Iraq had a particularly negative effect on recruiting as potential recruits held concerns about the potential of being injured or killed while serving in combat, which coupled with a healthy economy made recruiting particularly difficult, especially for the army and marine corps.[5] According to Curtis Gilroy, who served as director of accession policy and oversaw recruiting for the Department of Defense, a decline in violence in Iraq in late 2008 had a positive effect on recruiting.[6] In 2008 Congress expanded the G.I. Bill, extending benefits to military personnel who had served at least ninety days on active duty since September 11, 2001; the bill approximately doubled the educational benefits, including money for tuition, housing, and books, available to service members and their families.[7] Together, these two factors made it easier to sell military service during wartime, rebalancing perceptions of military service as a benefit that was worth the risk. At the same time the 2008 recession drove greater numbers of vulnerable people toward military service.

High unemployment and economic precarity have made recruiting easier throughout the AVF and are fundamental to the exploitation of vulnerability at the center of tactical inclusion. During the Great Recession, which at the time was the most extended period of economic decline since the Great Depression, a number of Americans were faced with unemployment, evictions, and foreclosures, the impacts of which were unevenly distributed and intensified systemic inequalities of gender and race.[8] As many Americans struggled to make ends meet, some saw the military as a unique site of economic security and opportunity. One report indicated that the 80 percent rise in youth unemployment between 2007 and 2009 may have increased high-quality enlistments by over 30 percent and assisted the military in meeting and exceeding its personnel goals.[9] In contrast to a stagnant civilian sector, the military was recruiting between 138,000 and 164,000 new active-duty recruits each year between 2008 and 2016. The military was not only meeting its numerical recruiting goals but it was also surpassing its goals for recruit quality, getting more high-quality recruits than it had for the previous two decades.[10] Furthermore, as unionized public-sector employees were attacked as "parasites of government" by right-wing pundits and politicians,[11] the military remained one of the only favorably viewed pathways to access government support. In short, the Great Recession intensified the biopolitics of vulnerability undergirding the AVF, driving increasing numbers of Americans toward military service during a time of war. As advertisers and recruiters found themselves in a favorable recruiting environment, efforts to target women and people of color—which in previous decades had often been guided by a dearth of young, White male recruits most desired by the military—were guided, in part, by strategic imperatives of the war on terror.

Military women were considered to be of particular importance for wars in Iraq and Afghanistan. More specifically, military women were vital for building rapport with local communities, for accessing women-only spaces crucial for intelligence gathering and helping "identify friend from foe."[12] Beginning in 2009 the army made plans to form cultural support teams composed of women service members tasked with engaging Afghan women and children while conducting raids and gathering intelligence. Cultural support teams were temporary units designed to respect Afghan culture and followed other strategies to utilize women service members in the wars in Iraq and Afghanistan, including the Lioness Program, which posted women soldiers and Marines at checkpoints to search Iraqi women for weapons and explosives, and an initiative to create female engagement teams, ad hoc teams created to improve relationships between the U.S. military and Afghan women.[13] The strategic imperatives driving military women's engagement in cultural support teams and female engagement teams were similar to the impetus behind the Military Accessions Vital to the National Interest (MAVNI) program. Initiated in 2009 MAVNI was designed to recruit skilled immigrants, including refugees, students, and visa holders. The goal of MAVNI was to target and recruit immigrants with linguistic and cultural knowledge seen to be of strategic importance and to recruit medical personnel.[14] In exchange for their service, service members were offered an expedited pathway to citizenship, albeit one that hinged upon completing one's term of service and receiving an honorable discharge.[15] Military officials viewed MAVNI as a resounding success that attracted unusually highly qualified recruits and fostered cultural awareness in overseas operations.[16] Programs like MAVNI and cultural support teams reveal how militarized diversity was rooted in the strategic imperatives of wars in Afghanistan and Iraq. As advertisers navigated a new focus on militarized diversity, they also were learning to adapt their strategies and messaging in a changing media landscape.

Since the beginning of the AVF, advertisers have sought to publish recruiting ads in a variety of media, including print magazines, television, and radio. Alongside these efforts, advertisers also regularly sought to reach potential recruits directly via mailings and programs in schools, universities, and professional organizations. Advertising in print magazines had long been considered a highly effective site for recruitment advertising, due to low cost, and was even found to be better at reaching high-quality enlistees than other forms of media.[17] However, as shifts in media technologies and consumer habits changed, so, too, did the strategies of advertisers. Advertising in traditional media, considered to include print media, radio, and broadcast television, was found to be less relevant in the middle of the first decade of the twenty-first century as potential recruits spent more time engaging with cable television, video games, and the internet.[18] Although advertisers didn't wholly abandon billboards, television, and print ads, new materials became important parts of the recruitment advertising landscape.

Immersive experiences, including the Army Experience Center complete with Humvee and helicopter simulators, marine corps-branded Humvees with built-in video-game consoles, and a $2.5 million army truck with multimedia displays touting medical occupations, became part of recruiting efforts.[19] These experiential advertisements coincided with increased military sponsorship of sporting events, including the X Games, and coordination with collegiate and professional sports teams for patriotic displays during games.[20] The military advertising industry also increased their focus on digital and social media. In 2008 the navy was concerned with reaching a younger generation via digital and social media and reviewed its partnership with

Campbell Ewald, which had been in charge of navy advertising since 2000.[21] By 2016 digital advertising, which the military defined as a diverse set of efforts including websites for all branches of the armed forces, the use of banner ads, geofencing, data mining, and extensive use of social media, including Facebook, Twitter, LinkedIn, and others, was increasingly important.[22] The national campaigns that once appeared in print magazines were more likely to be found on branch websites, YouTube channels, and social media. Official advertising campaigns circulated alongside social-media posts made by local recruiting offices, public relations materials celebrating diversity, and other militarized media. As part of a larger project of cultural production, the development of an array of militarized media both expanded and muddled the efforts of the military advertising industry as advertisers sought to create appeals that could travel across an increasingly fragmented mediascape.[23]

Militarism and Stories of Progress

Although the project of tactical inclusion had been underway for decades, the cultural and political context of Obama's administration influenced the terms and conditions under which advertisers sought to target new recruits. As several scholars have noted, Obama's election as the first Black president catalyzed a proliferation of discourses celebrating America as postracial.[24] Postracial narratives had been present in recruitment ads years before but the concept of postrace gained greater cultural currency in the first two decades of the twenty-first century. In terms of militarized media, postrace was often represented alongside postfeminism, in a configuration feminist media studies scholar Mary Vavrus refers to as "postpolitics," which was crucial in aligning the military with broader narratives of cultural and social progress.[25] The melding of militarism and progress was key to how Obama positioned himself as a candidate and to policies instituted during his administration.

During the 2008 presidential campaign Obama framed himself as an alternative to George W. Bush's brand of militarism and called for an end to the war in Afghanistan and the closure of the detention center at Guantanamo Bay Naval Base, Cuba.[26] However, any view of Obama as less invested in militarism was quickly dispelled. In 2009 the Obama administration pledged to increase the size of the military by ninety-two thousand service members and oversaw a troop surge in Afghanistan.[27] During the Obama administration, drone warfare proliferated and was institutionalized as part of the expanded war on terror.[28] Scholars have argued that Obama's presidency rearticulated links among militarism, masculinity, and American exceptionalism, essentially functioning to maintain American militarism while providing it with a different set of justifications rooted in soft power and benevolence.[29] Ideas of renewed American global leadership and a commitment to humane war were crucial to a narrative of progress contrasting the Obama administration with previous moral failures of the war on terror, including the exposure of torture at the Abu Ghraib prison complex in Iraq, the extralegal detainment of suspects at Guantanamo Bay, and erroneous justifications for invading Iraq. In addition to a broader aura of progress, four major policy shifts significantly altered the trajectory of tactical inclusion and contributed to militarized diversity: the formation of the Military Leadership Diversity Commission (MLDC), the repeal of DADT, the end of the combat ban for women, and the end of the ban on transgender service members. While each of these policies will be further discussed in relation to associated recruiting efforts, a brief overview of them is offered here.

In the 2009 National Defense Authorization Act, the MLDC was established to evaluate and assess diversity efforts among military leadership. In the words of their report, the MLDC was meant to "support the U.S. military's continuing journey of becoming a preeminently inclusive institution."[30] Seen as part of a lineage of committees dedicated to military inclusion dating back to the 1940s, the MLDC focused specifically on gender and racial representation in the officer corps.[31] The MLDC instituted a uniform definition of diversity, catalyzing an official embrace of militarized diversity that replaced terms like "equal opportunity" and "multiculturalism," widely used in the military advertising industry previously, with that of "diversity."

In December 2010 Obama issued a statement celebrating the DADT Repeal Act, which ended the 1994 policy that had effectively barred gay, lesbian, and bisexual service members from openly serving in the military. In his statement Obama situated sexual orientation in lineage with race, gender, and religion as virtuous characteristics emblematic of patriotic service and American exceptionalism.[32] The DADT Repeal Act officially sutured sexual orientation, narrowly defined as being gay, lesbian, or bisexual, to militarized diversity and marked an unprecedented embrace of homonationalism as an explicitly militarized endeavor.

The end of the direct ground-combat exclusion rule for military women was announced in 2013 by secretary of defense Leon Panetta. The change opened over 230,000 positions to women and began a three-year process in which each military branch was required to devise plans to fully include women in all occupations.[33] Despite resistance, namely, from the marine corps, which asked for an exemption from the new policy, defense secretary Ash Carter issued a memorandum in 2015 that opened all military occupations to women, in effect closing the decades-long debate about women's military inclusion in combat positions. In 2016 Carter ended policies allowing for the discharge, separation, or denied reenlistment of transgender service members, allowing transgender service members to openly serve.[34]

Together, these policy shifts marked a significant expansion of tactical inclusion not seen since the initial years of the AVF and firmly entangled militarism, state violence, and liberal quests for rights as defining traits of Obama's presidency. The superficially progressive bona fides of the Obama administration, including his receiving the Nobel Peace Prize in 2009, though seemingly indicative of a contradictory pairing of inclusion with violence and war, reveal how the constitutive logics of tactical inclusion resonated in broader political discourses and mark the limits of social progress when tethered to extant state structures. The most publicized shifts in military policy focused on gender and sexuality, as seemingly the last walls of military exclusion. However, advertisers embraced a broader view of militarized diversity characterized by campaigns celebrating difference as manifest in various forms, including race, religion, and gender. The general aura of social progress and equality the Obama administration espoused and an ongoing commitment to militarism provided an opportunity for advertisers to sell potential recruits a new vision of the military as a wall-breaking organization and critical actor in shaping a new political era of inclusion and equality.

The Officially Diverse Military

In 2011 the MLDC released its report *From Representation to Inclusion: Diversity Leadership for the 21st-Century Military*. The first recommendation in the report is for the military to uniformly adopt the following definition of diversity: "Diversity is all the different characteristics and attributes of individuals that are consistent with Department of Defense core values, integral to overall readiness and mission accomplishment, and reflective of the Nation we serve."[35] In defining diversity, albeit doing so in vague terms that elide any reference to specific differences, such as those of race, gender, and sexuality, the report catalyzed two important shifts for thinking about the project of tactical inclusion: the first being the formal adoption of "diversity" as *the* term for thinking about and managing difference in the military and the second being an inducement for advertisers to create and promote materials that actively embraced militarized diversity. This section traces the circulation of diversity in various iterations across the military advertising industry, including as policy language, a representational form, and a production logic.

The MLDC had two objectives: to develop demographically diverse military leadership and to broaden the understanding of diversity in order to enhance military performance. Its report, *From Representation to Inclusion*, focused on the representation of racial and/or ethnic minorities and women in leadership positions and provided a standard definition of diversity. The generative power of militarized diversity to promote both inclusion and militarism was enabled by the particular way diversity was defined by the MLDC. As noted, the definition of diversity ignores any specific differences, seemingly subsuming any array of possible differences within a more vague and capacious definition. Diversity is defined solely in institutional terms; differences were considered part of diversity provided they were consistent with existing core values of the Department of Defense. As such, diversity functioned as normative, as a way to marshal differences in alignment with existing institutional values, and as a performative gesture, a way to signal that the military was attuned to social, cultural, and demographic shifts without requiring any serious consideration of institutional inequalities.[36] Diversity was put to work as "a vital strategic military resource" by framing it in terms of representativeness, readiness, and mission accomplishment.[37] Throughout the report, diversity is viewed as key to maintaining the military's competitive advantage, a reason to explore untapped recruiting markets, and a strategy through which the military could better respond to unconventional warfare in the twenty-first century. Cultivating diversity is framed as synonymous with the further refinement of state violence and as a symbol of America's unique commitments to democracy, equality, and militarism. In other words, diversity is operationalized to leverage a renewed investment in state violence.

A variety of recruiting and public relations materials, including websites, brochures, and ads for the different branches of the military, contributed to the emergence of militarized diversity.[38] The air force's website detailed how diversity made the military stronger by emphasizing how America's diverse populace needed to be leveraged to face the challenges of the day, while a series of brochures for the navy detailed exactly which groups were targeted as part of that diverse populace. The diversity page of the air force website featured the slogan "Excellence through diversity" and claimed, "There is no other country in the world so widely diverse, yet so deeply committed to being unified as the United States of America."[39] Echoing and rearticulating the myth of America as an exceptional melting pot, diversity was mobilized to expand recruiting efforts: "The challenges we face today are far too serious, and the implications of failure far too great, for our Air Force to do less than fully and inclusively leverage our nation's greatest strength—our remarkably diverse people." Diversity is imbricated with the identification, targeting, and a persuasion of a "remarkably diverse people." Rather than a form of exploitation or a consequence of a free-market model of military service, reaching out to new recruiting targets is framed as an expression of excellence and a reflection of America's strength. Militarized diversity is made a national imperative, crucial to national defense, and a specific inducement to hail a broader spectrum of potential recruits. While the air force made clear that diversity is militarized—a video on the website states that "diversity and inclusion are not just buzzwords, diversity and inclusion are warfighting imperatives"—little information was conveyed regarding exactly who was envisioned as a desirably diverse recruit.[40]

Six brochures featured on the diversity page of the navy's website detailed who exactly was seen an embodying diversity and elucidated the representational contours of militarized diversity. Four of the brochures focus on different racial groups—African Americans, Asian Pacific Americans, Hispanics, and Native Americans—while one focuses on women and the last focuses on religious diversity in the navy (see fig. 5.2). The brochures all share the phrase "A global force for good," the navy's slogan from 2009 to 2014, a slogan consistent with visions of the military as a benevolent global actor driven by humanitarian impulses.[41] Each brochure discusses the history of different groups, featuring notable individuals emblematic of the navy's commitment to including women and sailors of different racial and religious backgrounds. While reproducing messaging strategies used in other recruiting materials, what made the brochures notable was an explicit detailing of which differences are valued within militarized diversity.

Racial difference is the most pervasive and detailed aspect of the navy's commitment to diversity. Groups long targeted in recruiting efforts, especially African Americans/Black Americans and more recently Hispanic/Latinx, remained central to militarized diversity and were included alongside groups less apparently targeted in tactical inclusion. Asian Americans and Pacific Islanders have a unique history of naval service, tied to imperialistic endeavors and practices of settler militarism throughout the Pacific Islands and Asia, yet have largely been ignored in recruitment advertising, especially in national campaigns.[42] Indigenous Americans, who have long served in the military, were similarly targeted in regionally specific recruiting efforts and direct mailings but largely ignored in national campaigns. The brochure on religious diversity discusses a variety of Christian denominations, Islam, Judaism, and Indigenous American spiritual traditions and details different chaplains from these faith backgrounds. The embrace of religious diversity is tied both to ideas of religious freedom as a national value and to images of racial and gender diversity.

In the religious diversity brochure, women and men, both White and of

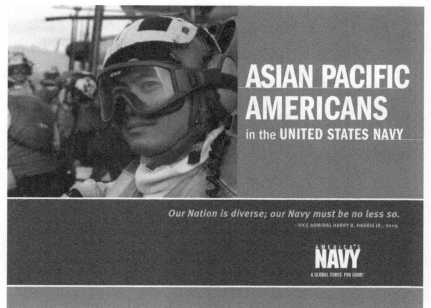

Figure 5.2. Navy diversity brochures. Source: U.S Navy, www.navy.com/who-we-are/diversity

Figure 5.2. (*continued*)

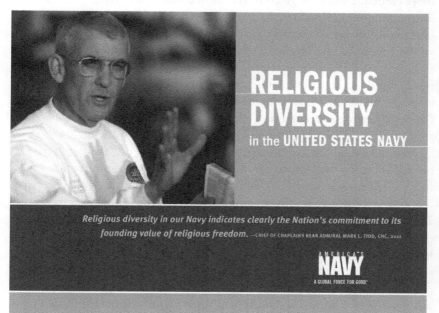

Figure 5.2. (*continued*)

color, are foregrounded as evidence of the navy's multicultural mosaic, a visual representation promoting faith as a form of diversity that simultaneously aided individual sailors and furthered the military mission. What was produced is an expression of religious exceptionalism, in which the war on terror, which both promoted and seized upon anti-Muslim sentiment, is recast as a war fought on behalf of religious freedom and tolerance. As argued by Atanasoski, the convergence of religious tolerance and multiculturalism has long animated U.S. military interventions around the world, including in the Balkans and the Middle East, framing them as humanitarian endeavors.[43] In militarized diversity, the conjunction of religious and racial diversity was made official and visible as important parts of the same whole.

The express inclusion of groups who had both been targeted by specific advertising campaigns—women, Black Americans, and Latinx—and generally ignored in national advertising campaigns—Asian Americans, Pacific Islanders, and Indigenous Americans—speaks to the ways militarized diversity relied on a strategic recognition and proliferation of difference. If diversity, especially racial diversity, was to be leveraged as a sign of America's strength, the more forms of difference that were explicitly named and made visible, the more credence could be given to claims of diversity as a national resource. The naming of racial and religious groups in the brochures doubled as a form of recognition and an extension of tactical inclusion. Mirroring dynamics at work in commercial advertising where difference becomes a source of value, increased visibility and representation in recruitment materials redefined newly visible groups as valuable markets for the maintenance of state violence. Militarized diversity entailed a proliferation of racial difference and connected increased recognition of different non-White groups to expanded recruitability and expressions of American exceptionalism.

Meanwhile, advertisers in charge of marine corps' ad campaigns drew on market research to construct militarized diversity as a production logic focused more on a message of convergence in which militarized diversity was attained through finding common ground in the military's mission. In 2012 the marines unveiled a new marketing campaign, "Toward the sounds of chaos."[44] The first video ad in the campaign begins with a shaky handheld shot of a smoke-filled sky over a dusty plain and the distant noise of screams and gunfire.[45] As dramatic orchestral music begins, the legs and feet of a Marine running come into frame. A voiceover begins: "There are a few who move toward the sounds of chaos, ready to respond at a moment's notice." At the same time, a montage shows marine corps helicopters, jets, and amphibious vehicles advancing toward an unseen objective. Following a brief pause in the music, during which the sounds of firearms being loaded dominate the soundscape, the montage continues as the voiceover says, "And when the time comes, we are the first to move toward the sounds of tyranny, injustice, and despair," and boxes with a printed American flag and the word "Aid" are shown on a convoy of trucks and in helicopters. As the advance of marines, trucks, and aircraft continues, the voiceover discusses the marines shown: "They are forged in the crucible of training. They are the few, the proud, the marines." The video ends with a close-up of a Black marine's face, as he runs toward chaos, looking over his shoulder, beckoning the viewer to follow his lead, as he yells, "Come on!" and the text, "Which way would you run?" appears on the screen.

The drama and gravitas of the ad marshal the full spectacle and might of the corps as the military's premier expeditionary force. The ad retains a vision of warrior masculinity long central to the corps' brand and redirects the military might of the corps toward justice, specifically the eradication of tyranny, injustice, and despair. While the ad certainly represents the corps' mission as coinciding with the dual pursuit of social justice and warfare, similar to the "Wall" ad discussed at the onset of the chapter, it is informed by research that saw such a message as meeting the demands and desires of the market.

Although advertisers contend that recruitment advertising is not driven by market research to the same extent as commercial advertising, market research is crucial to the military advertising industry.[46] In a 2010 study on advertising strategy, advertisers at the J. Walter Thompson agency found that there existed a gap in views between those who tended to join the ground forces—a term referring to troops whose mission is ground based, in the case of the U.S. military this refers to the marine corps and the army—and those who don't.[47] Advertisers named this gap the Rambo/Bono gap. The Rambo side of the gap is associated with a mostly White demographic and is characterized by terms like the heartland, rural, masculine, and nationalism. Alternatively, the Bono side of the gap is associated with a more racially diverse demographic and terms like coastal, urban, feminine, and global citizenship.[48] Advertisers viewed their challenge as producing a message that could appeal to both sides of the divide. Traditional symbols of patriotism like flags, though seemingly well poised to speak to a variety of potential recruits, were found to be too politicized and indicative of Whiteness.[49] As such, advertisers crafted visions of a marine corps that still transformed young men into brave warriors, willing to run toward chaos, but who did so to deliver aid and help those in need. As a production logic, militarized diversity was guided by collapsing difference, racial difference associated with geographical, political, and gender differences, into a singular representation.[50] In contrast to a proliferation of difference, as seen in the navy brochures discussed, the resulting ad foregrounds the military's mission. In other words, it doesn't matter if the military isn't composed of diverse service members representative of the nation provided their mission is guided by an imperative of eradicating tyranny, injustice, and despair.

In conducting widespread market research and accounting for race as an important variable, advertisers reframed racial difference through a message of convergence, as a way to translate patriotic service across an array of groups through a message of moral and militaristic unity.[51] Such a view of difference was easily subsumed within narratives of militarized diversity and American exceptionalism, both of which reflected and contributed to a broader political and cultural rhetoric during the years from 2008 to 2016. Militarized diversity was crafted as official language, representational form, and a production logic in the military advertising industry as it became an institutional imperative for the military. That diversity was so easily co-opted and adapted by the military, with its mission of state violence, and by the military advertising industry, with its industrial logics of capitalism and vulnerability, reveals the perils of diversity as an alleged path to liberation. Militarized diversity fits neatly within the larger trajectory of tactical inclusion, providing a new term and justification for expanding recruiting efforts and furthering state violence.

There Are No Female Marines

In February 2016 the U.S. Senate Armed Services Committee held a hearing on implementing the decision to open all combat positions to women. During the hearing much of the conversation centered on the military's personnel needs, physical standards, and women as an untapped talent pool. At one point Senator Angus King (I–Maine) said, "We need people. And the secret of the success of this country in my opinion is access and opening up access to more and more people. And I have no doubt that limiting access to any job, eliminating 50 percent of the talent pool is always a bad policy."[52] Ending the combat ban on women was seen as good policy, a continuation of a progressive legacy of inclusion, and a means to meet military personnel needs. More so than other aspects of militarized diversity, the end of the combat ban on women was viewed as a remedy to a difficult recruiting environment—the Armed Services Committee hearing also regularly included mention of the fact that only one out of four American youth met military enlistment standards.[53] The idea that fully opening the military to women would remedy recruiting challenges, though haunted by notions of gender essentialism, physical standards, and questions of unit cohesion in a mostly male military, fit neatly within the larger progress narrative of Obama's presidency.

As postracial discourses proliferated in popular culture following Obama's election, they converged with feminist and postfeminist discourses. Obama's willingness to show emotions, to express gratitude for the strong women in his life, and to identify himself as a feminist contributed to a convergence of postfeminist and postracial discourses. As noted by Vavrus, one of the primary ways this convergence manifested in militarized media was through martial postfeminism, an ideology that endorses war and views the military as the solution to problems faced by women and girls while also rejecting critiques of racial inequality.[54] Similar to ideas of postrace, martial postfeminism is a regime of representation that promotes visibility in lieu of structural critiques of sexism and war. Just as Obama's election was seen as a signal of the purported end of racism, the end of the combat ban on women was seen as a sign of the end of sexism, at least within the military.

The way advertisers targeted women in the late part of the first decade of the twenty-first century and the 2010s differed from previous recruiting appeals in important ways. Images of women in civilian clothes and spending off-duty time with their children or families were replaced with images of women in uniform, steadfast and resolute in their dedication to military service. As the end of the combat ban gave women the opportunity to access the operational heart of the military, ads represented women as closer to the ideological heart of the military. During the same time period, representations of women as martially competent circulated in other media spaces, particularly news stories, which, as Vavrus argues, were key to constituting military women as warriors and as postfeminist and postracial subjects.[55] While news stories rendered gender difference as a positive thing, recruiting ads, particularly for the marine corps, constructed a logic of gender equality in which gender was no longer relevant, a construction I refer to as "postgender militarism." I read postgender militarism as a particular instantiation of martial postfeminism, one constructed and embraced by the military advertising industry as they grappled with expanding efforts to recruit women. Recruiting ads portrayed women as empowered by the military when their gender became irrelevant, a logic influenced by a long history of the military disavowing difference.

A well-known saying in the marine corps, dating back to the 1970s, is that there are no Black Marines or White Marines, only green Marines, an idiom that fit neatly into discourses of colorblindness and continued to influence corps culture and military culture more broadly. In regards to women, when Captain Kristen Griest and First Lieutenant Shaye Haver became the first women to complete the grueling and prestigious Army Ranger School in 2015, a fellow service member said, "As far as the whole gender thing goes when you're out in the field you really don't see a difference."[56] The invisibility of gender was furthered by media images of Griest and Haver with shaved heads and wearing fatigues, fully immersed in Ranger training, representations that would have been unthinkable years earlier. As cultural and political discourses of postgender militarism proliferated and the end of the combat ban was planned for and implemented, the military continued to regulate the gender presentation of service members to create clear distinctions between women and men. Through policies on hair, makeup, uniforms, and billeting, the military maintained strict standards that made women service members easily distinguishable and separate from their male counterparts. In the midst of this tension, in which women's access to combat positions was predicated on a symbolic and rhetorical erasure of gender while the military insisted on maintaining a rigid gender binary, military advertisers constructed postgender militarism as a way women could see themselves as fully included in the military for the first time.

In fall 2015 a colleague stopped by my office at the University of Oregon to tell me that marine corps recruiters were on campus. I quickly made my way to the front of the student union building and found three recruiters, a corps-branded Humvee, tent, and pull-up bar. After a quick tour of the Humvee, complete with a built-in X box console, I started talking about efforts to recruit women with a public affairs officer who handed me two flyers: one focused on recruiting enlisted women, the other on recruiting women for the officer corps. The flyers were uniquely situated in the timeline of ending the combat ban, published following the order to end the combat ban but prior to its implementation. One flyer specifically states that women were not permitted to serve in ground combat occupations; both flyers signal how women could become and be marines equal with their male counterparts. Each flyer detailed that the path to becoming a marine would be filled with obstacles but that "gender will not be one of them." The flyers combined a narrative of equal opportunity with an expression of postgender militarism.

Both flyers assert that women in the corps were marines first and foremost: "There are no female marines. Only marines," and "We are not female marines. We are marines" (see fig. 5.3). The insistence that there are no female marines is accompanied by images of marine corps women in camouflage fatigues, standing at attention and holding firearms. In contrast to ads from the 1990s that insisted army women were still women, the flyers represented military women as beyond gender, as having left their gender behind as they became marines. The notion of postgender militarism functions in conjunc-

Figure 5.3. Marine corps brochure. Source: U.S. Marine Corps, 2015

tion with postpolitics of gender and race, obfuscating structural and systemic inequalities, making an analysis of sexual violence and gender discrimination in the military unintelligible. Such a view of postgender militarism promotes a masculinist norm—there have never been male marines, only marines—and perpetuates a view of gender-neutral meritocracy within the ranks, a view that is disputed by exhaustive accounts of the discrimination, harassment, and violence military women face.

In addition to the material inequities and violence that postgender militarism disavows, it also coincides with a requisite acknowledgement of gender. The flyer for the officer corps very clearly states "Female Officer" on the first page and goes on to tell potential recruits, "It matters not whether your commands are followed by 'Yes, Sir' or 'Yes, Ma'am'—as a leader of Marines, your commands will be followed." While it might not matter whether you are called sir or ma'am in terms of your commands being followed, it matters that there are two gendered options. The flyer for enlisted recruits urges women to follow a legacy of marine corps women: "For a century, women have

Walls Always Fall   173

answered the call to be one of the Few." While military women are viewed through a postgender lens, be it in the form of gender-neutral standards or recruiting ads that erase the word "female," women's experiences in the military remained fundamentally shaped by the masculinist, violent legacies of militarism as a gendered construct. From the seemingly innocuous, like being called ma'am and gender-specific uniforms, to the traumatic harm of sexual harassment and violence, it matters deeply when marines and other service members are women. To erase gender invalidates the ways that being a woman in the military comes with a set of unique obstacles and vulnerabilities. The queer possibilities of a genderless world are quickly subsumed by a military context long defined by masculinist violence. Postgender militarism shows how the representation of tactical inclusion as an opportunity or a way to leave gender behind—a strong affective pull that hints at being able to leave sexism behind, as well—coincides with experiences of inclusion that can be and often are harmful, violent, and traumatic.

The logic of postgender militarism, a representation that claims to leave gender behind in the military while also retaining an investment in securing the gender binary, also informed the production of recruiting ads. In May 2017 the marine corps released a video ad, "Battle Up." While the ad was released following the end of the Obama administration and its focus on militarized diversity, it reveals how the logic of tactical inclusion carried on unabated even as it contradicted the Donald J. Trump administration's focus on exclusion in the interest of expanding recruiting efforts and maintaining needed military personnel.

The one-minute ad follows a woman's trajectory to becoming a marine, beginning in elementary school and ending with her being a marine. In various settings, the woman embodies "the fighting spirit" of the corps. She stops bullies from picking on a younger child, breaks through a tackle on the rugby field, completes grueling training exercises, returns fire when her convoy is under attack, and helps unhoused people. The voiceover brings all these elements together, "No one knows where it comes from. Why some have it and some don't. It's the fighting spirit, and it needs to be fed. It consumes fear, self-doubt, and weakness. It stands ready to protect those in danger. And to fight, whatever shape the battle takes. Because as long as there are battles, there will always be marines." While the transformational narrative and emphasis on the traits valued and embodied by the corps are certainly not new, the ad is novel in its choice to center a woman. While other ads for the marine corps and other branches had long featured women, "Battle Up" shows a woman fully transformed into a marine and firing a

Figure 5.4. Captain Erin Demchko preparing to fire her weapon in a firefight in the ad "Battle Up." Source: "Battle Up," https://www.youtube.com, May 12, 2017

weapon (see fig. 5.4), a first that resulted from a particular production process and led to a unique resonance among audiences.

Advertisers in charge of corps advertising indicated that when all military roles were opened to women, it was important to not make ads for women but, rather, to makes ads featuring women.[57] This distinction undergirds "Battle Up," which was initially designed to feature a male infantry marine and was considered by advertisers to be a recruiting ad featuring a woman, rather than a "female ad." An ad featuring a woman instead of a "female ad" is the production equivalent of there being no female marines, only marines. Furthermore, the choice to cast a woman—specifically, Captain Erin Demchko—required a specific representation, as at the time there were no women serving in the combat arms. As such, advertisers, working closely with the marine corps, developed a realistic scenario in which a logistics officer would have to fire a weapon, returning fire when under attack. The firefight scene, which lasts for ten seconds of the sixty-second ad, does a lot of symbolic work under a larger narrative of protection and compassion in showing military women as directly included in the most violent aspects of warfare.

Throughout the ad, the woman's fighting spirit is guided by a sense of protecting those less fortunate. Captain Demchko fires her weapon because she has to and because she is committed to protecting those in danger and is guided by a sense of purpose that is just as easily fulfilled by standing up to bullies or helping unhoused people. The ad bolsters a narrative of militarized diversity, in which the goals of warfare and humanitarianism become one and the same. Women's participation in military violence—albeit, specifi-

Walls Always Fall   175

cally, not in a combat position—is framed as one aspect of a larger narrative of care. Joining the military is a way that women who possess the fighting spirit can care for those less fortunate than themselves.

The "Battle Up" ad, perhaps unsurprisingly, elicited a backlash among viewers. On the marine corps' recruiting page on YouTube, a number of commenters lament how the corps bowed to political pressure, social justice warriors, and feminists. While other ads, including the "Wall" ad discussed at the onset of the chapter, elicited similar comments from viewers, the comments on "Battle Up" were met with a response from the official marine corps recruiting account:

> Fans, this is not "Social Justice Warrior" stuff—just warrior stuff. The Marine Captain protagonist of the film is not being portrayed as an infantry officer—she's being portrayed as a logistics officer, which she is. She's portrayed reacting under fire like all Marines are trained to do, which she's done in real life, in a real firefight. Her story, service and dedication to our country is no less than any of yours because she happens to be a woman.[58]

The response reinforced postgender militarism and foregrounded the martial and masculinist legacy of the corps. The ad is "warrior stuff" that happens to feature a woman. Captain Demchko's identity and service as a marine is highlighted, and her gender is framed as a happenstance occurrence: "She happens to be a woman." The strong reactions the ad garnered not only point to the audience's investment in maintaining an exclusively male vision of the corps—as well as the misogynist climate of internet comments boards, more generally—but also to postgender militarism as a logic that influenced production, representation, and interpretation of recruiting ads.

Together, the marine corps flyers and "Battle Up" ad show how the tactical inclusion of women within representations of militarized diversity reinforced institutional norms in the military. As gender is rhetorically and representationally erased or minimized, so, too, is the possibility for structural critiques of sexism and misogyny within the military. Postgender militarism, in symbolically minimizing and erasing gender while still targeting women as potential recruits, shows how women's military inclusion does not change the military, an argument often forwarded by promilitary feminists in which military women would soften and humanize the military. Rather, women are included under the terms of masculinist, imperialist violence, which requires both the erasure of gender and a reinstantiation of gender inequality. This is not to say that radical imaginings of androgynous futures are invalid but that the contexts in which gender is erased matter deeply. The idea of a genderless military as holding any potential for liberation or equality is quickly dispelled by the ongoing investment in an institution whose norms, culture, and functions are founded on a rigid investment in the gender binary and masculinist violence.

Homomartial Pride

In December 2010 the 111th Congress voted to pass the Don't Ask, Don't Tell Repeal Act allowing gay, lesbian, and bisexual service members to openly serve in the military. The passage of the act followed years of activism by various groups, including the Human Rights Campaign and the Palm Center, among others, and was quickly accompanied by a statement from President Obama. In the statement Obama connected the repeal of DADT with national security, strength, and military readiness and situated the military inclusion of gay and lesbian Americans as the latest chapter in a story of national progress.[59] The repeal of DADT was framed as a crucial aspect of a larger investment in militarized diversity, yet did not catalyze efforts to create and target a recruiting market composed of gay, lesbian, and bisexual Americans. Unlike with the formation of the MLDC and the end of the combat ban on women, there wasn't a proliferation of recruiting materials recognizing and celebrating LGB service members, and sexual orientation is conspicuously absent from the plethora of diversity materials that circulated in military media. This is not to say that the repeal of DADT did not resonate through and inform recruitment advertising and tactical inclusion. Rather, the military's rigid investment in gender normativity resulted in more-diffuse and uneven representations of LBG service members, which were largely articulated via the emergence of homomartial pride.

Stemming from the same assimilationist and nationalist impulses as homonormativity and homonationalism, homomartial pride is a convergence of narrow expressions of gay pride, tied to Whiteness, maleness, and class privilege, and patriotic military pride guided by gender normativity. As discussed by queer and feminist scholar Lisa Duggan, homonormativity developed as a form of sexual politics in the 1990s that upheld heteronormative institutions and viewed equality as access to existing institutions.[60] Building on Duggan's work, Puar identifies homonationalism as the emergence of a national homosexuality corresponding with U.S. imperialism post-9/11 tied to Whiteness, sexual exceptionalism, and the limited incorporation of some homosexual subjects into the biopolitical reproduction of the nation.[61] Both Duggan and Puar point out the privileged position the military occupies in assimilationist politics, which also reinforce exclusive norms of citizenship. Gender studies scholar Liz Montegary argues that calls to repeal DADT were rooted in framing gay service members as productive citizens, marked by the physical, emotional, and mental capability to defend freedom at a moment when national security was at the forefront of the national consciousness post-9/11, a framing that reproduced an investment in militarized modes of national belonging.[62] Renewed investments in national security and martial citizenship, with attendant links to Whiteness, maleness, and able-bodiedness, were crucial to repealing DADT.[63] Homomartial pride explicitly marked the military as an exemplary site of inclusion, valorizing militarism and nationalism as pathways to equality in a moment when militarized diversity was paradigmatic of mainstream progressive politics.

Homomartial pride mobilized existing symbols of gay pride, specifically, pride parades and the rainbow pride flag, and imbued them with militarized meanings. Homomartial pride emerged primarily in California, specifically in San Diego and San Francisco, two locales with unique political, social, and martial geographies. Sanctioned by the repeal of DADT and by a small number of national level events, homomartial pride was largely restricted to specific geographical and institutional locations and cordoned off from the military advertising industry's broader recruiting efforts. Homomartial pride functioned as a boundary-making concept, detailing the parameters through which LGB service members became legible to the military and sequestering their visibility from broader representations of militarized diversity. Within the broader project of tactical inclusion, homomartial pride regulated what forms of sexual difference were intelligible in and acceptable to the military. The emergence of homomartial pride was also shaped by the particular regional and local contours at work in San Diego and San Francisco, cities with distinct sexual politics and legacies of militarism.[64]

In 2011 San Diego became the first city in the nation to formally have a contingent of military service members and veterans in its annual pride parade.[65] A year later, San Diego Pride became the first pride event at which service members could march while in uniform.[66] These occurrences were inescapably bound to the martial and political contours of San Diego: by its reputation as a military town, its proximity to the border, and the inescapable military presence in the form of bases, veterans, and service members.

San Diego County is bordered by Camp Pendleton—a marine corps base home to forty-three thousand Marines, sailors, and civilians and the largest employer in North San Diego County since the 1960s—to the north and the U.S.-Mexico border to the south.[67] San Diego is also home to Naval Base San Diego, the primary homeport for the navy's Pacific Fleet, and to the marine corps' Air Station Miramar, once known as Fightertown USA and made famous in the 1986 film *Top Gun*. San Diego has among the highest concentrations of military personnel in the country. In 2016 one out of every six navy sailors and one out of every four marines resided in San Diego.[68] The large-scale military presence in San Diego contributes to an expression of nationalism, a boundary-making project marking the city as distinctly American in contrast with the queer, unruly allure just south of the border, with Tijuana having long been a destination for the off-duty exploits of American service members.

The martial geography of San Diego, with associated assertions of nationalism and gender normativity tied to the military, is imbricated with a history of conservative racial and sexual politics. Former San Diego mayor Pete Wilson, who served in the marine corps, became governor of California in 1994 and was an outspoken supporter of Proposition 187, the so-called Save Our State initiative that contributed to anti-immigrant sentiment.[69] In 2008 a majority of voters in San Diego County voted in favor of Proposition 8, a measure to amend California's state constitution to restrict marriage to between a man and a woman. That San Diego, as a geographical, sexual, racial, and martial borderland long invested in maintaining boundaries tied to Americanness, Whiteness, and heteronormativity, was the first city with an official military contingent in Pride contributed to the normative contours of homomartial pride.

In 2011 many service members marched in San Diego Pride and wore T-shirts bearing the name of the branch in which they served. An image from 2011 shows two active-duty navy women, wearing rainbow armbands on their forearms and kissing as they march in gray T-shirts with the word "Navy" printed across the chest. One of the women has her sleeves rolled up to her shoulders, making visible her tattooed arms. The image foregrounds queerness with a connection to the military made apparent only by the plain letters of the word "Navy" on the women's shirts. In contrast to an image of queer love accompanied by a subtle marker of military association, as the military allowed service members to wear uniforms and eventually permitted the color guard—a group of soldiers in full dress uniform carrying branch flags and an American flag—any vestiges of queerness were overwhelmed by martial imagery. In 2012 and subsequent years, images of service members— some of whom still choose to wear T-shirts rather than march in uniform— were more likely to be orderly and restrained, creating a visual rubric of homomartial pride (see fig. 5.5).

The American flag, flags of the different military branches, and the rainbow pride flag coalesced into a coherent expression of homomartial pride,

Figure 5.5. Service members marching in pride parades in San Diego, California. Source: sdpix.com

in which military service, patriotism, and gay pride converged. Crisp, clean uniforms and service members walking in loosely formed lines gave a sense of order to the military contingents of Pride. While perhaps considered casual according to military standards, homomartial pride was markedly disciplined and orderly when contrasted with previous years and other sections of the parade. These sober expressions of homomartial pride followed a Pentagon event celebrating LGBT Pride Month in 2012 that not only paved the way for service members to march in uniform but also for the construction of homomartial subjects.

The event, broadcast to military bases around the world, featured a panel "The Value of Open Service and Diversity."[70] The panel situated the recognition of Pride Month firmly within militarized diversity, with its language of diversity—in this case, sexual orientation—leveraged to provide value to the military. However, whatever value was afforded by marking LGBT Pride Month—albeit, at a time when transgender service members were banned from serving—was secondary to privileging the martial aspect of homomartial pride. Among the speakers at the Pentagon event was marine corps Captain M. Matthew Phelps, who told attendees, "I happen to be gay, but more importantly, I'm a Marine."[71] Being gay is a happenstance occurrence subsumed by and not inhibiting Phelps's becoming and being a marine. The privileging of martial identity, as something unimpeded by the happenstance of being gay, was echoed in the tenor of the event, described as "sober and strict," a far cry from any unruly queerness.[72] In celebrating LGBT Pride Month, the event produced a strictly regulated homomartial subject, whose sexual identity is subsumed by martial identity and whose embodied performance is guided by military traditions.

The very actions required of service members, from standing at attention and saluting to rules regulating behavior while in uniform, are tied to maleness, Whiteness, and able-bodiedness and meant to display a level of discipline and productivity at odds with any notions of queer disruption or transgression. In these instantiations, homomartial pride regulates queerness, promoting a traditional vision of the military and placing it within the context of Pride celebrations. Just as San Diego functions as both a military town and a border town, homomartial pride is a boundary-making project. The institutional culture and representation of the military, tied to gender normativity, Whiteness, able-bodiedness, and productive citizenry, are held intact and protected from queerness, both from within by virtue of uniforms and behavioral regulations and from without by virtue of the spatial distinction between military contingents and portions of the parade featuring drag queens and scantily clad queers. Furthermore, as will be elaborated on, the highly localized nature of recruiting efforts targeting recruits at Pride parades protected an image of the military as a rigidly heteronormative institution.

The emergence of homomartial pride at parades, which as a form of commemoration have become hallmarks of Pride celebrations, further illustrates how homomartial pride builds on an exclusionary expression of sexual politics, guided more by legitimacy and institutional assimilation than by radical, transgressive queer politics.[73] As Pride parades have proliferated, the involvement of corporate sponsors, police, and official military contingents has furthered the parades' homonormative and homonational tendencies. As such, a Pride parade in a relatively politically conservative military town, such as San Diego, marked an ideal site through which the military could hone its ostensibly inclusive bona fides through investments in gender normativity. While it seems counterintuitive that San Diego would be at the vanguard of a new form of sexual politics, particularly, when contrasted with its larger neighbor to the north, Los Angeles or with the progressive San Francisco Bay Area it was the unique convergence of militarism, nationalism, and local politics in San Diego that shaped homomartial pride and enabled its emergence. However, not to be outdone, recruiters in San Francisco quickly capitalized on Pride as a recruiting opportunity.

In 2013 the California National Guard set up two recruiting booths at San Francisco's Pride parade, marking the first time the military had officially been involved in SF Pride. Recruiting at SF Pride was driven primarily by two concerns: a pragmatic recognition of the size of the event and a desire to achieve community representativeness. Organizers of SF Pride estimated that one million people would be in attendance: a large-scale event recruiters simply could not pass up. In the words of an Air National Guard recruiting officer, "This gives us the biggest bang for our buck. . . . When we looked at how many people we'd get a chance to talk to, the Pride events looked ideal to us."[74] The potential return on investment made Pride an ideal recruiting event, revealing the crass market logic of homomartial pride and of recruiting, more generally. This is unsurprising given the market logic undergirding recruiting and marks a distinction from other elements of militarized diversity. While militarized diversity was leveraged to specifically target Black Americans, people of color, and women as market groups—a practice that built on long-standing practices of recruiting at events like annual conventions for the National Association for the Advancement of Colored People (NAACP) and the National Council of La Raza—recruiting at Pride seemed more haphazard, guided by the sheer volume of potential recruits in attendance rather than those potential recruits' specific characteristics.

Efforts to recruit LGB service members were guided by a limited scope of tactical inclusion, seeking to show attendees at SF Pride that the military was just inclusive enough to be worthy of consideration.

Recruiters discussed this form of tactical inclusion as revolving around achieving community representativeness. A public affairs officer for the California National Guard told a reporter, "We're a community-based organization, too.... So we need to look like our community."[75] This view parallels the larger goal of militarized diversity to develop a military that reflects the nation it serves, and this view maps representativeness onto a perspective of San Francisco as a city characterized by a particular form of sexual politics. A number of scholars have chronicled the queer history of the San Francisco Bay Area from its reputation as a "wide-open town" and a hotbed of homophile organizations to the Castro, arguably being the most famous gay neighborhood in the country.[76] Alongside the city's reputation as a queer epicenter, sexual politics in San Francisco have also been marked by more moderate political approaches to those in other cities, an inclination tied to Whiteness and affluence further exacerbated by intense gentrification.[77] This is not to say that moderate sexual politics, Whiteness, and affluence characterize all of queer life in San Francisco but that such a form of politics was easily mobilized within articulations of homomartial pride. After all, homomartial pride is guided not by what queer folks think of the military but by the way the military thinks about queer folks and, as such, remains bound to the institutional norms of the military.

The emphasis on visibility, the military's need "to look like our community," is of particular interest for thinking about sexuality. The military wanted to look accepting of LGB service members without looking queer. Homomartial pride is as much about containment and compartmentalization as it is about inclusion. The visual dimensions of homomartial pride are generally indistinguishable from other military representations of soldiers, the only distinction being the occasional presence of the rainbow flag in military contingents at pride events. While the military claims to want to look like their community, within homomartial pride is an inducement for LGB service members to look like gender normative soldiers. Homomartial pride is a gender normative project, making clear that although the military is accepting and including some homosexuals, it remains deeply invested in disciplining queerness and promoting cisgender norms. As Puar notes in a discussion of the Israeli defense forces, "the homosexuals hailed by the nation-state are not gender queer or gender nonconforming—they are, rather, the ones recreating cisgender norms through, rather than despite, homosexual identity," a dynamic reproduced in the U.S. military.[78] In homomartial pride, homosexual service members re-create dominant norms of both gender and militarism, and pride is garnered through adherence to martial and gender normativity. The persistent investment in gender normativity undergirding homomartial pride was furthered through military policies on transgender inclusion.

In June 2016 secretary of defense Carter announced that transgender service members would be able to openly serve in the armed forces.[79] The new policy, begun with the development of a working group in 2015 and required to be implemented by July 2017, is framed within a broader embrace of militarized diversity. In his statement, Carter calls the new policy "the right thing to do for our people and for the force," saying, "We can't allow barriers unrelated to a person's qualifications prevent us from recruiting and retaining those who can best accomplish the mission."[80] Resistance to the inclusion of transgender service members quickly became a hallmark of conservative politics, despite the military's general acceptance of the order—a sign less of a sexually progressive institution but, rather, a pragmatic acknowledgment that the military couldn't afford to turn away or discharge anyone who wanted to serve. Given the political volatility surrounding transgender service members, the military advertising industry largely avoided any discussion of targeting and recruiting transgender Americans. However, the military's policies and guidelines surrounding transgender service members reproduced a rigid investment in gender normativity and when put in conversation with the emergence of homomartial pride illuminated the entanglement of gender normativity and sexuality within the military. The tactical inclusion of transgender service members was seen both as a way to increase the scope of recruiting efforts and a step along the path of militarized diversity. Specific aspects of the military's transgender inclusion policy indicate how gender normativity shapes the inclusion of transgender service members.

The policy requires an official process through which service members can transition.[81] Service members must receive a diagnosis from a military medical provider indicating medical necessity and must transition in a way that adheres to rigidly gendered standards. Specifically, military standards of grooming, uniform, and physical readiness meant that service members who were transitioning would generally be required to transition off-duty until their transition allowed them to fully fit within the rigid gender normative framework of military standards. Furthermore, the policy indicated that for transgender recruits to enlist, they must be "stable" in their gender for at least eighteen months prior to joining the military. The military's transgender inclusion policy not only reinforced the gender normative demands of the medical institution, as discussed in detail by a number of transgender studies scholars,[82] but also did so in a way that framed transgender service members as exemplary adherents to homomartial pride, through their dual commitment to the military and the gender binary. When taken along with other expressions of homomartial pride, the inclusion of transgender service members demonstrates how the tactical inclusion of LGBT service members, when properly achieved, is made invisible. Any queerness or gender noncomformativity is disciplined, displaced, or erased in representations of homomartial pride, allowing for the inclusion of LGBT service members to ultimately reproduce gender normativity.

Despite the repeal of DADT, or perhaps because of it, military culture both as experienced by service members and as envisioned by military advertisers remained incommensurate with queerness.[83] The repeal of DADT was subsumed within a larger frame of militarized diversity in which the military could engage in a limited show of support for the LGBT community while making clear that queerness remains the third rail of tactical inclusion, untouched and disavowed due to the military's unwavering investment in gender normativity. Homomartial pride provides sexualized cover for the continued pursuit of empire, as pride celebrations with military contingents and recruiting booths seek to legitimate the military with some communities and perpetuate the myth of U.S. sexual exceptionalism. However, homomartial pride did not increase targeted recruiting efforts focused on LGBT Americans as a distinct market,[84] seemingly not exposing LGBT Americans to an increased vulnerability to tactical inclusion in the form of increased recruiting. Perhaps, the vulnerability of inclusion for LGBT service members is more complex. Queer people have long been vulnerable to state violence, whether as service members or as survivors of state violence in various forms, including police violence, incarceration, and neglect. In espousing a new form of visibility, homomartial pride increases vulnerability to violence within a deeply antiqueer institution for select LGBT Americans and at the same time leveraging the visibility of LGBT service members to legitimate the military and the ongoing war on terror. Furthermore, images like that of service members carrying a rainbow flag implicate LGBT equality with the pursuit of state violence in the past, present, and future.

Violence and progress are made synonymous, a pairing that is crystallized when one considers the experiences of LGBT service members. Gay soldiers recount receiving death threats after disclosing their sexuality following the repeal of DADT, and over 80 percent of LGBT service members report being sexually harassed while serving,[85] a shockingly high rate even when compared with the already high rates of sexual violence within the military. The outcome of homomartial pride and tactical inclusion is an increased risk of violence, limited recognition, and complicity in state violence, an outcome that reveals that militarized diversity—while offering inclusion to groups who have long fought for it—is certainly not a pathway to liberation.

The Success of Tactical Inclusion

In many ways the years between 2008 and 2016 mark the ideal culmination of the decades-long project of tactical inclusion. Militarized diversity emerged from the convergence of different interests, including those of advertisers, politicians, citizens, and the military itself. While some military and political components, including the marine corps and conservative politicians and pundits, were resistant to policies mandating increased military inclusion, there seemed to be a recognition that militarized diversity, ultimately, helped the military meet its personnel needs, gain cultural and social legitimacy with citizens who hadn't been particularly supportive of the military in prior wars, and continue unabated in their mission as a war-fighting organization. The various forms militarized diversity took in recruiting materials contribute to a vision of the military as a war-fighting organization whose capacity for violence was strengthened through increased inclusion. Taken together, recruiting efforts and materials in the Obama era reveal militarized diversity to be an assimilationist and normative project that makes difference visible in narrow ways to bolster the military; its institutional norms of gender, sexuality, and race; and reinforce state violence.

At the end of the Obama administration, the decades-long project of tactical inclusion seemed to have reached its zenith. While the economic recovery from the 2008 recession created a more challenging recruiting environment, the military maintained a consistent level of high-quality recruits despite a better economic outlook. In 2016 the four major branches of the armed forces had a higher percentage of high-quality enlistees than in 2008.[86] At the same time the military in 2016 was the most diverse in the history of the AVF. The percentage of military women was at its highest level ever, both for enlisted women and officers.[87] The rates of new Black recruits had recovered from the low levels in the first decade of the twenty-first century, and the military was more racially diverse than the civilian population.[88]

At the same time, the military was also the most trusted American institution. A 2016 Gallup poll found that 73 percent of Americans had a great deal or quite a lot of trust in the military, a rate of trust far surpassing Americans' trust in other institutions, like Congress, the presidency, news media, and medical and financial systems.[89] Furthermore, 79 percent of Americans trusted that the military would act in the best interests of the public.[90] The combination of the military's unprecedented diversity and its status as the most trusted institution in the country speaks to what is, perhaps, the greatest accomplishment of tactical inclusion.

Trust in the military as an increasingly diverse institution, both in its composition and in its representation in recruiting materials, spanned the nation's deep political and cultural divisions and demonstrates how both sides of a deeply divided body politic are mobilized within militarized diversity. Through a framing of diversity as a warfighting imperative, a way to bolster national security, and ensure the continued dominance of the United States as a global power, politicians and civilians in favor of national security and military power could continue to support the military, increased defense budgets, and ongoing military actions. Other politicians and civilians historically more in favor of diplomacy and wary of militarism could applaud the steps to make the military more diverse, equitable, and inclusive and, as such, could support the military for its seemingly progressive bona fides. Ultimately, militarized diversity expanded both the pool of potential recruits

and the array of ideological justifications for supporting the military. The resolution of seemingly discordant goals of social progress and state violence within representations of militarized diversity allows for the military to be seen as an exemplary wall-breaking institution, invested equally in realizing liberal quests for equality and inclusion and imperial quests for domination and violence. The military's unique status as a diverse and lauded institution sets it apart from other American institutions, revealing an ongoing privileging of martial power in American culture and reflecting the success of tactical inclusion.

Conclusion
Beyond Tactical Inclusion

Much of this book was written during the years of the Trump administration, during which a number of incidents underscored the central role an exclusionary vision of the military played in calls to "make America great again." Renewed calls to ban transgender service members and orders to discharge noncitizen service members spoke to an emphasis on maintaining a military exclusively rooted in White, patriarchal heteronormativity. The pardoning of former Navy SEAL Eddie Gallagher, whom colleagues referred to as "freaking evil," for war crimes and Trump's repeated emphasis on military men straight out of "central casting" revealed an obsession with White military masculinity and gratuitous violence.[1] This embrace of an exclusionary vision of the military, one tied to a broader emphasis on xenophobia, White nationalism, and heteropatriarchal toughness, occurred alongside a proliferation of vehemently exclusionary and violent policies targeting queer and transgender folks, women, immigrants, Indigenous people, Black people, and people of color during the late 2010s and early 2020s. As the resonances of a politics of violent exclusion materialized and shaped the political and cultural landscape, I often felt deep ambivalence about critiquing inclusion and diversity as institutional and national imperatives.

Recruiting ads and military policies that a few years earlier seemed so blatant in their manipulation of tactical inclusion in service of state violence began to take on a nostalgic quality, an affective pull I found deeply unsettling. Time and time again, I would look at ads, official statements, and policies and find myself longing for a time when tactical inclusion was part of our national narrative. This affective pull helped me realize how deeply successful tactical inclusion has been. The military did not emerge as an exemplary inclusive institution in reaction to an egregiously exclusive administration but, rather, crafted itself as such by, over the course of decades, exploiting vulnerabilities and fashioning tactical inclusion as the realized promise of equality and a pragmatic strategy for recruiting within the inequities of capitalism. Vulnerabilities to tactical inclusion have continued unabated and have even been exacerbated, as the consequences of vulnerability—to systemic inequities in a pandemic, to police violence, to White nationalist, xenophobic, and antiqueer politics—have been increasingly laid bare in recent years. When I feel the affective pull of tactical inclusion, I am reminded that when the military becomes a model of equality, equality and violence become inseparably bound.

This conclusion begins with a brief synthesis of the project of tactical inclusion and its primary manifestations since the implementation of the AVF in 1973. Turning then to a discussion of the ongoing resonances and consequences of tactical inclusion, the focus is on three events from the summer of 2020: the role the military played in state responses to Black Lives Matter protests, the release of a statement calling for an antiracist military academy issued by recent graduates of West Point, and the murder of Army Specialist Vanessa Guillen. These events took place beyond the formal bounds of the military advertising industry, yet were firmly tethered to tactical inclusion as an industrial strategy and political narrative that resonates and shapes state violence in broader ways.

Tactical Inclusion during the AVF

This book traces tactical inclusion as an industrial and representational strategy that constructs subjects as vulnerable to recruiting appeals and maintains state violence. Ranging from appeals reaching out to women, Black Americans, Latinx Americans, people of color, and select members of the LGBTQIA+ community, tactical inclusion has not meant inclusion writ large but, rather, has been constructed with very clear limits tied to military culture, policies, and associated legacies of Whiteness, maleness, and heterosexism. In offering a brief discussion of the major permutations of tactical inclusion in the years since the implementation of the AVF in 1973, the conclusion seeks to highlight the continuity of tactical inclusion as a strategy and cultural narrative that influences our understandings of vulnerability, difference, and militarism.

The implementation of the AVF in 1973 radically altered meanings of military service and recruitment strategies as the concept of the citizen-soldier was replaced by that of the free-market volunteer. In this new model of military service, in which the military could no longer rely on the draft to motivate and procure new recruits, advertisements emphasized what the military could do for potential recruits. Recruitment ads represented the military as a recuperative institution aiding in the production of successful economic citizens by defining military service in relation to the free market, a process I refer to as marketization. Advertisers cemented connections between economic vulnerability and recruitability through three primary figures: the soldier laborer, the martial feminist, and the good Black soldier. Blending appeals emphasizing the market value of military service with claims to gender and racial inclusion, recruiting ads framed the military as a remedy to gender, racial, and economic vulnerabilities. As the military grew more diverse in terms of race and gender, questions of recruit quality—a term technically used to refer to test scores and educational background but more often deployed as a metonym for concerns about increasing numbers of women, Black Americans, and people of color in the ranks—led to a backlash against the marketization of military service and a rearticulation of tactical inclusion in the 1980s.

The industrial strategies rooted in vulnerability developed in the early years of the AVF continued throughout the 1980s but were represented in ways that framed the military and military service members as exceptional. Represented in alignment with Reagan-era narratives of the supremacy of a promilitary, profamily, capitalist nation, new figures of tactical inclusion including Black pilots, martial capitalists, and proud military families were constructed to portray a remasculinized military. The military was no longer represented as a place where those in need could access benefits but, rather, as an institution emblematic of America at its best, where young Americans deserved and earned the benefits of military service by virtue of hard work and commitments to high-tech militarism, capitalism, and racialized heteronormativity. Tactical inclusion in the 1980s and early 1990s showed how advertisers made room for women, Black Americans, and people of color within visions of an exceptional military that remained invested in manliness, Whiteness, and heteronormativity.

Following the Persian Gulf War in 1991, advertisers grappled with the effects that the war had on recruiting and with cultural pressures to portray a multicultural military. As youth were both wary of the risks of enlisting and expected to see cultural diversity in recruiting ads, advertisers were forced to rethink who was seen as the military type. Black men and Latinx men were portrayed as military types when transformed into embodiments of state authority and warriors. In contrast, women, though granted access to new military positions, were shown as not being transformed by the military but, rather, remaining recognizable as women within narrow confines of the gender binary and hetero-romance. Such representations made clear that newly included military women didn't change the military and its gendered and heterosexualized investments but, rather, reinforced them in the wake of DADT. As new military types were constructed, the risks of tactical inclusion were exposed through the Gulf War and other military operations in places like Somalia and Kosovo as well as revelations of widespread sexual assault in the military. The portrayal of the military at the end of the twentieth century as an institution dually committed to multiculturalism and violence set the stage for new expressions of tactical inclusion in the 2000s.

Faced with recruiting difficulties in the late 1990s that some saw as an existential threat to the AVF and highly unpopular wars in Afghanistan and Iraq in the first decade of the twenty-first century, advertisers sought to redefine what military service meant. Advertisements emphasized what the military did for the world through representations of multicultural benevolence. Composed of images and narratives of racial inclusion, heteropatriotism, and racialized martial maternity, multicultural benevolence provided military service with a set of compelling meanings linked to humanitarianism and moral clarity. A variety of new figures—including heteropatriotic families, exceptional Black service members from the World War II era, and Black military women—were deployed to frame military service as a way diverse groups of potential recruits could enlist and make the world a better place. The success of tactical inclusion meant that the most diverse military to date was responsible for and subject to vast numbers of casualties and the largest proliferation of violence since the implementation of the AVF in 1973.

The eight years between 2008 and 2016 marked a culmination of the decades-long project of tactical inclusion. Guided by a broader sense of social progress associated with Obama's election, often cast as postracial and postfeminist, military violence was melded with an official commitment to diversity, a configuration I refer to as militarized diversity. Diversity became the lingua franca for recruitment advertising and the military, more broadly, as ads sought to convey the military's primary mission as one dedicated to social justice and equality. Represented across an array of recruiting materials, militarized diversity sought to show how diversity was good for the military and the nation. Policy changes, including an unprecedented opening of the ranks to women, gay, lesbian, bisexual, and transgender service members, influenced new articulations of tactical inclusion. Representations of a military where military women were fully included in combat and of select members of the LGBTQIA+ community as symbols of homomartial pride framed the military as a wall-breaking organization, crucial to broader political narratives of inclusion and progress.

Between 1973 and 2016, tactical inclusion took on different forms and was expressed in a variety of ways, from marketization to militarized diversity. Responsive to shifts in military policy, market research, and political context, tactical inclusion has at times promoted military service as a job, a patriotic commitment, a humanitarian endeavor, and a personal calling and portrayed an array of potential recruits as soldiers, airmen, coast guardsmen, sailors, and marines. The breadth of such representations speaks to the adaptability of tactical inclusion as an industrial strategy and cultural narrative. Perhaps with more success than any other industry, the military advertising industry has marketed and sold the U.S. military and military service to a diverse array of recruits. While the various permutations of tactical inclusion changed over time, the foundational elements of tactical inclusion have been remarkably consistent.

Tactical inclusion is a mechanism of power, a normative project that forces service members to inhabit and embody the gendered, racialized, and sexualized parameters demanded by the military, parameters that though shifting over time remain inescapably bound to state violence. At the same time, tactical inclusion is also a representational form, a cultural production that recasts vulnerabilities as opportunities. The decades-long project of tactical inclusion reveals how forces of economic inequality, militarism, and inclusion, though perhaps viewed as having contradictory goals, bolster one another, rendering new populations as vulnerable to, valuable to, and subject to state violence.

Resonances of Tactical Inclusion

In the early 2020s, tactical inclusion continued unabated. Advertisers, highly cognizant of increased political polarization and debates about race and inequality, remained committed to making the different brand stories of the military branches—the army, air force, marine corps, navy, and coast guard—appealing to more American youth. As such, despite less pressure from the Trump administration to diversify the ranks than during the Obama administration, the military advertising industry continued to make and target new recruiting markets, create new appeals to reach those groups, and portray the military as a nationally representative organization. As tactical inclusion has accrued such momentum since the shift to the AVF, its effects shaped how we think of the military and state violence in broader ways. During the summer of 2020, as related forces of systemic police violence, the unmanaged COVID-19 global pandemic, and public health crisis converged to catalyze the most widespread social protest movements in the United States since the 1960s and 1970s, resonances of tactical inclusion rose to the surface.

In early June 2020 over twenty-six-thousand National Guard members were activated in various parts of the United States in response to Black Lives Matter protests, which spread across the country following the murder of George Floyd at the hands of police in Minneapolis. Described by military personnel as civil-unrest operations, the deployment of National Guard forces on city streets catalyzed debates about military power, authority, state violence, and racial inequality, perhaps no more so than in Washington, D.C. At the behest of President Trump, in a call to "dominate the streets," the D.C. National Guard was deployed in the nation's capital. While the deployment of the D.C. Guard and subsequent actions, which included the use of military helicopters, including those designated for medical use, to intimidate and scatter protestors, raised critical questions, the focus here is on how their deployment revealed particular consequences of tactical inclusion.

The D.C. National Guard in many ways represented the success of tactical inclusion, at the time being composed of 60 percent service members of color.[2] However, media discourses of the guard's deployment demonstrated how a diverse military, advertised as having a mission rooted in equality and justice, remains an ultimately repressive and violent institution called upon to maintain a political status quo rooted in patriarchal White supremacy. News stories reported that Black guard members objected to being deployed to quell protests in their own communities and that some guard members were so ashamed of their role that they didn't tell their families of their deployment.[3] Images of Black guard members standing toe-to-toe with Black protestors and social-media videos of Black guard members chanting along, under their breath, with protestors elucidate the ways Black service members and other service members are required to act in the interests of the state, even when those interests go against those of themselves, their families, and their communities. The military may want to look like the nation and the communities they recruit from, but when ordered to service members are bound to protect the status quo from the demands of those very communities.

The deployment of military personnel in American cities in response to protests against systemic racism and police violence laid bare how the function of the military, even and especially a diverse and inclusive military, is ultimately to uphold and defend the state and its power dynamics rooted in patriarchy, White supremacy, and heterosexism. Furthermore, the fact that the racial composition of the D.C. Guard was a point of concern when thinking about the role the military played domestically in the summer of 2020, but the racial and gender composition of the military is a point of pride when thinking about military interventions abroad points to a contradiction at the heart of tactical inclusion. Tactical inclusion justifies state violence abroad, giving it a veneer of liberal progressivism, but makes clear how state violence runs counter to calls for liberation at home. While the deployment of military personnel in American cities is seen as an extraordinary event, relegated to a tumultuous summer or to past protests from earlier decades, the dynamics of tactical inclusion and state violence echo beyond the military.

A 2012 RAND Corp. report argues that U.S. law enforcement agencies needed to increase minority representation and embrace diversity to increase effectiveness and bolster community legitimacy.[4] The report goes on to point out similarities between police forces and the military and how law enforcement agencies could learn valuable lessons from the military's handling of representation and diversity. While research indicates that police violence and distrust of police stems from systemic racism built into policing and the culture of police departments, pushes to diversify police departments have been framed as a solution to problems of police violence and community distrust.[5] That law enforcement agencies are looking to the military and military advertising industry shows how tactical inclusion, as an industrial and institutional strategy, travels and bolsters state power in spaces beyond the military. Militarism and diversity travel together, strengthening one another, suturing violence and inclusion. At the same time as incidents of militarized policing, whether by members of the National Guard or police forces, catalyzed discussions of diversity, policing, and militarization in the summer of 2020, graduates of West Point called on the army to challenge a history of White supremacy.

On June 25, 2020, nine graduates of the U.S. Military Academy at West Point emailed a policy proposal to academy leadership calling for an antiracist West Point.[6] Following the urges of George Washington, Alexander Hamilton, John Adams, and others, West Point was founded in 1802.[7] West Point is the nation's oldest military academy, and its graduates make up what is known as the long, gray line, a lineage of military officers including some of the most celebrated American military leaders, including Generals Douglas MacArthur, Dwight Eisenhower, and George Patton. In the proposal for an antiracist West Point, there is an acknowledgment that the vaunted history of the academy is saturated with racism. As such, the proposal calls for action in three major areas to create an antiracist West Point: an end to systemic racism, an antiracist education, and an antiracist institution.

The policy draws on the Anti-Racism Digital Library, an online resource created by Anita S. Coleman in 2016, to define "antiracism" as "some form of focused and sustained action, which includes inter-cultural, inter-faith, multi-lingual and inter-able (i.e., differently abled) communities with the intent to change a system or an institutional policy, practice, or procedure which has racist effects."[8] Framed as a way to explicitly discuss race and racism in response to academy leadership embracing diversity and inclusion while doing little to dismantle institutional racism, antiracism is situated as a corrective, a method of calling attention to the lived experiences of Black cadets by acknowledging and discussing race and moving past an ideology of colorblindness and postrace. As such, the proposal details the authors' experiences of racism at West Point and foregrounds a number of action items, including statements from West Point leadership, regular diversity and inclusion reports, hiring more Black faculty, removing references to Confederate figures, and the creation of a core course on race, ethnicity, gender, and class. While some of these action items align with broader demands of the Movement for Black Lives and ask for steps that move beyond the inclusion of more diverse bodies in West Point to consider curricula and knowledge production, others promote bureaucratic steps to incorporate diversity into the existing structures of the institution, steps that scholars like Ahmed have demonstrated do little to change systemic inequalities.[9] Rather than delve into the specific implications of each of the various action items, a consideration of what it means to situate an antiracist education within a military academy is presented next.

Several of the actions proposed to promote an antiracist education at West Point advocate for the inclusion of pedagogical materials attentive to the viewpoints and histories of Black, Latinx, and other marginalized peoples. Such forms of inclusion, while certainly a major shift in an institution so deeply dedicated to an overwhelmingly White, patriarchal lineage of military leadership, align with what Ferguson calls "adaptive hegemony," in which state and academic institutions incorporate minority difference within their own aims and objectives.[10] When considered within the broader context of the academy's curriculum and explicit militarism, the development of an antiracist education at West Point echoes dynamics of tactical inclusion. All cadets at West Point are required to take part in two parallel curricula. The first is a traditional academic program consisting of a variety of majors and minors, including somewhat typical majors like English, sociology, computer science, and engineering, and the second is a military program consisting of basic training, military instruction, military leadership courses, and physical training, including military movement, boxing, and combat applications. At the end of their time at West Point, graduates receive a Bachelor of Science and are then commissioned as second lieutenants in the army, where they must serve a minimum of eight years. The imagined antiracist West Point the proposal calls for seamlessly melds a pedagogy in warfighting and militarism with that of antiracism.

An antiracist West Point would become a place where the goals of antiracism and American militarism are codified as one and the same. Certainly, an antiracist West Point and the presumably antiracist officers it would produce are better than a racist military academy. Yet, we need to be wary of moments where goals of liberation and militarism appear to happily meet. An antiracist West Point would join its place in line with militarized diversity, multicultural benevolence, and other manifestations of tactical inclusion. Recruiting at West Point operates in a very different fashion from recruiting in general; admission to West Point is highly exclusive, dependent on requirements like a nomination from a congressperson or service member and an interview. Despite this difference, just as recruitment advertising leveraged symbols of tactical inclusion to increase its recruiting pool, so, too, could West Point. However, the risk of tactical inclusion is much more acutely focused on actionable items that provide antiracist cover for proliferating militarism. In an antiracist West Point, racism is framed as the enemy, an enemy fought alongside whoever or whatever else is deemed the enemy at the time. Antiracism, then, is militarized. It doesn't displace or disrupt the primary function of the military; it simply aligns antiracism with state violence. The statement calling for an antiracist West Point was both inspired by and a response to the same nationwide protests that led members of the National Guard to be deployed in American cities. These related events reveal how questions of vulnerability, power, and violence at the heart of tactical inclusion resonate both in and beyond the military. At the same time, the disappearance and murder of Army Specialist Vanessa Guillen, which elicited protests and outrage over sexual harassment and violence within the military, exposed the personal consequences of tactical inclusion.

Guillen, a twenty-year-old army specialist stationed at Fort Hood, Texas, went missing in late April 2020.[11] Months after Guillen was last seen, her remains were found, and her disappearance had become an international news story.[12] In many ways Guillen represented the ideal recruit in an age of militarized diversity, particularly vulnerable to tactical inclusion as a young Latinx woman who had excelled as a high school athlete and long dreamed of joining the military. Concurrently, as a Latinx woman in an institution defined by violence and imbued with legacies of White supremacy and patriarchy, Guillen was particularly vulnerable to harassment and violence. Soldiers at Fort Hood described a culture of sexual harassment and bullying, and Guillen's family alleged that Guillen was sexually harassed prior to her disappearance and murder. On October 20, an army investigation found that Guillen had died in the "line of duty" and as such her family was entitled to military honors at her funeral, final pay and allowance, and a death gratuity.[13] While framed as a way to compensate and empathize with her family, the military's categorizing Guillen's murder as in the line of duty reveals the costs of tactical inclusion.

Just as joining the military entails the potential for injury and death resulting from combat, it also entails the potential for injury and death resulting from sexual and racial violence within the ranks. In fact, for soldiers stationed at Fort Hood, the base in Texas has been particularly lethal, with more soldiers killed on and around the base since 2016 than killed in combat.[14] For soldiers like Specialist Guillen, death at the hands of fellow soldiers is part of the risk of joining the military. By categorizing her murder at the hands of another soldier as in the line of duty, the army acknowledged that when Specialist Guillen signed up to join the army, she wouldn't just be defending her country but would be defending herself from harassment and violence. Additionally, by framing Guillen's death as in the line of duty, violence in combat and violence in the ranks are made synonymous, and these dual threats of violence are simply costs of being included in the military. In November 2020 the commanding general at Fort Hood announced plans to name a memorial gate after Specialist Guillen.

Guillen's death at the hands of the military institution will become fully incorporated into the institution itself, and new recruits, who will be vulnerable to the same violence that killed Guillen, may very likely pass under a gate bearing her name as they become soldiers. Within a logic of tactical inclusion, the fear is that memorializing Guillen will become the end of the military's response, the gate bearing her name will be entirely symbolic, and the culture of sexual harassment, bullying, and violence at Fort Hood will continue unabated. Ultimately, thinking of tactical inclusion as an exploitation of vulnerability that continues once included in the military requires an acknowledgment that the military can never be a space free from exploitation and violence. The tragic murder of Vanessa Guillen makes clear the deadly consequences of tactical inclusion for military service members seen as ideal recruits in an age of militarized diversity. Calls for investigations into Specialist Guillen's murder and the army's response, which included investigations by the Federal Bureau of Investigation and Department of Justice, were framed as a way to ensure that her murder was not "swept under the rug," to quote President Trump in a meeting with Guillen's family in July 2020.[15] Although twenty-one army officers were disciplined, including some who were relieved of their commands, in connection with Specialist Guillen's murder, the army acknowledged that leaders failed to take seriously accusations of sexual harassment prior to Guillen's being murdered.[16] Rather than being "swept under the rug," Guillen's name will be placed on a gate, forever included in a military that ultimately killed her.

* * *

It has been many years since my relationship to military recruiting began. However, as was made clear when I recently went for a jog around my neighborhood in Milwaukee, Wisconsin, it is an ongoing relationship. On one of my jogging routes along the shores of Lake Michigan, I regularly pass a rack of blue bicycles that are part of a nonprofit bike-sharing program in the city, some of which have advertisements for the army ROTC printed on the rear fender. More than twenty years after I was required to take the ASVAB exam and over fifteen hundred miles from the high school where my classmates and I were sorted into divergent paths, one leading me away from the military, the other directing some of my classmates toward the military, military recruiting stubbornly remains part of my daily life.

Recruitment advertising is a pervasive part of the media and cultural landscape across the United States. As demonstrated in this book, everyday encounters with military advertising, whether on billboards, social media, or the backs of bicycles, are profoundly imbued with vulnerabilities and violence. Tactical inclusion has been the primary industrial and representational strategy for reaching out to ever-expanding groups of potential recruits. Inflected, at times, by highly visible debates over military policy and military actions, tactical inclusion remains a largely quotidian project, expressed through industrial language of demographic changes and market research and represented in recruiting ads for a military that very few Americans have any tangible and material connection to. The consistent and even habitual nature of tactical inclusion obfuscates the consequences of its violence and contributes to a view of select moments like the end of the combat ban for women, the repeal of DADT, and the end of the transgender ban as exceptional moments of social progress. However, viewing inclusion as a tactic, as a strategy imbued with power and exploitative of inequalities, allows us

to recognize tactical inclusion not as the realization of promises of equality but, rather, as a decades-long project of exploiting vulnerabilities and perpetuating state violence.

Appendix

Table 1: Active-duty accessions by year

Year	Army	Navy	Marine Corps	Air Force	Total
1973	169,517	93,648	48,946	93,539	405,650
1974	179,968	90,051	45,323	73,376	388,718
1975	180,311	98,455	57,122	73,870	409,758
1976	178,916	91,380	51,484	71,582	393,362
1977	216,883	129,280	57,579	91,367	495,109
1978	122,399	78,060	38,146	67,039	305,644
1979	128,289	76,980	38,726	66,684	310,679
1980	158,630	88,536	42,085	71,494	360,745
1981	109,209	85,995	38,830	70,472	304,506
1982	120,114	80,095	37,956	67,294	305,459
1983	132,650	73,909	36,628	60,274	303,461
1984	129,682	77,161	39,119	59,101	305,063
1985	119,082	82,930	34,051	64,954	301,017
1986	126,740	88,315	34,669	64,053	313,777
1987	120,376	87,753	33,528	54,668	296,325
1988	105,728	89,779	34,960	40,777	271,244
1989	112,091	89,606	32,941	43,182	277,820
1990	84,516	70,559	32,901	35,749	223,725
1991	77,638	68,472	29,635	29,756	205,501
1992	76,573	58,464	31,768	34,817	201,622
1993	73,937	63,154	34,735	31,289	203,115
1994	61,401	53,496	31,756	29,756	176,409
1995	57,401	47,152	31,946	30,788	167,287
1996	69,910	46,144	32,531	30,548	179,133
1997	75,727	49,131	33,949	30,088	188,895
1998	68,321	46,726	33,450	31,534	180,031
1999	67,007	51,436	32,998	32,327	183,768
2000	66,399	49,338	30,232	32,864	178,833

Table 1: (continued)

Year	Army	Navy	Marine Corps	Air Force	Total
2001	69,109	49,870	30,147	33,850	182,976

2002	69,591	43,500	31,972	36,447	181,510
2003	67,940	40,204	32,078	36,186	176,408
2004	72,710	39,416	30,156	33,690	175,972
2005	63,324	37,729	32,015	19,092	152,160
2006	69,758	35,840	31,362	30,429	167,389
2007	62,896	34,565	34,040	27,745	159,246
2008	69,345	37,951	37,010	27,738	172,044
2009	63,668	35,223	30,934	31,780	161,605
2010	70,081	34,049	28,018	28,363	160,155
2011	61,942	33,356	29,751	28,265	153,314
2012	58,891	36,275	30,504	28,757	154,527
2013	66,427	39,898	32,083	26,266	164,674
2014	55,157	33,637	25,974	24,134	138,902
2015	56,990	34,864	29,389	24,027	145,270
2016	58,693	30,485	30,283	31,929	151,390

Source: *Population Representation in the Military Services 2019*, https://www.cna.org/pop-rep/2019/index.html, accessed March 29, 2022.

Note: Accessions refers to new enlistees into the armed forces. Historical data for the U.S. Coast Guard is not included in *Population Representation in the Military Services*.

Table 2: Primary slogans in print advertisements published in *Cosmopolitan*, *Ebony*, and *Sports Illustrated*

Military branch	Slogan	Years in use

Branch	Slogan	Years
Air Force	Find yourself in the Air Force.	1973
	Look up. Be looked up to.	1974–1975
	A great way of life	1976–1985
	Aim high.	1986–1995
	Cross into the blue.	2002–2008
Armed Forces	Freedom isn't free.	1978
	It's a great place to start.	1982–1984
	Opportunity is waiting for you.	1990
	Stand up. Stand out.	1991–1992
	Make it happen.	1995–1996
	Today's military	1997–2012
Army	Today's army	1973–1974
	Join the people who've joined the Army.	1974–1980
	Be all you can be.	1981–2000
	An Army of one	2001–2006
	Army Strong	2007–2009
Coast Guard	Help others. Help yourself. Join the lifesavers.	1973–1975
	Help others. Help yourself.	1976–1981
	Be part of the action.	1992–1996
	Jobs that matter	1997–2000
	Born ready.	2011–2014
Marine Corps	We're looking for a few good men.	1973–1987
	The few. The proud. The Marines.	1988–2014
Navy	The Navy's not just sayin' it, they're doin' it!	1973–1974
	Be a success in the new Navy.	1973
	Be someone special. Join the Navy.	1974–1975
	The opportunity is for real . . . and so are we.	1974–1975
	Build your future on a proud tradition	1975
	It's not just a job. It's an adventure.	1976–1986
	Live the adventure.	1987
	You are tomorrow. You are the Navy.	1988–1989
	Full speed ahead	1990–1995
	Let the journey begin.	1996–2000
	Accelerate your life.	2001–2009

Note: There are some years where no ads for a particular branch in the sample were published. Additionally, ads published in the 2010s often did not contain a specific slogan but, rather, referred recruits to a branch's website, such as marines.com or airforce.com.

Table 3: Advertising agencies with primary contracts for recruitment advertising, 1973–2016

Military Branch	Agency	Years with Contract
Air Force	D'Arcy, MacManus, and Maisus	1973–1986
	Bozell	1987–2000
	GSD&M	2001–2016
Armed Forces / Department of Defense / Joint Recruitment Advertising Program	Grey Advertising	1980–1990
	Bates Worldwide/Backer Spielvogel Bates	1991–1993
	Mullen	2003–2013
Army	N. W. Ayer	1973–1986
	Young and Rubicam	1987–1999
	Leo Burnett Worldwide	2000–2005
	McCann Worldgroup	2006–2016
Coast Guard	Bates Worldwide/Backer Spielvogel Bates	1992–1993
	Cosette Communications	2008–2010
	Paskill, Stapleton, and Lord	2012–2013
Marine Corps	J. Walter Thompson	1973–2016
Navy	Grey Advertising	1973
	Bates Worldwide/Backer Spielvogel Bates	1974–1986
	Batten, Barton, Dustine, and Osborne (BBDO)	1987–1995
	Campbell Ewald	2000–2014
	VMLY&R	2015–2016

Sources: Advertising Age, The Standard Advertising/Marketing Redbooks, The Advertising Red Books, and archival sources, Advertising and Marketing History, Hartman Center for Sales, Duke University

Note: For many years between 1973 and 2016 there is no record of advertising agencies awarded primary contracts for military recruitment advertising. Additionally, several of the agencies listed above subcontracted with other specialty agencies, including agencies specializing in reaching non-White markets, while managing military accounts. Sporadic information about subcontracting was found but not with enough consistency or frequency to be reliably included above.

Notes

Introduction

1. First offered to high school students in 1968, the ASVAB was administered in 54 percent to 79 percent of American high schools between 1980 and 2011. Gregory V. Humble, "Why Schools Do Not Release ASVAB Scores to Military Recruiters" (thesis, U.S. Army Command and General Staff College, 2012); Janie H. Laurence, Janet E. Wall, Jeffrey D. Barnes, and Michelle Dela Rosa, "Recruiting Effectiveness of the ASVAB Career Exploration Program," *Military Psychology* 10, no. 4 (1998): 225–38, https://doi.org/10.1207/s15327876mp1004_1_2. While the military cannot require students in any school to take the ASVAB, schools may require students to do so. Humble, "Why Schools Do Not Release."

2. Registering for the Selective Service System, which maintains a registry of men eligible for a draft, became a requirement for all male citizens ages eighteen through twenty-five in 1980 and is a condition of eligibility for student financial aid and employment with the federal government.

3. A number of scholars have discussed these forces in more detail. My conceptualization of vulnerability is particularly indebted to a lineage of scholarship including Roderick A. Ferguson, Jasbir Puar, Grace Kyungwon Hong, and Dean Spade, among others. Ferguson, *Aberrations in Black: Toward a Queer of Color Critique* (Minneapolis: University of Minnesota Press, 2004); Puar, *Terrorist Assemblages: Homonationalism in Queer Times* (Durham, NC: Duke University Press, 2007); Hong, *Death beyond Disavowal: The Impossible Politics of Difference* (Minneapolis: University of Minnesota Press, 2016); and Spade, *Normal Life: Administrative Violence, Critical Trans Politics, and the Limits of Law*, rev. expanded ed. (Durham, NC: Duke University Press, 2015). These authors detail how neoliberal economic policies and shifting understandings of gender, race, sexuality, and ability created groups of people exposed to varying levels of

vulnerability and insecurity while selectively incorporating some gendered, racialized, and sexualized subjects into reproductive respectability and protectable life.

4. The coast guard occupies a unique position in relation to the military. While officially a part of the Department of Homeland Security and previously housed in the Department of Transportation, the coast guard operates as a military branch during times of war or at the direction of the president. While not always considered as part of the military, given their recruiting efforts during the AVF, the coast guard is included alongside other branches of the military in this book. The space force, formed in 2019 and housed in the Department of the Air Force, is not included in this analysis as its formation and subsequent recruiting materials fall outside the time frame focused upon.

5. "Population Representation in the Military Services Fiscal Year 2019," *Office of the Under Secretary of Defense, Personnel and Readiness*, 2019, https://www.cna.org/pop-rep/2019/contents/contents.html.

6. I use the term "advertiser" to refer to advertising professionals who work closely on military recruitment advertising. These advertisers, some of whom have been veterans, are employed by advertising agencies that are then awarded contracts with various branches of the military. Use of the term "advertiser" does not mean advertising professionals in general but specifically refers to advertising professionals who work within the military advertising industry.

7. Spade, *Normal Life*.

8. Jennifer C. Nash, *Black Feminism Reimagined: After Intersectionality* (Durham, NC: Duke University Press, 2019).

9. Roderick A. Ferguson, *The Reorder of Things* (Minneapolis: University of Minnesota Press, 2012).

10. Keeanga-Yamahtta Taylor, *Race for Profit: How Banks and the Real Estate Industry Undermined Black Homeownership* (Chapel Hill: University of North Carolina Press, 2019).

11. Taylor, *Race for Profit*.

12. Sara Ahmed, *On Being Included: Racism and Diversity in Institutional Life* (Durham, NC: Duke University Press, 2012).

13. Sara Ahmed, *Living a Feminist Life* (Durham, NC: Duke University Press, 2017); Ahmed, *On Being Included*.

14. Daniel Martinez HoSang, *A Wider Type of Freedom: How Struggles for Racial Justice Liberate Everyone* (Berkeley: University of California Press, 2021).

15. HoSang, *Wider Type of Freedom*.

16. Herman Gray, "Subject(Ed) to Recognition," *American Quarterly* 65, no. 4 (2013): 771–98, https://doi.org/10.1353/aq.2013.0058.

17. Sarah Banet-Weiser, *Empowered: Popular Feminism and Popular Misogyny* (Durham, NC: Duke University Press, 2018).

18. "Confidence in Institutions," *Gallup*, June 22, 2007, https://news.gallup.com/poll/1597/Confidence-Institutions.aspx.

19. Kimberley L. Phillips, *War! What Is It Good For? Black Freedom Struggles*

and the U.S. Military from World War II to Iraq (Chapel Hill: University of North Carolina Press, 2012); Dean Spade and Aaron Belkin, "Queer Militarism?!" *GLQ: A Journal of Lesbian and Gay Studies* 27, no. 2 (2021): 281–307, https://doi.org/10.1215/10642684-8871705.

20. Ilene Rose Feinman, *Citizenship Rites: Feminist Soldiers and Feminist Antimilitarists* (New York: New York University Press, 2000).

21. W. E. B. Du Bois, *Black Reconstruction in America, 1860–1880* (New York: Free Press, 1998); Hector Amaya, "Dying American or the Violence of Citizenship: Latinos in Iraq," *Latino Studies* 5, no. 1 (2007): 3–24.

22. Each of the five terms is used by the different military branches to describe both men and women service members. For example, the terms "airman" and "coast guardsman" are used to refer to both women and men in the air force and coast guard.

23. Nirmal Puwar, *Space Invaders: Race, Gender, and Bodies out of Place* (Oxford: Bloomsbury Academic, 2004).

24. Such categories, though often conceptualized in recruitment advertising in simplistic and homogenous ways, are not homogenous. The ways categories of gender, race, and sexuality have been conceptualized in the military advertising industry and the military more broadly have contributed to a series of intersectional erasures.

25. Melissa T. Brown, *Enlisting Masculinity: The Construction of Gender in US Military Recruiting Advertising during the All-Volunteer Force* (Oxford: Oxford University Press, 2012).

26. "A Proposal for an Integrated Research Program for the U.S. Armed Forces," account files, J. Walter Thompson Co., John W. Hartman Center for Sales, Advertising, and Marketing History, David M. Rubenstein Rare Book and Manuscript Library, Duke University, Durham, North Carolina. Hereafter the Thompson Co. account files are referred to as Thompson Co. files.

27. Vulnerability is also reliant on whom the military will accept. The military maintains a series of requirements for enlistment, including requirements based on age, citizenship, education, entrance exam scores, and physical fitness. Potential recruits can be disqualified from serving for a variety of reasons, including medical issues, mental health issues, criminal records, and moral character. Enlistment standards have been debated in relation to the success of recruiting and maintaining an all-volunteer military for decades. In 2016 it was predicted that 31 percent of all youth aged seventeen through twenty-four would be disqualified from military enlistment for one or more reasons. While enlistment requirements are clearly delineated in military policy, in practice exceptions are often made during times of high personnel needs. I focus on the tension between whom the military wants and who the military can persuade as the primary tension undergirding recruitment advertising and tactical inclusion. With the exception of age, advertisers aren't particularly interested in crafting target markets based on enlistment standards, leaving it to military recruiters to do the work of sorting out which interested recruits are actually eligible to enlist. As such, further exploration of how enlistment requirements contribute to and influence tactical inclusion is beyond the scope of this book but represents an interesting avenue for further study.

28. The two primary attitude and awareness surveys used during the AVF have been the Youth Attitude Tracking Study (YATS) and the Joint Advertising Market Research and Studies (JAMRS) Advertising Tracking System. YATS was an annual telephone survey of sixteen- through twenty-year-old men and women conducted between 1975 and 1999 and designed to collect information about youth views on the military and recruiting and ultimately to measure propensity, the likelihood that one expects to enlist in the military. Shelley Perry and Jerry Lehnus, "The Youth Attitude Tracking Study (YATS) In-Depth Interviews with Young Women: A Methodological Overview," Defense Technical Information Center report, Navy Advancement Center, Pensacola, Florida, 1998, https://apps.dtic.mil/sti/citations/ADA362444. Initially only surveying young men, YATS surveys were separated by gender and often used to measure distinctions in attitudes between racial groups, most notably differences between White youth, Black youth, and Latinx youth. YATS surveys were replaced in 2000 with the JAMRS Advertising Tracking System, which similarly sought to measure youth attitudes toward the military. Bernard D. Rostker, Jacob Alex Klerman, and Megan Zander-Cotugno, "Recruiting Older Youths: Insights from a New Survey of Army Recruits," RAND Corp. report (Santa Monica, CA: National Defense Research Institute, 2014).

29. Jackson Lears, *Fables of Abundance: A Cultural History of Advertising in America* (New York: Basic Books, 1995); Roland Marchand, *Advertising the American Dream: Making Way for Modernity, 1920–1940* (Berkeley: University of California Press, 1985); Arlene Dávila, *Latinos, Inc.: The Marketing and Making of a People* (Berkeley: University of California Press, 2001).

30. Jerald G. Bachman et al., "Does Enlistment Propensity Predict Accession? High School Seniors Plans and Subsequent Behavior," *Armed Forces & Society* 25, no. 1 (1998): 59–80, https://doi.org/10.1177/0095327X9802500104; S. G. Berkowitz et al., "Career Plans and Military Propensity of Young Men: Interviews with 1995 Youth Attitude Tracking Respondents," DMDC report (Arlington, VA: Defense Manpower Data Center, 1997); Brenda L. Moore, "The Propensity of Junior Enlisted Personnel to Remain in Today's Military," *Armed Forces & Society* 28, no. 2 (2002): 257–78, https://doi.org/10.1177/0095327X0202800205; David R. Segal et al., "Propensity to Serve in the U.S. Military: Temporal Trends and Subgroup Differences," *Armed Forces & Society* 25, no. 3 (1999): 407–27, https://doi.org/10.1177/0095327X9902500304; Mady W. Segal et al., "Gender and the Propensity to Enlist in the U.S. Military," *Gender Issues* 16, no. 3 (1998): 65–87, https://doi.org/10.1007/s12147-998-0022-0.

31. A number of scholars have discussed the uneven distribution of economic precarity in relation to race, gender, and sexuality, whether through discussions of racial capitalism, the feminization of poverty, or the production of certain populations as surplus labor. Ferguson, *Aberrations in Black*; Hong, *Death beyond Disavowal*; Diana Pearce, "The Feminization of Poverty: Women, Work and Welfare," *Urban and Social Change Review* 28 (1978): 28–36; Cedric J. Robinson, *Black Marxism: The Making of the Black Radical Tradition* (Chapel Hill, NC: University of North Carolina Press, 2000).

32. David Harvey, *A Brief History of Neoliberalism* (Oxford: Oxford University Press, 2005).

33. Harvey, *Brief History*.

34. Spade, *Normal Life*.

35. Lisa Duggan, *The Twilight of Equality? Neoliberalism, Cultural Politics, and the Attack on Democracy* (Boston: Beacon, 2004); Ferguson, *Aberrations in Black*; Hong, *Death beyond Disavowal*.

36. Jodi Melamed, *Represent and Destroy: Rationalizing Violence in the New Racial Capitalism* (Minneapolis: University of Minnesota Press, 2011); Michelle Alexander, *The New Jim Crow: Mass Incarceration in the Age of Colorblindness* (New York: New Press, 2012); Roopali Mukherjee, *The Racial Order of Things: Cultural Imaginaries of the Post-Soul Era* (Minneapolis: University of Minnesota Press, 2006); David L. Eng, *The Feeling of Kinship: Queer Liberalism and the Racialization of Intimacy* (Durham: Duke University Press, 2010).

37. Hong, *Death beyond Disavowal*.

38. Jasbir K. Puar, *The Right to Maim: Debility, Capacity, Disability* (Durham: Duke University Press, 2017).

39. Hong, *Death beyond Disavowal*.

40. Cynthia H. Enloe, *Does Khaki Become You?* (London: Pluto, 1983); Cynthia Enloe, *Bananas, Beaches, and Bases: Making Feminist Sense of International Politics*, 2nd ed. (Berkeley: University of California Press, 2014); Cynthia Enloe, *Maneuvers: The International Politics of Militarizing Women's Lives* (Berkeley: University of California Press, 2000); Cynthia Cockburn, "Gender Relations as Causal in Militarization and War: A Feminist Standpoint," *International Feminist Journal of Politics* 12, no. 2 (2010): 139–57; Feinman, *Citizenship Rites*.

41. Phillips, *War*; Brenda L. Moore, *To Serve My Country, to Serve My Race: The Story of the Only African-American WACS Stationed Overseas during World War II* (New York: New York University Press, 1997); Charissa J. Threat, *Nursing Civil Rights: Gender and Race in the Army Nurse Corps* (Urbana: University of Illinois Press, 2015); Allan Bérubé, *Coming Out under Fire*, 20th anniv. ed. (Chapel Hill: University of North Carolina Press, 2010); Aaron Belkin, *Bring Me Men: Military Masculinity and the Benign Facade of American Empire, 1898–2001* (New York: Columbia University Press, 2012); Steven Rosales, *Soldados Razos at War: Chicano Politics, Identity, and Masculinity in the U.S. Military from World War II to Vietnam* (Tucson: University of Arizona Press, 2017); Máel Embser-Herbert, *Camouflage Isn't Only for Combat: Gender, Sexuality, and Women in the Military* (New York: New York University Press, 1998).

42. Susan Jeffords, *The Remasculinization of America: Gender and the Vietnam War* (Bloomington: Indiana University Press, 1989); Susan Jeffords, *Hard Bodies: Hollywood Masculinity in the Reagan Era* (New Brunswick, NJ: Rutgers University Press, 1993); Mary Douglas Vavrus, *Postfeminist War: Women in the Media-Military-Industrial Complex* (New Brunswick, NJ: Rutgers University Press, 2018); Beth Bailey, *America's Army: Making the All-Volunteer Force* (Cambridge, MA: Harvard University

Press, 2009); Jennifer Mittelstadt, *The Rise of the Military Welfare State* (Cambridge, MA: Harvard University Press, 2015).

43. Wendy M. Christensen, *Mothers of the Military: Support and Politics during Wartime* (Lanham, MD: Rowman and Littlefield, 2018); Stephanie Szitanyi, *Gender Trouble in the U.S. Military: Challenges to Regimes of Male Privilege* (London: Palgrave Macmillan, 2020); Brown, *Enlisting Masculinity*.

44. Brown, *Enlisting Masculinity*.

45. Brown, *Enlisting Masculinity*.

46. Kimberlé Crenshaw, "Demarginalizing the Intersection of Race and Sex: A Black Feminist Critique of Antidiscrimination Doctrine, Feminist Theory, and Antiracist Politics," *University of Chicago Legal Forum* (1989): 151–52.

47. Marsha G. Henry, "Problematizing Military Masculinity, Intersectionality, and Male Vulnerability in Feminist Critical Military Studies," *Critical Military Studies* 3, no. 2 (2017): 182–99, https://doi.org/10.1080/23337486.2017.1325140, and "Why Critical Military Studies Needs to Smash Imperial White Supremacist Capitalist Heteropatriarchy: A Rejoinder," *Critical Military Studies* 6, no. 1 (2020): 107–10, https://doi.org/10.1080/23337486.2018.1429049.

48. Ahmed, *On Being Included*, 13, emphasis in original.

49. The United States had relied on drafts to procure military service members during times of war since the 1860s, with national drafts being instituted during the Civil War and again during World War I. Following the first, and short-lived, peacetime draft in 1940 and 1941, another peacetime draft was initiated in 1948 and continued until the implementation of the AVF in 1973.

50. Bailey, *America's Army*.

51. Phillips, *War*; Lorena Oropeza, "Antiwar Aztlán: The Chicano Movement Opposes U.S. Intervention in Vietnam," in *Window on Freedom: Race, Civil Rights, and Foreign Affairs, 1945–1988*, ed. Brenda Gayle Plummer (Chapel Hill: University of North Carolina Press, 2003).

52. James E. Westheider, *The African American Experience in Vietnam: Brothers in Arms* (Lanham, MD: Rowman and Littlefield, 2008).

53. Prior to and during the AVF, a variety of movements have advocated for women's military inclusion whereas others have opposed further inclusion as an extension of militarism. Feinman in *Citizenship Rites* proposes a framework based on two primary approaches, feminist antimilitarism and feminist egalitarian militarism. Phillips in *War* discusses the role race plays in shaping Black women's views on military inclusion, particularly in regards to broader Black freedom struggles. These examples make clear the complicated dynamics regarding women's military inclusion, which are defined not by a homogenous group of women but, rather, a variety of views shaped by dynamics of gender, race, class, and sexuality.

54. Phillips, *War*.

55. Phillips, *War*, 258.

56. Bailey, *America's Army*; Harvey, *Brief History of Neoliberalism*; Mittelstadt, *Rise of the Military Welfare State*.

57. Bailey, *America's Army*.

58. Richard Nixon, "Remarks on the CBS Radio Network: 'The All-Volunteer Armed Forces,'" October 17, 1968, The American Presidency Project, *UC Santa Barbara*, pid 123922, http://www.presidency.ucsb.edu/; Phillips, *War*; Mittelstadt, *Rise of the Military Welfare State*.

59. Willard Latham, *Modern Volunteer Army: The Modern Volunteer Army Program: The Benning Experiment, 1970–1972*, CMH 90-2 (Washington, DC: Department of the Army Publications, 2010).

60. Bernard D. Rostker, *I Want You! The Evolution of the All-Volunteer Force* (Santa Monica, CA: RAND, 2006).

61. Mady Wechsler Segal et al., "Hispanic and African American Men and Women in the U.S. Military: Trends in Representation," *Race, Gender & Class* 14, nos. 3–4 (2007): 48–64.

62. Segal et al., "Hispanic and African American."

63. Eileen Patten and Kim Parker, "Women in the U.S. Military: Growing Share, Distinctive Profile," blog, December 22, 2011, *Pew Research Center*, 2023, http://www.pewsocialtrends.org/.

64. The decrease in the military's size can be attributed to a number of factors, including changes in military technologies, strategies, and tactics.

65. Planners of the AVF paid little attention to the potential impacts an AVF would have on women, Latinx, or other people of color.

66. Mittelstadt, *Rise of the Military Welfare State*.

67. Bailey, *America's Army*.

68. Eliot A. Cohen, "Twilight of the Citizen-Soldier," *Parameters* 31, no. 2 (2001): 23–28.

69. Bailey, *America's Army*.

70. "The President's Commission on an All-Volunteer Armed Force" (Washington, DC: Library of Congress, February 1970), 6.

71. Latham, *Modern Volunteer Army*.

72. "Operation and Maintenance Overview: Fiscal Year 2016 Budget Estimates," Office of the Under Secretary of Defense (Comptroller)/Chief Financial Officer, February 2015. Different branches of the military categorize advertising budgets in different ways. Some branches have budgets dedicated exclusively to advertising, whereas others combine advertising with recruiting, training, and testing expenses. Furthermore, data on advertising spending is often inconsistent depending on whether it is reported by the advertising industry, the Department of Defense, Congress, or think tanks like the RAND Corp.

73. Nick Dyer-Witheford and Greig De Peuter, *Games of Empire: Global Capitalism and Video Games* (Minneapolis: University of Minnesota Press, 2009); Jonna Eagle, *War Games* (New Brunswick, NJ: Rutgers University Press, 2019); Nina B. Huntemann and Matthew Thomas Payne, *Joystick Soldiers: The Politics of Play in Military Video Games* (New York: Routledge, 2009); Tanner Mirrlees, *Hearts and Mines: The US Empire's Culture Industry* (Vancouver, Canada: University of British Columbia

Press, 2016); Roger Stahl, *Militainment, Inc.: War, Media, and Popular Culture* (New York: Routledge, 2009); Vavrus, *Postfeminist War*.

74. Lears, *Fables of Abundance*; Marchand, *Advertising the American Dream*.

75. Raymond Williams, "Advertising: The Magic System," *Advertising and Society Review* 1, no. 1 (2000), https://doi.org/10.1353/asr.2000.0016.

76. James Dertouzos and Steven Garber, "Effectiveness of Advertising in Different Media: The Case of U.S. Army Recruiting," *Journal of Advertising* 35, no. 2 (2006): 111–22.

77. Stahl, *Militainment, Inc.*

78. "I. Technical Proposal," Thompson Co. files; "U.S. Coast Guard Recommended Media Plan," client files, Bates Worldwide, John W. Hartman Center for Sales, Advertising, and Marketing History, David M. Rubenstein Rare Book and Manuscript Library, Duke University, Durham, North Carolina (hereafter referred to as Bates Worldwide files).

79. Jason Chambers, *Madison Avenue and the Color Line: African Americans in the Advertising Industry* (Philadelphia: University of Pennsylvania Press, 2009); Robert Weems, *Desegregating the Dollar* (New York: New York University Press, 1998).

80. Laurel R. Davis, *The Swimsuit Issue and Sport: Hegemonic Masculinity in Sports Illustrated* (Albany: State University of New York Press, 1997).

81. Davis, *Swimsuit Issue and Sport*.

82. Thomas P. Oates, *Football and Manliness: An Unauthorized Feminist Account of the NFL* (Urbana: University of Illinois Press, 2017); Samantha King, "Offensive Lines: Sport-State Synergy in an Era of Perpetual War," in *The NFL: Critical and Cultural Perspectives*, ed. Thomas P. Oates and Zack Furness (Philadelphia: Temple University Press, 2014), 191–204.

83. Brown, *Enlisting Masculinity*.

84. "The United States Marine Corps Advertising Tracking Study," "U.S. Marine Corps Year One Paid Advertising Media Proposal," "Awareness and Attitude Tracking Study: Wave XXIV," and "USMC Media Symposium," all Thompson Co. files.

85. "U.S. Marine Corps Year One Paid Advertising Media Proposal," "The United States Marine Corps Advertising Tracking Study," and "FY97 RAP," all Thompson Co. files.

86. Chambers, *Madison Avenue and the Color Line*; Noliwe Rooks, *Ladies' Pages: African American Women's Magazines and the Culture That Made Them* (New Brunswick, NJ: Rutgers University Press, 2004).

87. E. James West, "A Hero to Be Remembered: Ebony Magazine, Critical Memory, and the 'Real Meaning' of the King Holiday," *Journal of American Studies* 52, no. 2 (2018): 503–27, https://doi.org/10.1017/S0021875816001365; Rooks, *Ladies' Pages*; Jason Chambers, "Presenting the Black Middle Class: John H. Johnson and Ebony Magazine, 1945–1974," in *Historicizing Lifestyle: Mediating Taste, Consumption and Identity from the 1900s to 1970s*, ed. David Bell and Joanne Hollows (London: Routledge, 2006), 54–69.

88. E. James West, "'I See Enough Queers Walking the Streets in This City': Ho-

mosexuality and Sexual Geographies in Black Consumer Magazines during the 1970s," *Souls: A Critical Journal of Black Politics, Culture, and Society* 18, nos. 2–4 (October 2016): 283–301, https://doi.org/10.1080/10999949.2016.1230826; Thaddeus Russell, "The Color of Discipline: Civil Rights and Black Sexuality," *American Quarterly* 60, no. 1 (2008): 101–28.

89. Rooks, *Ladies' Pages*.

90. Laurie Ouellette, "Inventing the Cosmo Girl: Class Identity and Girl-Style American Dreams," *Media, Culture, and Society* 21, no. 3 (1999): 359–83, https://doi.org/10.1177/016344399021003004.

91. Ouellette, "Inventing the Cosmo Girl."

92. In April 2019 I conducted a four-hour in-depth, semi-structured interview with two advertising professionals from the agency J. Walter Thompson. Questions were devised by myself and a research assistant, Clark Brinson. The interview also included advertisers sharing the onboarding presentation given by J. Walter Thompson to marine corps leadership to familiarize them with the corps brand. In order to maintain confidentiality, the interviews are cited and referred to using the generic term "advertising professionals."

93. "United States Marine Corps Recruitment Advertising Plan FY '80," Thompson Co. files.

94. "The Forces of Change: Technical Proposal," Thompson Co. Files.

95. James Dertouzos, "The Cost-Effectiveness of Military Advertising" RAND Corp. report (Santa Monica, CA: National Defense Research Institute, 2009).

Chapter 1. We'll Hire You

1. Brown, *Enlisting Masculinity*; Jeanne Holm, *Women in the Military: An Unfinished Revolution*, rev. ed. (Novato, CA: Presidio, 1992).

2. Brown, *Enlisting Masculinity*.

3. Beth Bailey, "The Army in the Marketplace: Recruiting an All-Volunteer Force," *Journal of American History* 94, no. 1 (2007): 4, https://doi.org/10.2307/25094776.

4. Advertising professionals, interview with author, April 25, 2019.

5. The number of new enlistees surpasses the total number of military personnel for the years between 1973 and 1980, which decreased from 2.19 million to 2.03 million. This variance is due to military service members leaving the armed forces and the need for a steady influx of new service members in order to maintain overall numbers of military personnel.

6. David R. Segal, *Recruiting for Uncle Sam: Citizenship and Military Manpower Policy* (Lawrence: University Press of Kansas, 1989); Bailey, *America's Army*.

7. Mittelstadt, *Rise of the Military Welfare State*.

8. Mittelstadt, *Rise of the Military Welfare State*.

9. Charles C. Moskos, "Institutional/Occupational Trends in Armed Forces: An Update," *Armed Forces and Society* 12, no. 3 (1986): 377–82; advertising professionals, interview.

10. Brown, *Enlisting Masculinity*.

11. Bailey, *America's Army*.

12. "U.S. Marine Corps Reserve: FY '74 Recruitment Advertising Communications Plan," Thompson Co. files.

13. Hadas Mandel and Moshe Semyonov, "Going Back in Time? Gender Differences in Trends and Sources of the Racial Pay Gap, 1970 to 2010," *American Sociological Review* 81, no. 5 (2016): 1039–68, https://doi.org/10.1177/0003122416662958.

14. Mittelstadt, *Rise of the Military Welfare State*.

15. A number of scholars have discussed the gendered division of labor in the military. Brown, in *Enlisting Masculinity*, notes how military women were limited to clerical, administrative, and medical positions. Enloe, in *Bananas, Beaches and Bases*, argues that the gendered division of labor in the military situates women at the margins of military culture to maintain and valorize military masculinity. While women were granted access to new positions and roles during the early years of the AVF, women were still restricted from positions associated with combat, limiting their advancement and maintaining the ideological center of the military as a bulwark of masculinity.

16. Brown, *Enlisting Masculinity*.

17. The ads indicate a clear gender hierarchy within the military but not a racial one. This speaks, perhaps, to the history of racial and gender inclusion in the military. In the mid-1970s, the military had been racially integrated for approximately twenty years, and military personnel were acutely aware of ongoing issues of racist discrimination and violence within the ranks. Given the pervasive racial violence in the military during the 1960s and 1970s, there certainly was an incentive to depict a harmonious vision of a racially diverse military. This is not to say that the ad accurately represented race relations in the army or that issues of racism were moot but, rather, that there was a longer-standing institutional awareness of race in the military than of gender. Women have served in the military since its inception, but in the mid-1970s the military was still very much grappling with what it meant to have women able to volunteer for military service and able to serve to a greater extent than ever before. I read the presence of a gender hierarchy and the absence of a racial hierarchy as reflecting institutional anxieties of gender and race, in which the military was concerned with showing that the military was not racist but more immediately concerned that military women didn't overly disrupt a masculinist culture and tradition.

18. Lizabeth Cohen, *A Consumers' Republic: The Politics of Mass Consumption in Postwar America* (New York: Knopf, 2008); Ronald Roach, "From Combat to Campus," *Black Issues in Higher Education* 14, no. 13 (1997): 26; Charles C. Moskos, *The American Enlisted Man: The Rank and File in Today's Military* (New York: Sage, 1970).

19. Bailey, *America's Army*; Dorit Geva, "Different and Unequal? Breadwinning, Dependency Deferments, and the Gendered Origins of the U.S. Selective Service System," *Armed Forces & Society* 37, no. 4 (2011): 598–618, https://doi.org/10.1177/0095327X09358654.

20. "United States Marine Corps Reserve Communications Plan FY '76,"; "United States Marine Corps Recruitment Advertising Plan FY '79," both Thompson Co. files.

21. Hong, *Death beyond Disavowal*; Ferguson, *Aberrations in Black*.

22. Cockburn, "Gender Relations"; Ramon Hinojosa, "Doing Hegemony: Military, Men, and Constructing a Hegemonic Masculinity," *Journal of Men's Studies* 18, no. 2 (2010): 179–94; George L. Mosse, "Shell-Shock as a Social Disease," *Journal of Contemporary History* 35, no. 1 (2000): 101–8, https://doi.org/10.1177/002200940003500109; Joane Nagel, "Masculinity and Nationalism: Gender and Sexuality in the Making of Nations," *Ethnic and Racial Studies* 21, no. 2 (1998): 242–69, https://doi.org/10.1080/014198798330007.

23. R. W. Connell, *Masculinities: Knowledge, Power, and Social Change* (Berkeley: University of California Press, 2005).

24. Brown, *Enlisting Masculinity*.

25. Brown, *Enlisting Masculinity*.

26. Brown, *Enlisting Masculinity*, 47–48.

27. Patrick J. Akard, "Corporate Mobilization and Political Power: The Transformation of U.S. Economic Policy in the 1970s," *American Sociological Review* 57, no. 5 (1992): 597–615, https://doi.org/10.2307/2095915; Ruth Wilson Gilmore, *Golden Gulag: Prisons, Surplus, Crisis, and Opposition in Globalizing California* (Berkeley: University of California Press, 2007).

28. Mittelstadt, *Rise of the Military Welfare State*.

29. Feinman, *Citizenship Rites*; Randy Shilts, *Conduct Unbecoming: Gays and Lesbians in the U.S. Military* (New York: St. Martin's, 1993).

30. Rostker, *I Want You*.

31. Rostker, *I Want You*.

32. Feinman, *Citizenship Rites*.

33. Brown, *Enlisting Masculinity*.

34. Herbert, *Camouflage Isn't Only for Combat*; Bérubé, *Coming Out under Fire*.

35. Enloe, *Maneuvers*; Enloe, *Does Khaki Become You*.

36. Threat, *Nursing Civil Rights*; Leisa Meyer, *Creating G.I. Jane* (New York: Columbia University Press, 1998).

37. Loren Miller, "Glamorous G.I. Girls: Constructing American Servicewomen's Identities during World War II" (PhD diss., American University, Washington, DC, 2015), https://doi.org/10.17606/08dq-3813.

38. Brown, *Enlisting Masculinity*.

39. Brown, *Enlisting Masculinity*.

40. Ouellette, "Inventing the Cosmo Girl."

41. Ouellette, "Inventing the Cosmo Girl"; David Machin and Joanna Thornborrow, "Branding and Discourse: The Case of Cosmopolitan," *Discourse and Society* 14, no. 4 (2003): 453–71, https://doi.org/10.1177/0957926503014004003.

42. Michaela Frischherz, "Cosmo Complaints: Reparative Reading and the Possibility of Pleasure in Cosmopolitan Magazine," *Sexualities* 21, no. 4 (2018): 552–68, https://doi.org/10.1177/1363460717713385; Amy Adele Hasinoff, "It's Socio-

biology, Hon!" *Feminist Media Studies* 9, no. 3 (2009): 267–83, https://doi.org/10.1080/14680770903068233.

43. Ouellette, "Inventing the Cosmo Girl."

44. Ahmed, *On Being Included*.

45. Mittelstadt, *Rise of the Military Welfare State*.

46. One notable exception and the only ad published in *Ebony*, *Cosmopolitan*, and *Sports Illustrated* to focus exclusively on a Black woman in the 1970s was published in *Ebony* in February 1973. The navy ad featured a large image of Evangeline Bailey holding a microphone and wearing a red polka-dot dress with a large white collar, a glint of one earring visible against a black background. Bailey is described as having served in the hospital corps before being reassigned to the show unit of the navy band following a successful audition, a trajectory that reinforces gendered segregation in the military. The ad uses the image of Bailey to tell readers that there's "real opportunity in the Navy" and that "your son or daughter *can* be Black *and* Navy too," a slogan used in other navy ads published in *Ebony* featuring images of Black men.

47. Brown, *Enlisting Masculinity*.

48. Charles Moskos, "Diversity in the Armed Forces of the United States," in *Cultural Diversity in the Armed Forces: An International Comparison*, ed. Joseph Soeters and Jan Van der Meulen (London: Routledge, 2007), 15–30.

49. Thomas E. Ricks, *Making the Corps* (New York: Simon and Schuster, 1998).

50. Westheider, *African American Experience*.

51. Mark J. Eitelberg, "Evaluation of Army Representation," technical report (Alexandria, VA: Army Research Institute for the Behavorial and Social Sciences, August 1977), 13.

52. Rostker, *I Want You*.

53. Chambers, *Madison Avenue and the Color Line*.

54. Chambers, *Madison Avenue and the Color Line*.

55. Phillips, *War*.

56. Phillips, *War*.

57. Christian G. Appy, *Working-Class War: American Combat Soldiers and Vietnam* (Chapel Hill: University of North Carolina Press, 1993).

58. Stokely Carmichael, *Black Power: The Politics of Liberation in America* (New York: Random House, 1967).

59. Ferguson, *Aberrations in Black*.

60. Hong, *Death beyond Disavowal*.

61. Westheider, *African American Experience in Vietnam*.

62. Roopali Mukherjee, "Rhyme and Reason: 'Post-Race' and the Politics of Colorblind Racism," in *The Colorblind Screen: Television in Post-Racial America*, ed. Sarah E. Turner and Sarah Nilsen (New York: New York University Press, 2014), 39–56.

63. Although military demographic reports don't include information on the gender of Black service members, a further sign that the military fails to think about intersecting dynamics of gender and race, the fact that women made up no more than

7.5 percent of active-duty service members in the 1970s indicates that the majority of Black service members were men. However, Black women made up a disproportionately large share of military women during the same time period.

64. Mittelstadt, *Rise of the Military Welfare State*.
65. Mittelstadt, *Rise of the Military Welfare State*.
66. Rostker, *I Want You*; Mittelstadt, *Rise of the Military Welfare State*.
67. Mittelstadt, *Rise of the Military Welfare State*, 92.
68. Jeffords, *Hard Bodies*.

Chapter 2. America at Its Best

1. Rostker, *I Want You*, 387.
2. Rostker, *I Want You*.
3. Maxwell Thurman, "Sustaining the All-Volunteer Force 1983–1992: The Second Decade," in *The All Volunteer Force after a Decade: Retrospect and Prospect*, ed. William Bowman, Roger Little, and C. Thomas Sicilia (Washington, DC: Pergamon-Brassey's, 1986), 266–85.
4. Rostker, *I Want You*, 388.
5. Thurman, "Sustaining the All-Volunteer Force," 269.
6. Mittelstadt, *Rise of the Military Welfare State*.
7. Mittelstadt, *Rise of the Military Welfare State*.
8. For a detailed discussion of the Montgomery G.I. Bill and its significance during the Reagan era, see chap. 4 in Mittelstadt, *Rise of the Military Welfare State*.
9. Jeffords, *Remasculinization of America*, xii; Jeffords, *Hard Bodies*.
10. Jeffords, *Remasculinization of America*.
11. Jeffords, *Remasculinization of America*.
12. Bailey, *America's Army*; Mittelstadt, *Rise of the Military Welfare State*.
13. Brown, *Enlisting Masculinity*.
14. Thurman, "Sustaining the All-Volunteer Force."
15. Susan Faludi, *Stiffed: The Betrayal of the American Man* (New York: Harper Perennial, 2000).
16. Jeffords, *Hard Bodies*.
17. Judy Wajcman, "Feminist Theories of Technology," *Cambridge Journal of Economics* 34 (2010): 143–52; Ruth Cowan, *More Work for Mother: The Ironies of Household Technology from the Open Hearth to the Microwave* (New York: Basic Books, 1999); Anne Balsamo, *Technologies of the Gendered Body: Reading Cyborg Women* (Durham, NC: Duke University Press, 1995).
18. Jeffords, *Hard Bodies*.
19. Holm, *Women in the Military*.
20. One ad for the army featured a woman in representations of military technology. The ad, published six times in *Ebony* between 1981 and 1983, portrayed a woman wearing a flight-crew helmet and working in army aviation. Through a combination of occupational opportunities and narratives of challenge, the ad represents women as

included in new ways in a protech military. However, such an appeal is most notable for its limited nature and the ways it was ultimately subsumed by broader shifts in the 1980s, including efforts to decrease recruiting efforts targeting women and policies limiting women's military inclusion.

21. Lisa Burgess, "Despite Recruitment Efforts, Few Black Pilots Land in Air Force, Navy Cockpits," *Stars and Stripes*, June 22, 2003, http://www.stripes.com/.

22. "Domestic Box Office for 1986," Box Office Mojo, *IMDb.com*, https://www.boxofficemojo.com/year/1986/?ref_=bo_yl_table_38, accessed January 22, 2019.

23. A sequel to *Top Gun*, *Top Gun: Maverick*, was released in 2022. The sequel was celebrated both for valorizing the military and for featuring a diverse cast of military pilots, a sign of the resonances of tactical inclusion in commercial militarized media.

24. Ronald H. Cole, "Operation Just Cause: The Planning and Execution of Joint Operations in Panama, February 1988–January 1990" (Washington, DC: Joint History Office, Office of the Chairman of the Joint Chiefs of Staff, 1995).

25. "Whetstone 1986," Thompson Co. files.

26. "Whetstone 1986."

27. As noted by Mary Dudziak, representations of American democracy as enabling progressive social change and as morally just, particularly in regards to race, were key to Cold War narratives comparing democracy and communism. Mary L. Dudziak, *Cold War Civil Rights* (Princeton, NJ: Princeton University Press, 2000).

28. Connell, *Masculinities*.

29. Connell, *Masculinities*.

30. Brown, *Enlisting Masculinity*.

31. A similar strategy of including a variety of service members, including Black men and women, Latinx men, and White women and men, in different versions of the same ad was utilized in other recruiting materials. A series of army ads published in 1985 featured images of different service members in different versions of an appeal rooted in ideas of a meritocratic military.

32. Thurman, "Sustaining the All-Volunteer Force," 278.

33. Wallace Turner, "Reagan Cuts $503 Million from the Budget Passed by California Legislature," *New York Times*, July 4, 1971, https://www.nytimes.com/; Deborah Rankin, "Your Money; Reagan Cuts in Student Aid," *New York Times*, October 24, 1981, https://www.nytimes.com/.

34. Mittelstadt, *Rise of the Military Welfare State*, 113.

35. In their book *Producers, Parasites, and Patriots: Race and the New Right-Wing Politics of Precarity* (2019), Daniel HoSang and Joe Lowndes argue that the racialized categories of the producer, the parasite, and the patriot are the frames through which various individuals and groups are rendered legible within contemporary racial politics. That military service members, despite being recipients of an array of state support, are largely accepted as patriots whose service should be lauded is certainly influenced by representations in recruiting ads that sought to show military service members as exceptional and deserving.

36. The use of the army ROTC as a contrast to affirmative action is particularly interesting given the historical use of ROTC programs as a way to increase the representation of racial minorities within the officer corps, specifically through relationships with historically Black colleges and universities. Isaac Hampton, *The Black Officer Corps: A History of Black Military Advancement from Integration through Vietnam* (New York: Routledge, 2013); Bryan W. Leach, "Race as Mission Critical: The Occupational Need Rationale in Military Affirmative Action and Beyond," *Yale Law Journal* 113, no. 5 (2004): 1093–141.

37. James Burk and Evelyn Espinoza, "Race Relations within the US Military," *Annual Review of Sociology* 38, no. 1 (2012): 401–22, https://doi.org/10.1146/annurev-soc-071811-145501; Military Leadership Diversity Commission (MLDC), *From Representation to Inclusion: Diversity Leadership for the 21st-Century Military*, March 15, 2011 (Arlington, VA: MLDC, 2011).

38. Melamed, *Represent and Destroy*; Mukherjee, *Racial Order of Things*; Alexander, *New Jim Crow*; Eng, *Feeling of Kinship*.

39. "RE: Subcontract No. 0224," client files, Bates Worldwide, John W. Hartman Center for Sales, Advertising, and Marketing History, David M. Rubenstein Rare Book and Manuscript Library, Duke University; "Navy Advertising Plan FY '87," Thompson Co. files.

40. "Whetstone 1986"; "RE: Subcontract No. 0224."

41. Ronald Reagan, "Proclamation 4882—National Family Week," November 3, 1981, *National Archives*, https://www.reaganlibrary.gov/research/speeches/110381c.

42. Feinman, *Citizenship Rites*.

43. Cynthia Enloe, *The Morning After: Sexual Politics at the End of the Cold War* (Berkeley: University of California Press, 1993), 17.

44. Enloe, *Morning After*.

45. Mittelstadt, *Rise of the Military Welfare State*.

46. Holm, *Women in the Military*, 387.

47. Feinman, *Citizenship Rites*.

48. Shilts, *Conduct Unbecoming*.

49. Bérubé, *Coming Out under Fire*; Shilts, *Conduct Unbecoming*.

50. Brown, *Enlisting Masculinity*.

51. "The Coldstream Conference: Recruiting Advertising for the 1980s," June 1983, Thompson Co. files.

52. It's interesting to note how notions of pride, which played an influential role in movements for gay rights, are redirected away from social movements advocating for equal rights toward an association with a heteronormative vision of the military.

53. Mittelstadt, *Rise of the Military Welfare State*; Kellie Wilson-Buford, *Policing Sex and Marriage in the American Military: The Court-Martial and the Construction of Gender and Sexual Deviance, 1950–2000* (Lincoln: University of Nebraska Press, 2018); Meyer, *Creating G.I. Jane*.

54. Mittelstadt, *Rise of the Military Welfare State*.

55. Jeffords, *Remasculinization of America*.

56. Mittelstadt, *Rise of the Military Welfare State*; Wilson-Buford, *Policing Sex and Marriage*.

57. Shilts, *Conduct Unbecoming*; U.S. Army Public Health Command, *A Guide to Female Soldier Readiness*, June 2010.

58. Ferguson, *Aberrations in Black*; Hong, *Death beyond Disavowal*.

59. Mittelstadt, *Rise of the Military Welfare State,* 167.

60. For a detailed discussion of family programs in the army, see chap. 6 of Mittelstadt, *Rise of the Military Welfare State*.

61. Kimberly Jade Norwood and Violeta Solonova Foreman, "The Ubiquitousness of Colorism: Then and Now," in *Color Matters: Skin Tone Bias and the Myth of a Postracial America*, ed. Norwood (New York: Routledge, 2014), 9–28; Cedric Herring, Verna Keith, and Hayward Derrick Horton, *Skin Deep: How Race and Complexion Matter in the "Color-Blind" Era* (Urbana: University of Illinois Press, 2004).

62. Radhika Parameswaran, "'Jamming' the Color Line: Comedy, Carnival, and Contestations of Commodity Colorism," in *Racism Postrace*, ed. Roopali Murkherjee, Sarah Banet-Weiser, and Herman Gray (Durham, NC: Duke University Press, 2019), 57–71.

63. Eduardo Bonilla-Silva and Austin Ashe, "The End of Racism? Colorblind Racism and Popular Media," in *The Colorblind Screen: Television in Post-Racial America*, ed. Sarah E. Turner and Sarah Nilsen (New York: New York University Press, 2014), 57–82.

64. Feinman, *Citizenship Rites*; Segal et al., "Hispanic and African American Men and Women."

65. Melamed, *Represent and Destroy*.

66. Mittelstadt, *Rise of the Military Welfare State*.

67. Richard W. Stewart, "War in the Persian Gulf: Operations Desert Shield and Desert Storm, August 1990-March 1991" (Washington, DC: Center of Military History, 2010).

68. Thomas A. Keaney and Eliot A. Cohen, "Gulf War Air Power Survey" (Fort Belvoir, VA: Defense Technical Information Center, January 1, 1993), ix, https://doi.org/10.21236/ADA273996.

69. Rostker, *I Want You*, 532. Rostker served as the director of selective service and was the appellant for the 1981 U.S. Supreme Court case *Rostker v. Goldberg*, discussed earlier in the chapter.

70. Nese F. DeBruyne, "American War and Military Operations Casualties: Lists and Statistics" (Washington, DC: Congressional Research Service, September 14, 2018). The total number of service members who died during the Persian Gulf War is 382, including those who died of wounds and accidents or were missing then presumed dead.

71. Rostker, *I Want You*.

Chapter 3. The Military Type

1. "The Forces of Change: Technical Proposal," account files, Thompson Co. files, 5.

2. "Handwritten Notes," client files, Bates Worldwide files, n.p.

3. "Forces of Change," 5.

4. "Handwritten Notes," n.p.; "Forces of Change."

5. "Nexus Conference," account files, Thompson Co. files.

6. Aaron Belkin, "Don't Ask, Don't Tell: Is the Gay Ban Based on Military Necessity?" *Center for the Study of Sexual Minorities in the Military*, July 1, 2003, http://escholarship.org/uc/item/0bb4j7ss.

7. The official policy known as "Don't Ask, Don't Tell" used three terms to categorize the sexual activities and propensities of service members: homosexual, heterosexual, and bisexual. In the policy the terms "gay" and "lesbian" are subsumed within the broader term of "homosexuality." The popular discourse, however, centered more upon the terms "gay" and "lesbian" to the exclusion of "bisexuality."

8. Bérubé, *Coming Out under Fire*.

9. Bérubé, *Coming Out under Fire*.

10. "Gender Issues: Information on DOD's Assignment Policy and Direct Ground Combat Definition," *United States Government Accountability Office*, 1998, https://www.gao.gov/products/nsiad-99-7.

11. Margaret C. Harrell and Laura L. Miller, *New Opportunities for Military Women*, MR-896-OSD (Santa Monica, CA: RAND, 1997).

12. Feinman, *Citizenship Rites*.

13. During the U.S. Supreme Court confirmation hearings for Clarence Thomas in October 1991, Anita Hill testified that Thomas had sexually harassed her when supervising her at the Department of Education. A number of scholars have detailed how Hill's testimony and the subsequent backlash and defense of Thomas were illustrative of intersectional dynamics of the sexual harassment of Black women and of tensions between antiracist and feminist movements. Kimberlé Crenshaw, "Race, Gender, and Sexual Harassment," *Southern California Law Review* 65, no. 3 (1992): 1467–76, and "We Still Have Not Learned from Anita Hill's Testimony," *UCLA Women's Law Journal* 26, no. 1 (2019): 17–20; Devon W. Carbado et al., "Intersectionality: Mapping the Movements of a Theory," *Du Bois Review* 10, no. 2 (2013): 303–12. One month prior to Hill's testimony, the 1991 Tailhook Convention, an annual convention of navy and marine corps aviators was held in Las Vegas; eighty-three women and eight men reported being sexually assaulted during the convention, assaults that came to light in an October 1991 *San Diego Union* article. Megan N. Schmid, "Combating a Different Enemy: Proposals to Change the Culture of Sexual Assault in the Military," *Villanova Law Review* 55, no. 2 (2010): 475–508. The 1992 election was deemed "The Year of the Woman" following an unprecedented number of women being elected to the U.S. Senate—five women, including one incumbent—and the U.S. House of Representatives, twenty-four new women were elected. Elizabeth Adell Cook, Sue

Thomas, and Clyde Wilcox, *The Year of the Woman: Myths and Realities* (Boulder, CO: Westview, 1994).

14. Pushkala Prasad et al., *Managing the Organizational Melting Pot: Dilemmas of Workplace Diversity* (Thousand Oaks, CA: Sage, 1997).

15. Wally Snyder, "Diversity: A Starting Point toward a More Diverse Industry," *Advertising Age*, February 17, 1997; Coltun Webster, "Multicultural: A High-Priority Goal of America's Leading Advertisers Is Winning Over a Rainbow of Cultures; but Methods to Reach the General and Ethnic Market Are Troublesome, and Emotions Run High over How Budgets Are Directed," *Advertising Age*, November 17, 1997.

16. Mary Eileen Morrison, "Multicultural: Burnett, Ethnic Shop Hits Goals along Different Paths: Multicultural Marketing Now 'Is a Train That Is Coming Down the Tracks at 100 Miles Per Hour,'" *Advertising Age*, November 17, 1997; Gail Baker Woods, *Advertising and Marketing to the New Majority* (Belmont, CA: Wadsworth, 1994); Coltun Webster, "Multicultural"; Snyder, "Diversity."

17. Alfred Schreiber, "Forum: Defining the 'New America': Ads Have Vital Role in Placing Growing Ethnic Groups in Media Mainstream," *Advertising Age*, August 3, 1998.

18. Elaine Swan, "Commodity Diversity: Smiling Faces as a Strategy of Containment," *Organization* 17, no. 1 (2010): 77–100, https://doi.org/10.1177/1350508409350043.

19. Stuart Hall, "Conclusion: The Multicultural Question," in *Un/Settled Multiculturalisms: Diasporas, Entanglements, Transruptions*, ed. Barnor Hesse (London: Zed, 2000), 209–41.

20. Mukherjee, *Racial Order of Things*; Melamed, *Represent and Destroy*.

21. Melamed, *Represent and Destroy*.

22. Neda Atanasoski, *Humanitarian Violence: The U.S. Deployment of Diversity* (Minneapolis: University of Minnesota Press, 2013), 71.

23. Angela Davis, "Gender, Class, and Multiculturalism: Rethinking 'Race' Politics," in *Mapping Multiculturalism*, ed. Avery Gordon and Christopher Newfield (Minneapolis: University of Minnesota Press, 1996), 40–48.

24. "Nexus Conference," n.p.

25. "Handwritten Notes."

26. "USCG Media Planning/Placement," client files, Bates Worldwide files.

27. "Joint Recruiting Advertising Program Launches First-Ever Recruitment Ad Campaign Aimed At Women," client files, Bates Worldwide files, n.p.

28. "Nexus Conference"; "USMC Recruitment Advertising Plan, 1995," account files, Thompson Co. files.

29. Ahmed, *On Being Included*; Gavan Titley and Alana Lentin, *The Politics of Diversity in Europe* (Strasbourg, France: Council of Europe, 2008).

30. "Nexus Conference," n.p.

31. "United States Marine Corps FY93 Recruitment Advertising Plan" and "USMC RAO Conference—Summer 1994," both account files, Thompson Co. files.

32. U.S. Senate, "Military Personnel: Services Need to Assess Efforts to Meet

Recruiting Goals and Cut Attrition," Report to the Chairman and Ranking Minority Member, Subcommittee on Personnel, Committee on Armed Services (Washington, DC: General Accounting Office, June 23, 2000); Mittelstadt, *Rise of the Military Welfare State*.

33. "Military Personnel."

34. Stahl, *Militainment, Inc.*

35. "USMC Awareness and Image Tracking Study, 1991," account files, Thompson Co. files.

36. "USMC Recruitment Advertising Plan, 1995."

37. Bailey, *America's Army*.

38. Bruce R. Orvis, Narayan Sastry, and Laurie L. McDonald, "Military Recruiting Outlook: Recent Trends in Enlistment Propensity and Conversion of Potential Enlisted Supply," 1996, *Rand Corp*, https://www.rand.org/pubs/monograph_reports/MR677.html.

39. DeBruyne, "American War and Military Operations Casualties."

40. Brown, *Enlisting Masculinity*.

41. Military police function as law-enforcement officers on bases and installations and are tasked with enforcing military laws and regulations.

42. There is a long history of policies that have facilitated the hiring of veterans into policing professions, and in 2017, 19 percent of police officers were veterans. Simone Weichselbaum, Beth Schwartzapfel, and Tom Meagher, "When Warriors Put on the Badge," *Marshall Project*, March 30, 2017 https://www.themarshallproject.org/. As police departments have sought to diversify their ranks, they have also turned to practices of military recruiting to determine best practices for targeting and persuading diverse recruits to join law enforcement.

43. Advertisers scholars, including Marchand in *Advertising the American Dream*, Michael Schudson in *Advertising, the Uneasy Persuasion: Its Dubious Impact on American Society* (New York: Basic Books, 1986), and Lears in *Fables of Abundance*, have argued that ads do not reflect reality but, rather, reflect aspirations and fantasies of the good life. The aspirational nature of advertising not only hinges upon lack, on audiences not already living the good life represented, but also aids ads in marketing consumer goods and conveying social values. Mark Anthony Neal developed legibility as a concept to address historical articulations of Black masculinity through two reductive tropes: the good Black man and the bad Black man. In the context of recruitment advertising, joining the military and taking advantage of the transformative opportunities on offer consolidate one's standing as a good Black man. Neal, *Looking for Leroy: Illegible Black Masculinities* (New York: New York University Press, 2013).

44. "Text Exhibits," account files, Thompson Co. files.

45. Robert K. Griffith, *The US Army's Transition to the All-Volunteer Force, 1968–1974*, Army Historical Series, CMH pub. 30–18 (Washington, DC: Center of Military History, U.S. Army, 1997).

46. Jorge Mariscal, "Latinos on the Frontlines: Again," *Latino Studies* 1, no. 2 (2003): 347–51, https://doi.org/10.1057/palgrave.lst.8600036; Rosales, *Soldados Razos at War*.

47. Jorge Mariscal, *Aztlán and Viet Nam: Chicano and Chicana Experiences of the War* (Berkeley: University of California Press, 1999).

48. In her work, including *Latino Spin: Public Image and the Whitewashing of Race* (2008) and *Latinos, Inc: The Marketing and Making of a People* (2001), Arlene Dávila offers a discussion of the role marketing and advertising played in the development of a Hispanic/Latinx market and consumer identity.

49. Irene Garza, "Advertising Patriotism: The 'Yo Soy El Army' Campaign and the Politics of Visibility for Latina/o Youth," *Latino Studies* 13, no. 2 (2015): 245–68, https://doi.org/10.1057/lst.2015.13.

50. "FY96 RAP," account files, Thompson Co. files, 23.

51. Mukherjee, *Racial Order of Things*; Daniel HoSang, *Racial Propositions: Ballot Initiatives and the Making of Postwar California* (Berkeley: University of California Press, 2010).

52. Gina M. Pérez, "How a Scholarship Girl Becomes a Soldier: The Militarization of Latina/O Youth in Chicago Public Schools," *Identities* 13, no. 1 (2006): 53–72, https://doi.org/10.1080/10702890500534346.

53. George Ramos, "Army Launches Campaign in L.A. to Recruit More Latinos," *Los Angeles Times*, June 5, 1999.

54. Garza, "Advertising Patriotism."

55. "Joint Recruiting Advertising Program Launches."

56. Inderpal Grewal, *Saving the Security State: Exceptional Citizens in Twenty-First-Century America* (Durham: Duke University Press, 2017).

57. Grewal, *Saving the Security State*.

58. Judith Halberstam, *Female Masculinity* (Durham, NC: Duke University Press, 1998).

59. "U.S. Coast Guard Recommended Media Plan," client files, Bates Worldwide files.

60. Makeup is highly regulated in the military, and policies have encouraged women to maintain a feminine appearance through recommendations regarding the use of makeup. Carol Burke, *Camp All-American, Hanoi Jane, and the High and Tight: Gender, Folklore, and Changing Military Culture* (Boston, MA: Beacon Press, 2004). For example, the marine corps required women to wear eye shadow and lipstick at a minimum during basic training in the 1980s, and the only kind of facial tattoos allowed in the army are permanent makeup tattoos on women soldiers.

61. Brown, *Enlisting Masculinity*.

62. Loren Miller, "Glamorous G.I. Girls."

63. Woods, *Advertising and Marketing*.

64. "USMC Awareness & Attitude Tracking Study-Fall 1994" and "United States Marine Corps Awareness & Attitude Tracking Study, Spring 1995," both account files, Thompson Co. files.

65. "USMC Awareness... Fall 1994."

66. C. J. Pascoe, *Dude, You're a Fag: Masculinity and Sexuality in High School* (Berkeley: University of California Press, 2007).

67. Gary L. Lehring, *Officially Gay: The Political Construction of Sexuality* (Philadelphia: Temple University Press, 2003).

68. Chandan Reddy, *Freedom with Violence: Race, Sexuality, and the US State* (Durham, NC: Duke University Press, 2011); Hong, *Death beyond Disavowal*.

69. Human Rights Watch, "Uniform Discrimination: The 'Don't Ask, Don't Tell Policy of the U.S. Military," January 2003, https://www.hrw.org/report/2003/01/06/uniform-discrimination/dont-ask-dont-tell-policy-us-military.

70. Herbert, *Camouflage Isn't Only for Combat*.

71. Carol Cohn, "Gays in the Military: Texts and Subtexts," in *The "Man" Question in International Relations*, ed. Marysia Zalewski and Jane Parpart (Boulder, CO: Westview, 1998), 129–49.

72. In 1996, there were reports that women trainees were sexually harassed and raped by army drill instructors at the Aberdeen Proving Grounds. Several army drill sergeants were convicted of rape and sexual harassment charges. Schmid, *Combating a Different Enemy*.

73. Atanasoski, *Humanitarian Violence*.

Chapter 4. Make the World a Better Place

1. George W. Bush, "Address to the Joint Session of the 107th Congress," September 20, 2001, *Selected Speeches of President George W. Bush: 2001–2008*, 70, The White House, https://georgewbush-whitehouse.archives.gov/infocus/bushrecord/documents/Selected_Speeches_George_W_Bush.pdf.

2. George W. Bush, "Address to the Nation on Operations in Afghanistan," October 7, 2001, *Selected Speeches of President George W. Bush: 2001–2008*, 75, The White House, https://georgewbush-whitehouse.archives.gov/infocus/bushrecord/documents/Selected_Speeches_George_W_Bush.pdf.

3. Lila Abu-Lughod, "Do Muslim Women Really Need Saving? Anthropological Reflections on Cultural Relativism and Its Others," *American Anthropologist* 104, no. 3 (2002): 783–90; Carol A. Stabile and Deepa Kumar, "Unveiling Imperialism: Media, Gender, and the War on Afghanistan," *Media, Culture & Society* 27, no. 5 (2005): 765–82, https://doi.org/10.1177/0163443705055734.

4. Puar, *Terrorist Assemblages*.

5. Cynthia A. Young, "Black Ops: Black Masculinity and the War on Terror," *American Quarterly* 66, no. 1 (2014): 35–67, https://doi.org/10.1353/aq.2014.0015; Erica R. Edwards, *The Other Side of Terror: Black Women and the Culture of US Empire* (New York: New York University Press, 2021).

6. Garza, "Advertising Patriotism"; Bailey, *America's Army*.

7. U.S. Senate, Subcom. on Personnel, Comm. on Armed Services, "Military Personnel: Services Need to Assess Efforts to Meet Recruiting Goals and Cut Attrition,"

Report to the Chairman and Ranking Minority Member, GAO/NSAID-00-146 (Washington, DC: General Accounting Office, June 23, 2000).

8. Bailey, *America's Army*.

9. Bailey, *America's Army*.

10. Bailey, *America's Army*.

11. Bailey, *America's Army*.

12. U.S. Senate and House Comms. on Armed Services, "Military Recruiting: DOD Needs to Establish Objectives and Measures to Better Evaluate Advertising's Effectiveness," GAO-03-1105 (Washington, DC: General Accounting Office, September 19, 2003); "A New Focus for Military Advertising and Market Research," Client Files, Bates Worldwide.

13. "Military Recruiting."

14. "Military Advertising," *Ad Age*, September 15, 2003, http://adage.com/article/adage-encyclopedia/military-advertising/98777/.

15. Jerald G. Bachman, Peter Freedman-Doan, and Patrick M. O'Malley, "Youth, Work, and Military Service: Finding from Two Decades of Monitoring the Future National Samples of American Youth" (Fort Belvoir, VA: Defense Manpower Data Center, June 2000).

16. John Eighmey, "Why Do Youth Enlist? Identification of Underlying Themes," *Armed Forces & Society* 32, no. 2 (2006): 307–28, https://doi.org/10.1177/0095327X05281017.

17. Eighmey, "Why Do Youth Enlist."

18. Eighmey, "Why Do Youth Enlist."

19. Julian E. Barnes, "A Nation Challenged: Proud Spirits; As Demand Soars, Flag Makers Help Bolster Nation's Morale," *New York Times*, September 23, 2001, https://www.nytimes.com/.

20. Stahl, *Militainment, Inc.*; Mirrlees, *Hearts and Mines*.

21. Stahl, *Militainment, Inc.*

22. Mary Douglas Vavrus, *Postfeminist War: Women in the Media-Military-Industrial Complex* (New Brunswick, NJ: Rutgers University Press, 2018); Young, "Black Ops."

23. Quoted in Bailey, *America's Army*, 244.

24. Beth J. Asch, Paul Heaton, and Bogdan Savych, "Recruiting Minorities," 2009, *RAND Corporation*, 1994–2023, https://www.rand.org/pubs/monographs/MG861.html.

25. Asch, Heaton, and Savych, "Recruiting Minorities."

26. Eighmey, "Why Do Youth Enlist."

27. Catherine Lutz, "US and Coalition Casualties in Iraq and Afghanistan," Watson Institute for International and Public Affairs, February 21, 2013, *Brown University*, https://watson.brown.edu/costsofwar/files/cow/imce/papers/2013/USandCoalition.pdf.

28. Lutz, "US and Coalition Casualties."

29. Lutz, "US and Coalition Casualties."

30. "Civilians Killed & Wounded," Watson Institute for International and Public Affairs, *Brown University*, https://watson.brown.edu/costsofwar/costs/human/civilians, accessed June 2, 2020.

31. Brown, *Enlisting Masculinity*.

32. Brown, *Enlisting Masculinity*; Bailey, *America's Army*.

33. Neta C. Crawford, "United States Budgetary Costs of the Post-9/11 Wars through FY2019: $5.9 Trillion Spent and Obligation," Watson Institute for International and Public Affairs, November 14, 2018, *Brown University*, https://watson.brown.edu/costsofwar/.

34. Donald H. Rumsfeld, "A New Kind of War," *New York Times*, September 27, 2001, https://www.nytimes.com/.

35. Thom Shanker and Eric Schmitt, "Rumsfeld Seeks Leaner Army and a Full Term," *New York Times*, May 11, 2005, https://www.nytimes.com/.

36. Bailey, *America's Army*.

37. To maintain the numbers of troops needed for operations in Afghanistan and Iraq, the military also engaged in other tactics, including calling up reserve and National Guard units and issuing stop-loss orders, which suspended discharges and kept service members in the military after their initial terms of commitment.

38. Gretchen Livingston, "Profile of U.S. Veterans Shifts as Their Ranks Decline," November 11, 2016, blog, *Pew Research Center*, http://www.pewresearch.org/.

39. National Research Council, Committee on the Youth Population and Military Recruitment—Phase II et al., *Evaluating Military Advertising and Recruiting: Theory and Methodology* (Washington, DC: National Academies Press, 2004); T. Reichert, J. Y. Kim, and I. Fosu, "Assessing the Efficacy of Armed-Forces Recruitment Advertising: A Reasoned-Action Approach," *Journal of Promotion and Management* 13, no. 3–4 (2007): 399–412.

40. Donna Miles, "Army Recruiting Campaign Focuses on Prospects, Influencers," August 30, 2005, *U.S. Department of Defense*, https://www.veteransadvantage.com/blog/military-veterans-news/army-recruiting-campaign-focuses-prospects-influencers.

41. Bailey, *America's Army*.

42. Stahl, *Militainment, Inc.*

43. Puar, *Terrorist Assemblages*, xxv.

44. John Hope Franklin et al., "Black History Month: Serious Truth Telling or a Triumph in Tokenism?" *Journal of Blacks in Higher Education* 18 (Winter 1997–98): 87–92, https://doi.org/10.2307/2998774; LaGarrett J. King and Anthony L. Brown, "Black History, Inc! Investigating the Production of Black History through Walmart's Corporate Web Site," *Multicultural Perspectives* 14, no. 1 (2012): 4–10, https://doi.org/10.1080/15248372.2012.646633.

45. Melton A. McLaurin, *Marines of Montford Point: America's First Black Marines* (Chapel Hill: University of North Carolina Press, 2007).

46. McLaurin, *Marines of Montford Point*.

47. McLaurin, *Marines of Montford Point*.

48. Du Bois, *Black Reconstruction*.

49. Robert K. Chester, "'Negroes' Number One Hero': Doris Miller, Pearl Harbor, and Retroactive Multiculturalism in World War II Remembrance," *American Quarterly* 65, no. 1 (2013): 31–61, https://doi.org/10.1353/aq.2013.0012.

50. Chester, "Negroes' Number One Hero."

51. Chester, "Negroes' Number One Hero."

52. Tanine Allison, *Destructive Sublime: World War II in American Film and Media* (New Brunswick, NJ: Rutgers University Press, 2018).

53. Allison, *Destructive Sublime*.

54. Roopali Mukherjee, Sarah Banet-Weiser, and Herman Gray, eds., *Racism Postrace* (Durham, NC: Duke University Press, 2019).

55. Lawrence P. Scott and William M. Womack, *Double V: The Civil Rights Struggle of the Tuskegee Airmen* (East Lansing: Michigan State University Press, 1998).

56. Allison, *Destructive Sublime*, 56.

57. Advertising professionals, interview.

58. Brown, *Enlisting Masculinity*.

59. M. W. Segal et al., "Hispanic and African American Men and Women."

60. Moore, *To Serve My Country*; Sandra M. Bolzenius, *Glory in Their Spirit: How Four Black Women Took On the Army during World War II* (Urbana: University of Illinois Press, 2018).

61. Bolzenius, *Glory in Their Spirit*.

62. Helene Cooper, "Army's Ban on Some Popular Hairstyles Raises Ire of Black Female Soldiers," *New York Times*, April 20, 2014, http://www.nytimes.com/; C. Chic Smith, "The Policing of Black Women's Hair in the Military," *Africology: The Journal of Pan African Studies* 12, no. 8 (2018): 14.

63. Markus J. Whitehead, "The Military Promotion Process: The Lived Experiences of African-American Women in the Military" (PhD diss., Wayne State University, Detroit, Michigan, 2021).

64. Phillips, *War*.

65. M. W. Segal et al., "Hispanic and African American Men and Women."

66. Julia Melin, "Desperate Choices: Why Black Women Join the U.S. Military at Higher Rates Than Men and All Other Racial and Ethnic Groups," *New England Journal of Public Policy* 28, no. 2 (2016): 1–14.

67. Jennifer Hickes Lundquist, "Ethnic and Gender Satisfaction in the Military: The Effect of a Meritocratic Institution," *American Sociological Review* 73, no. 3 (2008): 477–96.

68. Melin, "Desperate Choices."

69. Brenda L. Moore, "African-American Women in the Military," *Armed Forces & Society* 17, no. 3 (1991): 363–84.

70. Brown, *Enlisting Masculinity*.

71. Miller, "Glamorous G.I. Girls." Black women may have been more consistently targeted as potential recruits in another publication, such as *Essence*. While archival

documents indicate that recruiting ads were published in *Essence* to a limited degree, Black women were still largely ignored in advertising plans for the armed forces, coast guard, navy, and marine corps.

72. Patricia Hill Collins, *Black Feminist Thought: Knowledge, Consciousness, and the Politics of Empowerment* (New York: Routledge, 2008).

73. Raka Shome, *Diana and Beyond: White Femininity, National Identity, and Contemporary Media Culture* (Urbana: University of Illinois Press, 2014).

74. Hill Collins, *Black Feminist Thought*.

75. That the ad shows a Black woman in a domestic setting speaks to an anxiety of representing Black women in the military. While previously deployed in the 1970s to offset concerns about combat in the wake of Vietnam, situating Black women in domestic settings—whether with their children or caring for others' children—allows military advertisers to render Black women intelligible within long-standing tropes of domesticity while also maintaining the military and its core mission of combat as a space dominated by Whiteness and maleness.

76. E. R. Edwards, "Sex after the Black Normal," *Differences* 26, no. 1 (2015): 148, https://doi.org/10.1215/10407391-2880636; Edwards, *Other Side of Terror*.

77. Natalie Fixmer-Oraiz, *Homeland Maternity: U.S. Security Culture and the New Reproductive Regime* (Urbana: University of Illinois Press, 2019).

78. Audre Lorde, *Sister Outsider: Essays and Speeches* (Berkeley, CA: Crossing, 2007).

79. Wendy M. Christensen, "Recruiting through Mothers: You Made Them Strong, We'll Make Them Army Strong," *Critical Military Studies* 2, no. 3 (2016): 193–209, https://doi.org/10.1080/23337486.2016.1162975.

80. Wendy M. Christensen, "The Black Citizen-Subject: Black Single Mothers in US Military Recruitment Material," *Ethnic and Racial Studies* 39, no. 14 (2016): 4, https://doi.org/10.1080/01419870.2016.1160139.

81. Ferguson, *Aberrations in Black*; Patricia Hill Collins, *Black Sexual Politics: African Americans, Gender, and the New Racism* (New York: Routledge, 2005).

82. Congressional Budget Office, *Recruiting, Retention, and Future Levels of Military Personnel*, pub. no. 2777, October 2006.

83. Linda Kerber, "The Republican Mother: Women and the Enlightenment-An American Perspective," *American Quarterly* 28, no. 2 (1976): 187–205.

84. Christina Sharpe, *In the Wake: On Blackness and Being* (Durham, NC: Duke University Press, 2016).

85. Alison Howell and Zoë H. Wool, "The War Comes Home: The Toll of War and the Shifting Burden of Care," Costs of War Project, June 13, 2011, Brown University, https://watson.brown.edu/costsofwar/papers/2011/war-comes-home-toll-war-and-shifting-burden-care.

86. Howell and Wool, "War Comes Home."

87. Neta C. Crawford, "War-Related Death, Injury, and Displacement in Afghanistan and Pakistan 2001–2014," May 22, 2015, and "Assessing the Human Toll of the Post-9/11 Wars: The Dead and Wounded in Afghanistan, Iraq, and Pakistan,

2001–2011," both Watson Institute for International and Public Affairs, Brown University, June 13, 2011, https://watson.brown.edu/costsofwar.

Chapter 5. Walls Always Fall

1. The use of the LGBT acronym reflects the military's narrow policy focus on lesbian, gay, bisexual, and transgender service members. A more inclusive acronym, such as LGBTQIA+, while more responsive to ongoing demands for recognition of various groups, including Two-Spirit, intersex, asexual, and queer individuals, would distort the exclusionary nature of the military's policy shifts. The narrow embrace of LGBT service members was predicated on an explicit exclusion of forms of queerness not intelligible within the military's rigid and absolute investment in the gender binary and associated gender presentations.

2. Lizette Alvarez, "More Americans Joining Military as Jobs Dwindle," *New York Times*, January 19, 2009, https://www.nytimes.com/; James Dao, "With Recruiting Goals Exceeded, Marines Toughen Ad Pitch," *New York Times*, September 17, 2009, https://www.nytimes.com/.

3. "Military Meets Recruiting Goals," Associated Press, *New York Times*, October 14, 2009, https://proquest.com.

4. Alvarez, "More Americans Joining Military."

5. Alvarez, "More Americans Joining Military"; Barbara Bicksler and Lisa Nolan, *Recruiting an All-Volunteer Force: The Need for Sustained Investment in Recruiting Resources—An Update* (Arlington, VA: Strategic Analysis, December 2009).

6. Alvarez, "More Americans Joining Military."

7. Bicksler and Nolan, *Recruiting an All-Volunteer Force*.

8. A greater percentage of Black and Latinx Americans lived in poverty during the Great Recession and were much more likely to have lost their homes to foreclosure than White Americans. Brian D. McKenzie, "Political Perceptions in the Obama Era: Diverse Opinions of the Great Recession and its Aftermath among White, Latinos, and Blacks," *Political Research Quarterly* 67, no. 4 (2014): 823–36. The Pew Research Center found that although men lost over 70 percent of jobs lost in the United States between December 2007 and June 2009, men gained jobs back more quickly as women continued to lose jobs. Furthermore, wealth inequality by race and ethnicity grew in the year following the recession as the economic recovery was more likely to benefit White men.

9. Bicksler and Nolan, *Recruiting an All-Volunteer Force*.

10. Michelle Norris, "A Weak Economy Is Good for Military Recruiting," *All Things Considered*, National Public Radio, July 29, 2011.

11. Daniel Martinez HoSang and Joseph E. Lowndes, *Producers, Parasites, Patriots: Race and the New Right-Wing Politics of Precarity* (Minneapolis: University of Minnesota Press, 2019).

12. Megan Katt, "Cultural Support Teams in Afghanistan," *Joint Force Quarterly*, 2014, 107.

13. Katt, "Cultural Support Teams."

14. Julia Preston, "U.S. Military Will Offer Path to Citizenship," *New York Times*, February 15, 2009, https://proquest.com.

15. "Military Accessions Vital to the National Interest (MAVNI) Recruitment Pilot Program," *Department of Defense*, ca. 2015, https://dod.defense.gov/news/mavni-fact-sheet.pdf.

16. Preston, "U.S. Military Will Offer Path"; Julia Preston, "Thriving Military Recruitment Program Blocked," *New York Times*, January 22, 2010, https://www.nytimes.com/.

17. Dertouzos, "Cost-Effectiveness of Military Advertising."

18. Dertouzos, "Cost-Effectiveness of Military Advertising."

19. Natalie Zmuda, "Are the Army's New Marketing Tactics a Little Too Kid-Friendly?" *Ad Age*, September 8, 2008, http://adage.com/.

20. Stahl, *Militainment, Inc.*; King, "Offensive Lines."

21. Ira Teinowitz, "Navy Puts Recruitment Ad Contract in Review," *Ad Age*, April 21, 2008, http://adage.com/.

22. "DOD Advertising: Better Coordination, Performance Measurement, and Oversight Needed to Help Meet Recruitment Goals," Report to Congressional Comms., GAO-16-396, U.S. Government Accountability Office, May 2016.

23. Dertouzos, "Cost-Effectiveness of Military Advertising"; advertising professionals, interview.

24. Sarah E. Turner, *The Colorblind Screen: Television in Post-Racial America*, ed. Sarah Nilsen (New York: New York University Press, 2014); Mukherjee, Banet-Weiser, and Gray, *Racism Postrace*.

25. Vavrus, *Postfeminist War*.

26. Cynthia Enloe, "The Risks of Scholarly Militarization: A Feminist Analysis," *Perspectives on Politics* 8, no. 4 (2020): 1107–11.

27. Cynthia Enloe, *Nimo's War, Emma's War: Making Feminist Sense of the Iraq War* (Berkeley: University of California Press, 2010); Mark Landler, "The Afghan War and the Evolution of Obama," *New York Times*, January 1, 2017, https://www.nytimes.com/.

28. Lisa Parks and Caren Kaplan, *Life in the Age of Drone Warfare* (Durham, NC: Duke University Press, 2017); Ronak K. Kapadia, *Insurgent Aesthetics: Security and the Queer Life of the Forever War* (Durham, NC: Duke University Press, 2019).

29. John C. Landreau, "Fighting Words: Obama, Masculinity, and the Rhetoric of National Security," *Thirdspace: A Journal of Feminist Theory and Culture* 10, no. 1 (2011), https://journals.lib.sfu.ca/index.php/thirdspace/article/view/landreau; Emma Cannen, "Avant-Garde Militarism and a Post–Hip-Hop President," *International Feminist Journal of Politics* 16, no. 2 (2014): 255–77, https://doi.org/10.1080/14616742.2013.780375.

30. MLDC, "From Representation to Inclusion."

31. Daniel P. McDonald and Kizzy M. Parks, *Managing Diversity in the Military: The Value of Inclusion in a Culture of Uniformity* (New York: Routledge, 2011).

32. Kori Schulman, "The President on the Don't Ask, Don't Tell Repeal Act of 2010: 'An Historic Step,'" December 18, 2010, *The White House*, https://www.whitehouse.gov/blog/2010/12/18/president-dont-ask-dont-tell-repeal-act-2010-historic-step.

33. Claudette Roulo, "Defense Department Expands Women's Combat Role," *American Forces Press Service*, January 24, 2013, https://www.nationalguard.mil/.

34. Struggles over the open inclusion of transgender service members has become a key point in political struggles in the years since 2016. President Donald Trump announced a ban on transgender service members in summer 2017, one of many openly and vehemently anti-trans policy changes the Trump administration made. Shortly after his inauguration in 2021, President Joe Biden repealed the ban.

35. MLDC, *From Representation to Inclusion*, 12.

36. Such a reading of diversity echoes Sara Ahmed's reading in *On Being Included* of diversity in higher education.

37. MLDC, *From Representation to Inclusion*, xv.

38. Each branch of the military created diversity materials, including diversity pages on their websites. For example, the army's diversity website featured the slogan "Strength In Diversity" and largely focused on racial and gender differences. However, in a series of "diversity messages" focusing on the stories of different soldiers, one story details the experience of Captain Scotty Smiley, who lost his eyesight when wounded in combat. Smiley's loss of sight is discussed as an injury that didn't prevent him from continuing to serve his country as a soldier. His story is unique in its focus on ability as an aspect of militarized diversity and notable given the military's strict and normatively ableist entrance standards but is not unique in regard to the prevalence of casualties suffered by service members during wars in Afghanistan and Iraq. The inclusion of Smiley's story is easily subsumed within a narrative of virtuous difference and patriotic service whereas other discussions of ability largely focus on exclusion, whether in terms of physical entrance standards, mental standards, or the use of ability as a mode of excluding women and transgender people from serving.

39. "Air Force Diversity & Inclusion," *United States Air Force*, https://www.af.mil/Diversity.aspx, accessed December 3, 2018.

40. "Air Force Diversity & Inclusion," 2016, *United States Air Force*, https://www.youtube.com/watch?time_continue=6&v=MpHrI3jg5-0&feature=emb_logo; the source is no longer available.

41. The "Global Force for Good" slogan was largely seen as ineffective and unpopular. It was also viewed as a catalyst for the navy ending its partnership with Lowe Campbell Ewald and seeking out a new advertising firm, Young and Rubicam, in 2015. Mark D. Faram, "Navy Dumps Unpopular Recruiting Slogan during Army Game," *Navy Times*, December 15, 2014, https://www.navytimes.com/news/pentagon-congress/2014/12/15/navy-dumps-unpopular-recruiting-slogan-during-army-game/; Geoff Ziezulewicz, "After a Long Wait, Navy Unveils a New Slogan," *Navy Times*, December 5, 2017, https://www.navytimes.com/news/your-navy/2017/12/05/after-a-long-wait-navy-unveils-a-new-slogan/.

42. Juliet Nebolon, "'Life Given Straight from the Heart': Settler Militarism, Biopolitics, and Public Health in Hawai'i during World War II," *American Quarterly* 69, no. 1 (2017): 23–45, https://doi.org/10.1353/aq.2017.0002; Jeremiah Favara, "The Recruiting Archipelago: U.S. Military Recruiting and Resistance in the Pacific," presentation, American Studies Association Conference, Honolulu, Hawaii, 2019.

43. Atanasoski, *Humanitarian Violence*.

44. James Dao, "Ad Campaign for Marines Cites Chaos as a Job Perk," *New York Times*, March 9, 2012, https://www.nytimes.com/.

45. "Marine Corps Commercial: Toward the Sounds of Chaos," 2012, *YouTube.com*, https://www.youtube.com/.

46. Advertising professionals, interview.

47. Advertising professionals, interview.

48. These two White men, both of whom embody imperialistic and neocolonial endeavors, albeit in different guises, represent the two sides of this gap. Rambo carries guns and uses brute force, whereas Bono carries humanitarian aid and uses capitalism and Western models of development. The use of such figures speaks to the cemented links between militarism, Whiteness, and manliness, even when thinking about diversity.

49. Advertising professionals, interview.

50. For a further discussion of the ways race informed production logics of marine corps recruiting ads during the late 2000s and 2010s, see Favara and Brinson, "'White at Heart': Making Race in Marine Corps Recruitment Advertising," *Communication, Culture, and Critique* 16, no. 1 (2023): 33–40.

51. At the same time as racial diversity was leveraged to promote messages targeting those bound by a shared investment in militarized diversity, advertisers continued to create targeted campaigns to specific racial groups. The marine corps was singled out for its extensive and highly successful efforts targeting Latinx markets, as evidenced in two iterations of their Hispanic Values campaigns. The Hispanic Values campaigns aligned cultural values of family, honor, courage, and commitment with military service to promote a vision of Latinx people as culturally inclined to military service. The success of the campaign has led to Latinx people being overrepresented in the marine corps, an overrepresentation tied to concerns about the risks of combat and death being inequitably borne by Latinx service members.

52. U.S. Senate, Armed Services Comm., "Implementation of the Decision to Open All Ground Combat Units to Women," February 2, 2016, 69, http://www.armed-services.senate.gov/hearings/16-02-02-implementation-of-the-decision-to-open-all-ground-combat-units-to-women.

53. "Implementation of the Decision."

54. Vavrus, *Postfeminist War*.

55. Vavrus, *Postfeminist War*.

56. Alan Yuhas, "First Female US Army Rangers 'Open up New Doors for Women,'" (New York) *Guardian*, August 20, 2015, http://www.theguardian.com/.

57. Advertising professionals, interview.

58. Marine Corps Recruiting, "U.S. Marine Corps Commercial: Battle Up:60," *Youtube.com*, 2017, https://www.youtube.com/.

59. Schulman, "President on the Don't Ask, Don't Tell." While the act allowed gay, lesbian, and bisexual service members to openly serve, Obama's statement only mentioned gay and lesbian Americans.

60. Lisa Duggan, "The New Homonormativity: The Sexual Politics of Neoliberalism," in *Materializing Democracy: Toward a Revitalized Cultural Politics*, ed. Russ Castronovo and Dana D. Nelson (Durham, NC: Duke University Press, 2002), 175–94.

61. Puar, *Terrorist Assemblages*.

62. Liz Montegary, "Militarizing US Homonormativities: The Making of 'Ready, Willing, and Able' Gay Citizens," *Signs: Journal of Women in Culture and Society* 40, no. 4 (2015): 891–915, https://doi.org/10.1086/680333.

63. Montegary, "Militarizing US Homonormativities."

64. While I focus on San Diego and San Francisco, local recruiting efforts focused on gay, lesbian, and bisexual recruits occurred in other places, as well. In the initial days and weeks following the repeal of DADT, there were a few instances of recruiters being invited to recruit at gay community centers and events. For instance, marine corps recruiters were invited to set up recruiting booths at a gay community center in Tulsa, Oklahoma, and in Pasadena, California. While recruiters from all five branches were also invited to set up recruiting booths in Tulsa the day after DADT was repealed, marine corps recruiters were the only recruiters who did so. These initial forays into recruiting LGB service members were notably not initiated by the military but were characterized as successful public relations events for the marine corps. Elisabeth Bumiller, "Marines Hit the Ground Running in Seeking Recruits at Gay Center," *New York Times*, September 20, 2011, https://www.nytimes.com/; Martha Groves, "Marine Recruits Reach out at Gay Pride Event in Pasadena," *Los Angeles Times*, October 9, 2011, https://www.latimes.com/.

65. "Military Department," blog, *San Diego Pride*, https://sdpride.org/military/, accessed July 20, 2020.

66. Julie Watson, "Troops Allowed to March in Gay Pride Parade," *Seattle (WA) Times*, July 16, 2011, http:/seattletimes.com/.

67. *San Diego Military Economic Impact Study 2019* (San Diego, CA: San Diego Military Advisory Council, 2019).

68. *San Diego Military Economic Impact Study 2016* (San Diego, CA: San Diego Military Advisory Council, 2016).

69. HoSang, *Racial Propositions*.

70. "Military Holds 1st Event Marking Gay Pride Month," June 26, 2012, *SFGate*, accessed October 26, 2016, http://www.sfgate.com/.

71. "Military Holds 1st Event."

72. "Military Holds 1st Event."

73. Beginning as a form of commemoration following the Stonewall riots in 1969, pride parades and their meanings have transformed as they have proliferated and gained more mainstream acceptance. Elizabeth Armstrong and Suzanna Crage argue

that the commemoration of Stonewall, rather than of earlier riots like that at Compton's Cafeteria in San Francisco in 1966, results from organizational capacities and the very form of the parade, as something replicable that promoted visibility. The emphasis on visibility, coming out, and pride itself is tied to a particular expression of queer identity, one that has operated via the exclusion of transgender folks, queers of color, and rural queers. Elizabeth A. Armstrong and Suzanna M. Crage, "Movements and Memory: The Making of the Stonewall Myth," *American Sociological Review* 71, no. 5 (2006): 724–51, https://doi.org/10.1177/000312240607100502; Carly Thomsen, "In Plain(s) Sight: Rural LGBTQ Women and the Politics of Visibility," in *Queering the Countryside: New Frontiers in Rural Queer Studies*, ed. Mary L. Gray, Colin R. Johnson, and Brian J. Gilley (New York: New York University Press, 2016), 244–66; Susan Stryker, *Transgender History: The Roots of Today's Revolution* (Berkeley, CA: Seal Press, 2008); Martin F. Manalansan, "In the Shadows of Stonewall: Examining Gay Transnational Politics and the Diasporic Dilemma," *GLQ: A Journal of Gay and Lesbian Studies* 2, no. 4 (1995): 427–38.

74. Justin Berton, "Military Will Have Robust Presence at Pride Events," June 24, 2013, *San Francisco (CA) Chronicle*, http://www.sfchronicle.com/, accessed November 29, 2016.

75. Berton, "Military Will Have Robust Presence."

76. Nan Alamilla Boyd, *Wide-Open Town: A History of Queer San Francisco to 1965* (Berkeley: University of California Press, 2003); Amin Ghaziani, *There Goes the Gayborhood?* (Princeton, NJ: Princeton University Press, 2015); John D'Emilio, *Sexual Politics, Sexual Communities: The Making of a Homosexual Minority in the United States*, 2nd ed. (Chicago: University of Chicago Press, 1998).

77. Armstrong and Crage, "Movements and Memory"; Scott James, "There Goes the Gayborhood," *New York Times*, June 21, 2017, https://www.nytimes.com/.

78. Schulman, "President on the Don't Ask, Don't Tell."

79. "Secretary of Defense Ash Carter Announces Policy for Transgender Service Members," June 30, 2016, *U.S. Department of Defense*, accessed November 29, 2016, http://www.defense.gov/.

80. "Secretary of Defense Ash Carter."

81. "In-Service Transition for Transgender Service Members," DoD Instruction 1300.28, June 30, 2016, *Department of Defense*, https://dod.defense.gov/.

82. Dean Spade, "Mutilating Gender," in *The Transgender Studies Reader*, ed. Susan Stryker and Stephen Whittle (New York: Taylor and Francis, 2006), 315–32; Sandy Stone, "The Empire Strikes Back: A Posttransexual Manifesto," *Camera Obscura* 10, no. 2 (1992): 150–76.

83. This is not to say that military service members aren't having same-sex sex, but, rather, as argued by both Aaron Belkin in *Bring Me Men* and Jane Ward, that same-sex experiences in the military actually bolster perceptions of straightness and White masculinity. Jane Ward, *Not Gay: Sex between Straight White Men* (New York: New York University Press, 2015).

84. As of winter 2023 there had not been any national recruiting campaigns por-

traying LGBT service members for any branch of the military. In spring 2021 the army created and released an animated ad, "The Calling," based on the experiences of Corporal Emma Malonelord, a soldier raised by two mothers. The ad was criticized by conservative politicians and pundits as a sign of a "woke" and weakened military for its depiction of a service member raised by lesbian parents.

85. Ashley C. Schuyler et al., "Experiences of Sexual Harassment, Stalking, and Sexual Assault during Military Service among LGBT and Non-LGBT Service Members," *Journal of Traumatic Stress* 33, no. 3 (2020): 257–66, https://doi.org/10.1002/jts.22506.

86. "Population Representation in the Military Services: Fiscal Year 2016 Executive Summary," Personnel and Readiness, *Office of the Under Secretary of Defense, Department of Defense*, n.d., https://www.cna.org/pop-rep/2016/summary/summary.html.

87. "Population Representation . . . 2016."

88. "Population Representation . . . 2016."

89. "Confidence in Institutions," *Gallup.com*, June 22, 2007, https://news.gallup.com/poll/1597/Confidence-Institutions.aspx.

90. Brian Kennedy, "Most Americans Trust Military and Scientists to Act in the Public's Interest," October 18, 2016, blog, *Pew Research Center*, https://www.pewresearch.org/, accessed November 23, 2020.

Conclusion

1. "Navy Seal Pardoned of War Crimes by Trump Described by Colleagues as 'Freaking Evil,'" *Guardian*, December 27, 2019, http://www.theguardian.com/; Daniel Dale, "'Central Casting': Trump Is Talking More Than Ever about Men's Looks," August 13, 2019, *CNN*, accessed December 2, 2020, https://www.cnn.com/.

2. Thomas Gibbons-Neff, Eric Schmitt, and Helene Cooper, "Aggressive Tactics by National Guard, Ordered to Appease Trump, Wounded the Military, Too," *New York Times*, June 10, 2020, https://www.nytimes.com/.

3. Gibbons-Neff, Schmitt, and Cooper, "Aggressive Tactics."

4. Abigail Haddad et al., "Increasing Organizational Diversity in 21st-Century Policing," 2012, *RAND Corporation*, https://www.rand.org/pubs/occasional_papers/OP385.html.

5. Elizabeth Hinton, *America on Fire: The Untold History of Police Violence and Black Rebellion Since the 1960s* (New York: Liveright, 2021); Alex S. Vitale, *The End of Policing* (London: Verso, 2018).

6. David Bindon et al., "Policy Proposal: An Anti-Racist West Point," June 25, 2020, *SlideShare from Scribd*, https://www.slideshare.net/TimothyBerry8/an-anti-racist-west-point?from_action=save.

7. Stephen E. Ambrose, *Duty, Honor, Country: A History of West Point* (Baltimore, MD: Johns Hopkins University Press, 1999).

8. Bindon et al., "Policy Proposal."

9. Ahmed, *On Being Included*.

10. Ferguson, *Reorder of Things*.

11. In May 2023, Fort Hood, which was named after the Confederate general John Bell Hood, was renamed Fort Cavazos. The renaming of the base honors the first Latinx four-star general, Richard Edward Cavazos, and follows in line with other efforts to rename bases and installations with links to members of the Confederacy.

12. Christina Morales, "'An Empty Presence in My Chest': Vanessa Guillen's Family Calls for Change in the Military," *New York Times*, July 6, 2020, https://www.nytimes.com/.

13. Patricia Kime, "Vanessa Guillen's Family Will Receive Military Death Benefits after New Army Ruling," October 20, 2020, *Military.com*, https://www.military.com/.

14. Manny Fernandez, "A Year of Heartbreak and Bloodshed at Fort Hood," *New York Times*, September 9, 2020, https://www.nytimes.com/.

15. "A #MeToo Moment in the Military," *New York Times*, July 31, 2020, https://www.nytimes.com/.

16. Lolita Baldor, "Army Disciplines 21 at Fort Hood in Probe of Soldier's Death," *AP NEWS*, April 30, 2021, https://apnews.com/.

Index

Note: Page numbers in *italics* denotes figures and tables.

9/11 attacks, 124, 127, 129–30, 135, 143, 149, 157, 177

Aberdeen Proving Grounds, 121, 225n72
able-bodiedness, 16, 178, 181, 205n3. *See also* disability
absent father, stereotype of, 57, 88, 150
Abu Ghraib, 160
Abu-Lughod, Lila, 124
active duty, 19, 33, 65–66, 81, 99, 131, 142, 157–58; women, 43, 179, 217n63
activism, 18–19, 81, 95, 97, 177
Adams, John, 195
Advertising Age, 96–97
advertising agencies, 5, 21, 34, *204,* 206n6. *See also individual advertisement agencies*
affirmative action, 7, 28, 64, 74, 80, 219n36
Afghanistan, 29, 124–25, 129–30, 132, 149, 151–53, 158–60, 192, 227n37, 232n38
African Americans, 7, 97, 135–36, 138, 164. *See also* Black feminism; Black pilots; Black women
AfroLatinx Americans, 94
AH-1F Cobra, 71
Ahmed, Sara, 7–8, 17, 48, 196
airmen, 10, 69, 193, 207n22. *See also* Tuskegee Airmen
Air National Guard, 182
Air Station Miramar, 178
airstrikes, 124–25
Allison, Tanine, 137, 141
all-volunteer force (AVF), 4–5, 65, 70, 74, 80, 132, 186, 206n4, 207n28, 210n53; and Black women, 142–44, 147, 151–52; and the Great Recession, 156–61; implementation of, 11–28, 31–34, 38–46, 50–62, 74, 210n49; and "minority market," 98–100, 105–7, 111, 122, 128–29, 211n65; and Persian Gulf War, 90–91; and tactical inclusion, 190–93, 207n27; and women, 92, 214n15
American Samoa, 5
American studies, 8, 137
America's Army (video game), 129
antihomosexuality, 82, 85, 95, 118, 120
antiracism, 16, 30, 97, 190, 195–97, 221n13
Anti-Racism Digital Library, 196
Anti–social welfare politics, 14, 79
antiwar movements, 17–19, 40
Armed Services Vocational Aptitude Battery (ASVAB), 1, 199, 205n1
Army Experience Center, 159
Army National Guard, 57, 63, 77, 85–88, 142, 194–95, 197
Army Ranger School, 171
army's inspector general, 120–21
"Army Strong," 150, *203*
Ashe, Austin, 88–89
Asian Americans, 5, 14, 97, 99, 131, 164, 168

Asian American studies, 14
assimilationism, 107, 109–10, 177, 181, 186
Atanasoski, Neda, 97, 123, 168
Atlanta, Georgia, 56

Bailey, Beth, 18, 31, 65
Bailey, Evangeline, 216n46
Balkans, 29, 168
Banet-Weiser, Sarah, 8
banner ads, 159
Bates Worldwide, 34, 63, 80, 92, 98, 111, 113, *204*
"Battle Up" video ad, 174–76
"Be all you can be," 1, 62, 128, *203*
Behind Enemy Lines, 129
Belkin, Aaron, 15
Berlin Wall, 90
Bethlehem Steel Corp., 77
billboards, 21, 26, 159, 199
biopolitics, 3, 12–14, 158, 177
bisexuals, 10, 29, 155–56, 161, 177, 192, 221n7, 230n1, 234n59, 234n64. *See also* LGBTQIA+ community; queerness; sexuality
Black Enterprise Magazine, 77
Black feminism, 16, 97, 146, 149
Black Hawk Down, 129
Black History Month, 135, 138
Black Lives Matter, 30, 190, 194
"black normal," 148
Black pilots, 64–66, 70–73, 89, 139, 141, 191. *See also* Tuskegee Airmen
Black power, 18
Black women, 7, 29, 60, 89, 125, 142, 210n53, 221n13; in ads, 36, 52, 115, 127, 216n46, 229n75; and martial maternity, 142–51; representation in military, 100, 217n63; as target market, 44, 52, 94, 111, 229n71
Bly, Robert, 61
bombs, 124, 130, 139
Bonilla-Silva, Eduardo, 88
boot camp, 9, 149
Bosnia, 122
Bright, Robert, 77
"bright future," 131, 134–35
Brown, Helen Gurley, 25
Brown, Melissa T., 11, 34, 45, 116, 130, 144, 214n15; on military masculinity, 15, 24, 36, 40, 66, 77, 82, 101
Brown University's Costs of War Project, 130, 152

Bush, George H. W., 90–91, 96
Bush, George W., 91, 124–26, 160

Caldera, Louis, 111, 131
California, 79, 106, 109–10, 178–79, 182; Hollywood, 129; Los Angeles, 107, 182; North San Diego County, 178; San Diego, 178, *180,* 234n64; San Francisco, 46, 178, 182–83, 234n64, 235n73; San Francisco Bay area, 107
California National Guard, 182
camouflage, 63, 101–3, 125, 150, 172
Campbell Ewald, 128, 159, *204*
Camp Pendleton, 178
Cannon, Timothy, 77
capitalism, 8, 12, 23, 39, 61, 170, 190, 233n48; and Black men, 57; and citizenship, 108; economy, 33, 38; golden age of, 41; legitimation of, 46; martial, 28, 63–66, 73–80, 89–90, 191; patriarchal, 52; racial, 208n31. *See also* martial capitalism
Carter, Ash, 161, 183–84
Central America, 73
Chambers, Jason, 53
Cheney, Richard Bruce, 91
Chester, Robert K., 137
Chicago, Illinois, 107
Chicanx people, 107
Chisholm, Shirley, 17
Christensen, Wendy M., 15, 150
Christianity, 81, 88, 164
citizenship, 2–3, 17, 31, 94, 108–10, 159, 169, 181, 207n27; and Black people, 24, 54, 56–57, 100, 105, 142, 144, 148, 150–51; and the citizen-soldier, 20, 190; economic, 27, 33, 39, 42–43, 60–61, 74, 77; martial, 9, 88–89, 137, 177–78; maternal, 85–86; norms of, 12, 15; and tactical inclusion, 189, 190
citizen-soldier, 20, 190
civil rights, 17–18, 23–24, 31, 53, 139
Civil War, 9, 210n49
Clarke, Jeffrey J., 90
class, 16–17, 20, 46, 66, 210n53; managerial, 74; middle, 24–25, 62, 81, 96, 108, 143; privilege, 2, 177, 196; working, 27, 32, 38, 43, 60. *See also* managerial class; middle class; working class
Clinton, Bill, 95, 99
Cockburn, Cynthia, 15
Cohn, Carol, 121

240   Index

Cold War, 89–91, 99, 218n27
Coleman, Anita S., 196
college, 2–4, 31, 75, 79–80, 101, 106–7, 118, 128, 132, 150
College Preview, 107
Collins, Patricia Hill, 146
colonialism, 18, 56, 88, 124, 233n48
colorblindness, 14, 53, 59, 138, 171, 196
colorism, 88–89
Combat Missions, 129
Commission on an All-Volunteer Armed Force, 18, 20
communism, 63, 73, 80–81, 90, 218n27
Confederacy, 196, 237n11
Connell, R. W., 40, 75
consumer market, 32, 54; Black, 24–25, 135
consumption, 24–25, 54, 97
Cosmopolitan, 24–26, 31, 34–37, 44–51, 81–82, 85, 118, 134, 144, 216n46
COVID-19, 194
Crenshaw, Kimberlé, 16
Crisis, The, 24
critical race theory, 7, 16
Cruise, Tom, 70
Cuba, 160
cultural memory, 137
cultural studies, 22, 97

D'Arcy, MacManus, and Masius, 34, 63, *204*
Davis, Angela, 97
Davis, Joseph, 57
Davis-Delano, Laurel, 24
D.C. National Guard, 194
Defense Race Relations Institute, 57
Demchko, Erin, *175,* 175–176
democracy, 28, 73, 81, 123–25, 137, 152, 163, 218n27
demographics, 11, 39, 42, 94, 98, 111, 122, 128, 169, 199; military, 19, 25, 61–62, 65, 144, 162–63, 216n63
detention, 124, 160
DeThorne, Ray, 129
digital media, 156–57, 159
direct ground-combat exclusion rule, 161
disability, 10, 14. *See also* able-bodiedness
displacement, 3, 124, 184, 197
Distinguished Flying Cross, 139
District of Columbia, 5
domesticity, 24–25, 82, 86, 88, 147, 229n75

Don't ask, don't tell (DADT), 94–95, 118, 120–21, 192, 221n7
Don't Ask, Don't Tell Repeal Act, 156, 161, 177–78, 185, 199, 234n59
Double V campaign, 9, 143
draft, 5, 39–40, 43, 45, 106, 128, 191, 205n2, 210n29; opposition to, 17–19, 53
drill instructors, 83, 136, 150, 225n72
drill sergeants, 102–3, 105, 225n72
Du Bois, W. E. B., 137
Duggan, Lisa, 177
duty, 31, 39, 43, 147, 198; off-, 116, 120, 171, 179, 184; patriotic, 3, 20, 60. *See also* active duty
Dyer, John, 56

Ebony, 34, 50–59, 67, 69, 75, 77, 87, *203,* 217n20; focus on Black men, 71, *72,* 101–4; focus on Black women, 144–50, 216n46; focus on women, 24–26, 36–37, 45, 85, 111–14, *114,* 118, 130, *133,* 134–136, *136,* 139, *140*
education, 6–8, 11–12, 20, 38–39, 74–75, 79, 196, 207n27; opportunities through military, 26–27, 31–33, 92, 118, 134, 157; publications, 107–8; requirements, 70, 128, 191. *See also* college; higher education; U.S. Military Academy at West Point
Edwards, Erica R., 125, 148
Eiffel Tower, 37
Eisenhower, Dwight, 195
elitism, 20, 27, 34, 38–39, 77, 82, 108–9, 125, 149
Elle, 111
Emancipation Proclamation, 9
Embser-Herbert, Máel, 15
empire, 6, 13, 22, 124–25, 148, 185
Enloe, Cynthia, 15, 44, 81, 214n15
equal opportunity, 7, 23, 33, 58, 91, 128, 161, 172; for women, 44, 49, 50, 98, 112–14, 118
Equal Opportunity Office, 121
equal rights, 18, 31, 48, 139, 219n52
Equal Rights Amendment (ERA), 43
ethnicity, 23, 99, 162, 196, 230n8
ethnic studies, 7
Europe, 38, 139
exceptional military, 28, 64–66, 86, 88–91, 153, 191
experiential advertisements, 157, 159
Exxon-Mobil, 77

Index 241

Facebook, 159
Fahey, Catherine, 77
families, 107, 109, 157, 171, 194, 198–99, 233n51; Black, 54–56, 57, 60, 147, 149; heteropatriotic, 127, 131–35, 152, 192; proud military, 28–29, 56, 64–65, 81–89, 131–35, 191. *See also* heteropatriotic families; proud military families
fatherhood, 86, 88; Black, 56–58, 150. *See also* absent father, stereotype of
federal student aid programs, 2, 79, 205n2
Feinman, Ilene Rose, 9, 81
femininity, 25, 44–46, 50, 64, 82, 107, 112–13, 116–21, 145
feminism, 18–19, 24, 81, 124, 176, 210n53, 221n13; Black, 16, 97, 146, 149; liberal, 44, 52, 114–15; martial, 27, 32, 43–53, 60, 191; post, 129, 160, 170–71, 192; security, 112–13
feminist studies, 7, 9, 97, 176–77; feminist media studies, 15, 17, 24, 46, 145, 149
Ferguson, Roderick, 7, 196
Fightertown USA. *See* Air Station Miramar
Fixmer-Oraiz, Natalie, 149
Floyd, George, 194
Focke-Wulf 190 fighter, 139
Fort Jackson (South Carolina), 31
Fortune 500 companies, 77
Foucault, Michel, 14
freedom, 8, 15, 20, 120, 124; religious, 164, 168, 177
free market, 5, 13–14, 18–20, 23, 32, 54, 74
Friedman, Milton, 13
From Representation to Inclusion: Diversity Leadership for the 21st-Century Military, 162

Gallagher, Eddie, 189
Gallup, 186
Garza, Irene, 111
Gates Commission. *See* Commission on an All-Volunteer Armed Force
gay people, 10, 118, 183, 185, 219n52, 230n1; bans against, 29, 95; and DADT, 121, 221n7; military inclusion of, 155–56, 161, 192, 234n59, 234n64; and pride, 177–79, 181. *See also* Don't ask, don't tell (DADT); Don't Ask, Don't Tell Repeal Act; homomartial pride; homosexuality; LGBTQIA+ community; queerness
Gebo, Carl, 77

Geiner, Vicki, 50
gender binary, 29, 112–13, 115, 156, 172, 174, 176, 184, 192, 230n1
gender studies, 14, 64, 112, 121, 177
General Accounting Office reports, 25
general equivalency diplomas (GEDs), 111
Germany, 139
G.I. Bill. *See* Montgomery G.I. Bill
Gilmore, Ruth Wilson, 41
Gilroy, Curtis, 157
global counterterrorism, 148
Goldwater, Barry, 18
good Black soldier, figure of, 27, 32, 53–54, 56–58, 60
Gray, Herman, 8
Great American Family Awards, 86
Great Depression, 157
Great Recession, 157–58, 186, 230n8
green Marines, 171
Greenspan, Alan, 13
Grewal, Inderpal, 112–13
Griest, Kristen, 171
Guam, 5
Guantanamo Bay Naval Base, 160–61
Guillen, Vanessa, 30, 190, 197–99
Gwyn, Jim, 56

Haiti, 29, 122
Hall, Charles B., 139
Hall, Stuart, 97
Hamer, Fannie Lou, 17
Hamilton, Alexander, 195
harassment, 3, 111, 121, 138; sexual, 96, 143, 173–74, 185, 197–99, 221n13, 225n72
Haver, Shaye, 171
hegemony, 7, 24, 28, 40, 196
Henry, Marsha G., 17
heroism, 31, 41, 83, 109, 130, 137
Herzegovina, 122
heteronormativity, 63–65, 81–82, 134–35, 151, 177, 179, 181, 189, 191, 219n52; and Black men, 24–25, 57; and diversity, 127, 131; and families, 85–86, 88–89; and homophobia, 95–96; and recruitment advertisements, 6, 10, 28, 61; and women, 44–46, 52, 93, 113, 115–16, 118
heteropatriarchy, 90, 189
heteropatriotic families, 127, 131–35, 152, 192. *See also* proud military families
heteropatriotism, 29, 125, 131, 134, 192
hetero-romance, 28, 95, 112, 115–16, 118, 120, 190

heterosexuality, 24–25, 45, 46, 112, 119, 192
hierarchy, 7, 10, 17, 214n17
higher education, 7–8, 38, 74–75, 79, 107, 232n36
high school, 1–4, 83, 92, 107–8, 111–12, 197, 199, 205n1
high-tech military, 65–73, 89, 191
high-tech soldiers, 28, 64, 66, 70, 89
Hill, Anita, 96, 221n13
Hirschman, Lieutenant Commander, 118
Hispanic Americans, 80, 97, 108, 164, 233n51
Hispanic Student USA, 107
Hispanic Times, 107
Holm, Jeanne, 81
homomartial pride, 29, 156, 177–85, 219n52
homonationalism, 124, 161, 177, 182
homophobia, 95, 120
homosexuality, 82, 85, 95–96, 118, 120–21, 124, 177, 183, 221n7. *See also* antihomosexuality; lesbians; LGBTQIA+ community; queerness
Hong, Grace, 14, 57
honorary whites, figure of, 89
HoSang, Daniel Martinez, 8, 109, 218n35
humanitarianism, 29, 63, 112, 122–23, 125, 145, 164, 168, 175, 192–93
Human Rights Campaign, 177
Humvees, 21, 159, 172

IEDs, 3
immigrants, 109–10, 158, 179, 189
Indigenous peoples, 5, 97, 99, 164, 168, 189. *See also* people of color
inequality, 7–8, 13–15, 18–20, 33, 97, 158, 163, 190, 193–94, 196; economic, 2, 43, 75, 230n8; gender, 80, 171–73, 176, 199; racial, 25, 43, 57
injury, 3, 12, 14, 100–101, 105, 129–30, 142, 151–52, 157, 198
intersectionality, 10, 16–17, 96, 113, 115, 134, 143–45, 207n24, 216n63, 221n13
Iraq, 3, 122, 157, 227n37
Iraq War, 9, 29, 124, 129–30, 132, 141, 149–53, 158–61, 192, 232n38
"Irresistible Force," 63
Israel, 183
Iwo Jima, 137

Jeffords, Susan, 64
Jet, 53

jets, 66–67, 118, 168
jobs, 3, 31–36, 38–39, 41–42, 54, 103, 108; civilian, 27, 36, 52, 73–74; military, 1–2, 49, 50, 62, 86, 143, 193; training, 12, 92, 122; for women, 111, 170
Johnson, John H., 24, 53, 54
Johnson, Kiesha, 111
Joint Advertising Market Research and Studies Group, 21, 207–8n28
Joint Recruiting Advertising Program, 21, 111, *204*
junior reserve officer training corps (JROTC), 4, 111
J. Walter Thompson agency, 11, 21, 26–27, 34, 63, 100, *204,* 213n92; targeting diverse audiences, 80, 92, 98, 108, 118

King, Angus, 170
King, Martin Luther, Jr., 17
King, Samantha, 24
Korean War, 31, 91
Kosovo, 122, 192
Kumar, Deepa, 124
Kuwait, 122

labor market, 14, 18, 27, 32–36, 40, 77, 143; soldiers, 39–43, 49, 54, 60, 74–75, 191, 214n15. *See also* soldier laborers
Lacey, Willis, 56
Lake Michigan, 199
Latinx peoples, 5, 9, 94–95, 196–97, 208n28, 211n64, 230n8, 237n11; exploitation of, 38, 53; recruitment of, 23, 28, 66, 98–99, 106–11, 128, 164, 168, 190–91, 233n51; service members, 15, 17, 19, 77–79, 91, 122, 131, 218n31. *See also* people of color
Lears, Jackson, 22
Leo Burnett Worldwide, 128
lesbians, 44, 50, 236n84; "specter of the dyke," concept of, 119–20. *See also* Don't ask, don't tell (DADT); Don't Ask, Don't Tell Repeal Act; homomartial pride; homosexuality; LGBTQIA+ community; queerness
lethality, 70
Lewis, John, 17
LGBT Pride Month, 181–85
LGBTQIA+ community, 10, 29, 155–56, 181, 183, 190, 192, 230n1. *See also* bisexuals; Don't ask, don't tell (DADT); Don't Ask, Don't Tell Repeal Act;

LGBTQIA+ community (*continued*)
gay people; homomartial pride; queerness; transgender people
liberal feminism, 44, 52, 114–15
liberalism, 7–8, 14, 18, 155, 162, 187, 195. *See also* neoliberalism
liberatory messaging, 17, 29, 52, 124, 170, 176, 185, 195, 197
LinkedIn, 159
Lioness Program, 158

MacArthur, Douglas, 195
Mademoiselle, 111
magazines, 1, 4
Maine, 170
Malcom X, 17
maleness, 2, 10, 61, 177–78, 181, 190, 229n75. *See also* masculinity
managerial class, 74
Marchand, Roland, 22
marketization, 27, 32–40, 43, 45, 52, 53–54, 60–62, 65, 191, 193
market research, 11, 21, 36, 52, 98, 118, 131, 168–70, 193, 199
marriage, 6, 64, 82, 86, 118, 179
martial capitalism, 28, 64–65, 74–80, 89, 191
martial feminism, 27, 32, 43–52, 60, 191
martial maternity, 29, 125, 127, 142–51, 192
martial normativity, 112, 115–16, 118–21
Martinez, Joaquin, 77, 79
masculinity, 9, 67, 75, 77, 95–96, 120, 160, 172–76, 214n17; and the Army, 49; Black, 54, 57, 58, 103–10, 223n43; and culture, 9; hegemonic, 24, 40; heteronormative, 52; and machinery skills, 36; military, 11, 15, 36, 38–44, 189; and violence, 29; warrior, 94, 105, 128, 169; and whiteness, 32, 66, 236n83. *See also* maleness; remasculinization
Mbembe, Achille, 14
media-military-industrial complex, 22. *See also* military-entertainment complex; U.S. empire's culture industry
media studies, 8, 22, 109, 124, 137; feminist, 15, 17, 24, 46, 145, 149
Melamed, Jodi, 89
meritocracy, 28, 56, 63–64, 73–80, 173, 218n31
meteorologists, 67
methodology of the book, 4–17, 24–30. *See also* American studies; Black feminism; critical race theory; cultural studies; ethnic studies; feminist studies; gender studies; intersectionality; media studies; political science; queer of color critique; sociology
Mexico, 110, 178; Tijuana, 179
middle class, 24–25, 62, 81, 96, 108, 143
Middle East, 154, 168
Military Accessions Vital to the National Interest program (MAVNI), 158–59
military-entertainment complex, 22. *See also* media-military-industrial complex; U.S. empire's culture industry
Military Leadership Diversity Commission (MLDC), 161–63, 177
military legitimacy, 4, 7–8, 17, 32, 195; and queerness, 181, 185–86; and race, 53, 58–60, 74, 110; and women, 43–46
military police (MP), 36, 38, 102–3, 105
military policies, 16, 36, 52, 62, 66, 70, 73, 120, 139, 223n42; and heteronormativity, 85, 183–84; and Obama, 29–30, 155, 160–61, 186; racist, 141, 143, 151; and Trump, 189–90; and women, 19, 44, 81–82, 95–96, 101, 111, 172, 218n20, 224n60
military-welfare state, 42, 66
Miller, Dorie, 137
Miller, Loren, 45
Milwaukee, Wisconsin, 199
Minneapolis, Minnesota, 194
minority advertising, 23, 98, 106
misogyny, 30, 121, 176
Mississippi Freedom Democratic Party, 17
Mittelstadt, Jennifer, 36, 42, 61, 65, 79
Montana, 1–2
Montana State University, 1
Montegary, Liz, 177
Montford Point Marines, 136–38
Montgomery G.I. Bill, 62, 79, 104, 118, 157
Moore, Brenda L., 15, 143
morality, 4, 88, 123–27, 135, 139–42, 149, 152, 170, 192; failures of, 33, 160; legitimacy through, 74, 218n27; superiority through, 29, 90
Morrison, Sarah, 111
Moynihan, Daniel Patrick, 55–57
Moynihan Report. *See* Moynihan, Daniel Patrick
Mukherjee, Roopali, 109
multicultural benevolence, 29, 125–31, 135, 138, 145, 147, 151–53, 192, 197

244 Index

multiculturalism, 4, 7, 14, 97, 110–12, 114–15, 137, 161, 164, 168; benevolence, 29, 125–31, 135, 138, 145, 147, 151–53, 192, 197; military, 28–29, 94, 96–101, 122–23, 149, 191
multicultural military, 28–29, 94, 96–101, 122–23, 149, 191

Nash, Jennifer C., 7
National Association for the Advancement of Colored People (NAACP), 182
National Chicano Moratorium, 17
National Council of La Raza, 182
National Defense Authorization Act, 95, 120, 161
National Family Week, 81
nationalism, 24, 30, 129, 177–78, 182, 189–90. *See also* homonationalism
national security, 18, 113, 130, 147, 149, 158, 177–78, 186
Native Americans. *See* Indigenous peoples
Navy Cross, 137
Nazism, 141
necropolitics, 14
neoliberalism, 13–14, 60, 205n3
New York City, 107, 124, 130; Harlem, 18
New York Fire Department, 130
New York Police Department (NYPD), 130
Nixon, Richard M., 13, 18, 61
Nobel Peace Prize, 162
North Macedonia, 122
Notre Dame University, 77
N. W. Ayer, 34, 62–63, *204*

Oates, Thomas P., 24
Obama, Barack, 5, 29, 153–56, 160–62, 170–71, 174, 177, 186, 192–93, 234n59
officers, 70–71, 73, 77, 141, 143, 175–76, 182, 186, 195, 197; army, 75, 85, 199; aviation, 96; Black, 57, 58; corps, 80, 98, 106–8, 161, 172–73, 219n36; multicultural, 23; navy, 118; white, 53
Operation Desert Shield, 90. *See also* Persian Gulf War
Ouellette, Laurie, 46

P-40 Warhawk, 139
Pacific Fleet, 178
Pacific Islanders, 5, 164. *See also* people of color
Pacific theater, 137

Palm Center, 177
Panama, 71, 73
Panetta, Leon, 161
Pascoe, C. J., 120
patriarchy, 6, 19, 49, 52, 57, 63–64, 69, 74–75, 144, 194–96. *See also* heteropatriarchy
patriotic mothers, 63–64, 85, 151
patriotism, 2–3, 11–12, 18, 20, 31, 34–35, 39, 129, 159, 193; and masculinity, 42, 108–10, 169–70; parenting, 132, 134–35; and race, 60, 138, 144–46, 218n35; and sexuality, 161, 177, 179. *See also* heteropatriotism; patriotic mothers; warrior patriotism
Patton, George, 195
Pearl Harbor, 137
Pell grants, 79
Penn State University, 77
Pennsylvania, 124
Pentagon, 157, 179, 181
people of color, 5–6, 9–10, 13, 64–66, 89–91, 128, 182, 189–91, 211n65; representation of, 19, 23, 80, 98, 113, 158. *See also* African Americans; AfroLatinx Americans; American Samoa; Asian Americans; Black feminism; Black pilots; Black women; Indigenous peoples; Latinx peoples; Pacific Islanders
Persian Gulf War, 28, 90–91, 94, 96, 99–100, 121–22, 191, 220n70. *See also* Operation Desert Shield
Peterson, L., 101
Phelps, M. Matthew, 181
Phillips, Kimberley, 15, 143
pilots, 67, 118, 218n23; Black, 64–66, 70–73, 89, 139, 141, 191. *See also* Black pilots
police, 9, 18, 36, 182, 195, 223n42; military (MP), 38, 102–3, 105, 223n41; New York, 130; violence by, 106, 149, 185, 190, 194
political science, 11
poster campaigns, 1, 21, 25–26
postracial discourse, 129, 137–38, 160, 170–71, 192, 196
post-traumatic stress disorder (PTSD), 3, 130
poverty, 14, 38, 55, 60, 208n31, 230n8
Presidential Commission on the Assignment of Women in the Armed Services, 96

Index 245

progressiveness, 6, 58, 95–98, 121, 125, 153, 170, 178, 218n27; liberal, 162, 187, 195; sexual, 182, 184
Project 100,000 program, 55
propensity, 11–13, 99–100, 128, 143, 208n28, 221n7
Proposition 187, 109–10, 179
proud military families, 28–29, 56–57, 64–65, 81–89, 131–35, 191. *See also* heteropatriotic families
Puar, Jasbir, 14, 124, 135, 177, 183
Puerto Rico, 5, 106

queerness, 6, 10, 13–16, 113, 120, 124–25, 179, 230n1, 235n73; homophobic/transphobic, 30, 189–90; regulation of, 156, 174, 181, 183–85. *See also* bisexuals; gay people; homosexuality; LGBTQIA+ community
queer of color critique, 16
queer studies, 177

racism, 7, 35, 58, 110, 137, 149, 151, 171; and the military, 57–58, 141, 143, 214n17; resistance to, 17–18; systemic, 171, 194–96. *See also* antiracism; colonialism; segregation; slavery; White supremacy
radio, 4, 21, 159
Rambo (movies), 63
Rambo/Bono gap, 169, 233n48
RAND Corp., 25, 129, 195, 211n72
Reagan, Ronald, 4, 13, 28, 61, 65, 67, 69–70, 73, 79, 90; pro-family politics of, 81, 85–86, 191
recession, 35, 41, 153–54; Great Recession, 157–58, 186, 230n8
recruitability, 2–3, 6, 11–14, 22, 80, 91, 122, 148–49, 168, 191
Reddy, Chandan, 120
"Reinvention of Government," 99
remasculinization, 28, 64–65, 67–69, 73, 82–90, 191
Risk Rule policy, 82
Robinson, Roderick, 125
Rooks, Noliwe, 24
Roosevelt, Franklin D., 141
Rosales, Steven, 15, 107
Rostker, Bernard, 90
Rostker v. Goldberg, 82
Rumsfeld, Donald H., 130

sailors, 10, 57–58, 164, 178, 193
Saigon, Vietnam, 18
Saludos Hispanos, 107
San Diego Pride, 178–82, 234n64
Saudi Arabia, 90, 122
Save Our State initiative. *See* Proposition 187
second job, military as, 36–38
Segal, M. W., 143
segregation, 36, 137, 141, 154, 216n46
Selective Service card, 1
servicewomen, 43, 96
Seventeen, 111
sexism, 17, 27, 35, 49, 143, 171, 174, 176; hetero-, 190, 195
sexual assault, 130, 143, 154, 173–74, 185, 197–99, 225n72; Tailhook assaults, 96, 121, 221n13. *See also* harassment
sexuality, 2, 13–19, 39, 85, 91, 207n24, 208n31; and DADT, 94–96; and military policy, 28, 162, 205n3; and queerness, 183–86; and women, 44, 50, 111–12, 120–21, 147, 210n53. *See also* Don't ask, don't tell (DADT); Don't Ask, Don't Tell Repeal Act; LGBTQIA+ community; queerness
sexual politics, 28, 64, 88–89, 177–83
Sherwin-Williams Co., 77
Shinsheki, Eric, 131
Shome, Raka, 145
Sicily, Italy, 139
slavery, 88, 151
slogans, 1, 26–27, 62, 86, 116, 128, 131, 163–64, *203,* 216n46. *See also individual slogans*
social conservatism, 81–82, 134
social media, 4, 25, 156–57, 159–60, 194, 199. *See also* Facebook; LinkedIn; Twitter; YouTube
social progress, 4, 6–7, 160, 162, 187, 199
social welfare programs, 14, 28, 64, 66, 74, 79, 96. *See also* military-welfare state
sociology, 24, 34, 40, 120, 196
soldier laborers, 27, 39–43, 49, 54, 60, 74–75, 191, 214n15
Somalia, 29, 100, 122, 192
South Carolina, 31
Soviet Union, 63, 65, 67, 69, 73, 81, 90
space race, 67–69
Spade, Dean, 7

246 Index

Spanish language, 106–9, 111
"specter of the dyke," concept of, 119–20
Sports Illustrated, 24–26, 34, 40, *41*, 67–71, 75–77, *78*, 130–35, *203*, 216n46; focus on Black men, 101, *102*, 125–126, *126*, 139, *140*, 150; focus on Black women, 51, 144, 216n46; focus on women, 38, 45, 63, 83, *84*, 92–93, *93*, 115–18, *119*
Stabile, Carol, 124
Stahl, Roger, 22
state authority, 28, 94, 101, 105, 120, 191
Student Non-Violent Coordinating Committee, 17
student-soldiers, 79
"support our troops," 134
Szitanyi, Stephanie, 15

tactical inclusion, definition of, 4
Tailhook sexual assaults, 96, 121, 221n13
Taylor, Keeanga-Yamahtta, 7
technical training, 27, 67, 71, 116, 143
technology, 11, 28, 40, 63–64, 66–73, 139, 211n64, 217n20
Teen, 111
television, 1, 4, 25–26, 100, 128–29, 159
Texas: Dallas-Fort Worth, 107; Fort Hood, 197–98; Houston, 107; San Antonio, 107
Thomas, Clarence, 96
Threat, Charrisa J., 15
Thurman, Maxwell R., 62–63, 79
Top Gun, 70, 178, 218n23
torture, 124, 160
toughness, 27, 103, 105, 189
transgender people, 181, 230n1, 232n38, 235n73; inclusion of, 9–10, 29, 155–56, 161, 183–84, 189, 192, 199, 232n34. *See also* Don't ask, don't tell (DADT); Don't Ask, Don't Tell Repeal Act; LGBTQIA+ community; queerness
trauma, 3, 12, 130, 152, 174. *See also* post-traumatic stress disorder (PTSD)
Truman, Harry, 141
Trump, Donald J., 30, 174, 189, 193–94, 199, 232n34
Ture, Kwame, 17
Tuskegee Airmen, 139–41
Twitter, 159

unemployment, 12–13, 41, 73–74, 80, 157–58
Union Army, 9
Union of Soviet Socialist Republics (USSR). *See* Soviet Union
universalism, 14, 80
University of California, Santa Barbara, 77–79
University of Idaho, 77
University of Oregon, 172
University of Texas at Austin, 77
upward mobility, 3, 11–13, 32, 34, 38–39, 42, 71, 90, 134, 142; for women, 46, 49
U.S. Congress, 124, 157, 177, 186
U.S. Department of Defense, 21, 82, 91, 152, 157, 162–63, 211n72
U.S. Department of Justice, 198–99
U.S. empire's culture industry, 22. *See also* media-military-industrial complex; military-entertainment complex
U.S. Federal Bureau of Investigation (FBI), 198
U.S. foreign policy, 90
U.S. Military Academy at West Point, 30, 190, 195–97
U.S. Naval Reserve, 145–148, *148*
U.S. Navy SEAL, 189
U.S. Senate Armed Services Committee, 170
U.S. Senate Judiciary Commission, 96
U.S. Special Forces, 125
U.S. Supreme Court, 82, 96, 221n13

Vavrus, Mary, 160, 171
Vibe, 111
video games, 4, 21, 129, 137, 159
Vietnam War, 4, 17–18, 23, 31–33, 35, 38, 40, 53–55, 73, 91
violence, 3–4, 12–17, 56–57, 120, 144, 151–52, 157, 189, 197–99; masculinist, 29, 40, 73, 104, 173–76; military, 154–55, 170, 192; police, 106, 149, 190, 193–95; racial, 31, 53, 138–39, 214n17; sexual, 96, 111, 121–22, 130; state, 6, 30, 43, 91, 110, 115, 126, 134–35, 162–63, 185–87. *See also* misogyny; police; sexual assault
Virginia, 124
Vista, 107
vocational training, 12, 27, 46
voters, 6, 18, 53, 81, 179

wages, 13, 18, 27, 32, 34–35, 39, 49, 52
Walker, Alice, 88
"Wall" video ad, 154–55, *155,* 169, 176
war on terror, 4, 28–29, 124–31, 134, 139–44, 147, 151–53, 156–60, 164, 185
Warren, Gary, 150
warrior patriotism, 28, 94, 107–10
Washington, DC, 194
Washington, George, 195
websites, 21, 25, 132, 159–60, 163–64, *203,* 232n38
welfare mother, stereotype of, 88
"White backlash," 18, 53
White supremacy, 18–19, 53, 59, 88, 96, 110, 137–38, 191, 194–95, 198
Williams, Raymond, 22
"womanpause" strategy, 70, 81

Woodson, Carter G., 135
working class, 27, 32, 38, 43, 60, 108
World War I, 106, 210n49
World War II, 9, 14, 45, 67, 95, 116, 127, 141–44, 192; memory of, 137, 139
Wunderman-Thompson. *See* J. Walter Thompson agency

xenophobia, 30, 189–90
X Games, 159

Year of the Woman (1992), 96
Young, Cynthia A., 125
Young and Rubicam, *204*
youth surveys, 11–12, 23, 100, 118, 128, 207–8n28
YouTube, 160, 176

JEREMIAH FAVARA is an assistant professor of communication studies at Gonzaga University.

The University of Illinois Press
is a founding member of the
Association of University Presses.

_____

University of Illinois Press
1325 South Oak Street
Champaign, IL 61820-6903
www.press.uillinois.edu